PUBLIC RELATIONS

PUBLIC RELATIONS

(For PG Diploma & Degree Courses in Journalism & Mass Media)

Seema Sharma

ANMOL PUBLICATIONS PVT. LTD.
NEW DELHI - 110 002 (INDIA)

ANMOL PUBLICATIONS PVT. LTD.
4374/4B, Ansari Road, Daryaganj
New Delhi - 110 002
Ph.: 23261597, 23278000
Visit us at: www.anmolpublications.com

Public Relations

First Published, 2005

ISBN 81-261-2335-4

PRINTED IN INDIA

Published by J.L. Kumar for Anmol Publications Pvt. Ltd., New Delhi - 110 002 and Printed at Mehra Offset Press, Delhi.

Contents

Preface

In Modern world, Journalism is one discipline, which attracts people like any thing, but, it is equally challenging and drastic in cases. Particularly, under the new world order and in current global scenario, its value has increased manifold.

Apart from being a glorious profession, Journalism, today is a full-fledged subject, mastery of which leads one to a successful career and an all powerful status in society.

As a discipline, Journalism requires proper training and a comprehensive course, if possible. Although, there is no defined qualification for appointment as a journalist, in any capacity, in any media organisation, yet it is always better to be properly qualified and well-equipped with all essential knowledge.

Of course, there are books on Journalism but not in a great number. And, if one goes selective, then only a few books would rest in hand, as there is still a dearth for exclusive and exhaustive books on several streams of Journalism.

This series of books on Journalism is an effort to fill the abovesaid vaccum only. Here are books on all subjects and topics, related to Journalism. The undersigned is confident enough that this humble endeavour would prove to be worthy on the basis of its merits and receive a warm acceptance by students of journalism, scholars and the working journalists, as well.

— **Editor**

Preface

In Modern world, Journalism is our discipline, which attracts people like anything, but it is equally challenging and critical in case. Particularly under the new world order and in current global scenario, its value has increased manifold.

Apart from being a famous profession, Journalism, today, is a full-fledged subject, mastery over which leads one to a successful career and an all powerful status in society.

As a discipline, Journalism requires proper training and a comprehensive course. It is possible that although there is no definite qualification for appointment as a journalist in any capacity in any media organisation, yet it is always better to be properly qualified and well equipped with all essential knowledge.

Of course there are books on Journalism but not in a great number. And if one goes over them, only a few books would rest in hand, as there is still a dearth of exhaustive and standard books on several streams of Journalism.

This series of books on Journalism is an effort to fulfil the demand of current days. Here are books on all major streams and topics related to Journalism. The undersigned is confident enough that the humble endeavour would prove to be worthy of the hopes of students and others who are interested in study of journalism, scholars and the working journalists as well.

— Editor

1

Introduction

The revolution in communication has created a whole new pattern of human dynamics. The current changes in society are basically because of shifts in public attitudes. It is because of this that Public Relations is rapidly gaining attention worldwide. The significance and dynamism of the concept of public relations is likely to increase in scope and effect.

The purpose of Public Relations practice is to establish a two-way communication to resolve conflicts of interest by seeking common ground or areas of mutual interest, and to establish understanding based on truth, knowledge and full information.

The scale of activity to promote good Public Relations may vary considerably according to the size and nature of the interested parties, but the philosophy, the strategy and the methods remain very similar, whether the Public Relations programme is designed to influence international understanding or to improve relations between a local company and its customers, agents and employees.

One of the earliest definitions of the term is coined by Denny Griswold, publisher of 'Public Relations News':

> "Public Relations is the management function which evaluates public attitudes, identifies the policies and procedures of an organization with the public interest, and executes a programme of action to earn public understanding and acceptance."

Another important definition is by two American Public Relations Professionals, Scot M. Cutlip and Allen H. Center:

> "Public Relations is the planned effort to influence opinion through good character and" responsible performance, based upon mutually satisfactory two-way communication."

The Institute of Public Relations in the U.K. has defined Public Relations as-"The deliberate, planned and sustained effort to establish and maintain mutual understanding between an organization and its public."

An interesting and modern definition of Public Relations is the Mexican statement made at an International Conference of Public Relations institutions held in Mexico city in 1978:

> "Public Relations practice is the art of social science of analysing trends, predicting their consequences, counselling organisation leaders, and implementing planned programmes of action which will serve both the organisation and the public interest."

This is a very helpful and practical definition. First of all, it introduces the need for research, to audit or assess the situation, and to consider the implications of what is discovered. Second, it stresses the advisory role of Public Relations, its service to management. Third, it shows that Public Relations programmes must be planned. Finally, it states that PR action must not only benefit its sponsors, but must also be in public interest, that is it should be socially responsible.

D.S. Mehta defines Public Relations as "an attempt, through information, persuasion, adjustment and contacts, to seek support for some activity, cause, movement, institution, product or service".

Nature and Scope : Public Relations as a process serves a number of functions. The nature of Public Relations indicates that it is essentially a task promoting rapport and goodwill between a person, firm or institution and the community at large through dissemination of information. Public Relations aims to bring about harmonious and mutually advantageous adjustment between an organization and the community through dissemination of ideas and also by providing feedback from the public to the management. It also evaluates public attitudes, identifies policies that interests public and executes the programme of communication. Good public relations implies a sound moral base i.e., communication must be sincere and based on facts.

Elements in Public Relations : Public Relations involves four major elements. They are inter-related and overlapping. Infact, one tends to lead to another.

Two-way Communication : Public Relations philosophy puts great emphasis on the need for two-way communication. It is now fairly well accepted that feedback is important. The foremost objective in any public relations programme is to improve existing channels of communication and to establish two-way flow of information.

Mutual Understanding : Mutual understanding requires, by definition, a two-way communication. A Public Relations policy for any organisation, should include both inward activity and intelligence to assess the policies and behaviour of the management, to see whether action is necessary to improve the organisation's image; and outward activity to inform the public about its achievement.

In any public relationship, there are at least two parties involved. First, there is the organisation which has something to promote, often in competition with others. Second, there are the 'publics' to which the organisation directs its efforts. Thus, there are two interests to be met: the private interest and the public interest. Generally, these interests are often in conflict. Resolving these conflicts is the essential part of Public Relations, which can only be done by achieving 'Mutual Understanding' between the organization and all the interests.

Caring for Public Opinion : Public Opinion is the consensus of individual opinions of the majority among the masses, based on their attitudes and widely held beliefs, moulded by public interest. Public Relations provides the necessary information to various public interest groups, in the interest of the organisations.

Social Responsibility : For the organisation to profit or gain through its efforts, it has necessarily to first achieve the acceptance and approval of the people for its role. Public Relations seeks to attune itself to the needs and aspirations of the community it serves and identifies the interests of the organization with that of the community's.

Scope of Public Relations Practice : Public Relations consists of a number of little things and a few big things. It is the daily application of common sense, common courtesy and common decency. Public Relations practice is still concerned with getting publicity, for somebody or something. Many Public Relations practitioners do little else. But publicity is not Public Relations, it is only a tool of Public Relations. Public Relation's scope extends to policy and strategy and counselling managements.

The broadness and non-specificity of the term "public relations" prevents it from becoming associated with any one type of function. As it is a general word, it remains suitable an "umbrella" term covering many types of functions that it performs.

The broad variety and scope of Public Relations functions, ranging from doing small favours for people, being just visible in a social gathering, to devising a broader strategy to gain public favour, can encompass, many things that come under the 'umbrella' term of Public Relations. But one thing should be borne in mind. No two Public Relations practitioner's programmes or functions are exactly the same. They differ from organisation to organisation and person to person.

Role of Public Relations : Public Relations serve a wide variety of institutions in society such as business, trade unions, government agencies, voluntary agencies, foundations, religious institutions, hospitals. To achieve their goals, these institutions must develop effective relationships with many different audiences or 'publics', such as employees, members, consumers, local communities, other institutions and with society at large.

The Public relations professional, is a specialist in communication and in public opinion.

Public Relations as Management Function : One of the most important role and function that Public Relations performs is identifying the 'public interest' and keeping the organization informed about it. But, in the final analysis, determining what is public interest, is a decision for the management. This leads to the conclusion that Public Relations is a management function. It is the Public Relations function to provide skilled assistance and advice to management to and from its publics, internally and externally.

Process of Communication : Public Relations practice is the continuing effort to effect a harmonious adjustment between an organization and the various interests it serves. This can be achieved through two-way communication resulting in mutual understanding at each other's interests. In this process, the Public Relations practitioner plays the role of communicator, catalyst and counsellor.

Public Relations Process and Tools of Communication : Public Relations today involves complete analysis and understanding of all the factors that influence people's attitudes toward an organization. This is achieved through what has been popularly called "Public Relation's Four-stage Process". The stages are:

Fact-finding : research analysis of opinion, environment.

Planning : policy formulation, programming, goal setting.

Communication : implementing planned communication activities, execution.

Evaluation : feedback and adjustment/course modification.

The gamut of Public Relations operations are-targeted towards diverse publics with varied information needs so as to help the publics have a right perspective of the organisations and its goal. The Public Relations practitioner works through the printed word, the spoken word and the image to communicate and interpret messages to the publics. The tools that can be used by the Public Relations person are House Publications, Letters and Bulletins, Bulletin Boards, Posters, Photographs and Billboards, Institutional advertising, Meeting, Speaker's Bureau, Public Address Systems, Films, Video and Slide Films, Displays and Exhibits, Visitors for Open House, Plan Tours, Staging Special Events, etc. Instead of listing targets strictly by publics, we shall group them according to the specialised media or other means of communication to reach them. Thus:

Public to be Reached	*Tools of Communication*
Stockholders	Annual and interim reports, meetings.
Financial Community	Financial Publications, Personal Meetings.
(brokers, security, analysts)	
Employees	House Journals, Bulletin Boards, Posters, Handbills, Target Charts, Letters, Video Films, Meetings.
Labour Unions	Bulletins and statements or policy.
Communities	Company Publications, Local Press, Radio and TV Outlets, Local Group Meetings, Meetings with Opinion Leaders, Exhibitions.
Government	House Publications, Reports, Brochures, Booklets.
Technical Group	Through Technical Magazines and Journals.

Trade Group	Through Tiade Magazines.
Competitors	Association Meetings, Direct Mail
Suppliers/Creditors	Credit and Banking Associations, Supplier's Meet.
Customers	Product Publicity Media, Press Releases, Advertising, POP Marketing, Direct Mail, Television Sponsored Programmes, Newspaper Cell etc.

Ethical Aspects

Public Relations has now become a vital function affecting management decisions and influencing public opinion in every non-profit or profit making organization.

In the early growth stages of Public Relations there were quite a few people posing a Public Relations persons but working as press agents who indulged in unethical practices to achieve their ends. It is a difficult task to describe what is ethical and what is unethical. There are a number of acts that could be classified as unethical, ranging from suppressing of news to misleading the audience. Unethical act may include:

— suppressing unfavourable news,

— misrepresenting facts,

— undercutting a competitor,

— purporting to serve a cause but actually serving some other interest,

— promising results that can not be obtained,

— use of undesirable methods towards pressurising editors for carrying publicity material.

Public Relations recognises a long-term responsibility and seeks to persuade and to achieve mutual understanding by securing the willing acceptance of attitudes and ideas. It can succeed only when the basic policy is ethical, and the means used are truthful.

In Public Relations, the ends can never justify the use of false, harmful or questionable means.

Impact of P.R. on Society : There are no suitable yardsticks by which Public Relations impact can be measured. Publication of Press Releases may be a tangible sign but still it doesn't mean that

— it has been read by the target audience;

— it has been understood as desired by source;

— it has brought about a change in the attitude of the receiver.

Practical Aspects

Information : One of the functions/role of Public Relations is to inform the public. But docs Public Relations really help to inform the public? There can be flaws in the kind of information given out and the kind of information suppressed. There can also be several ethical aspects to the content, timing of message and the channel used.

Another aspect often criticised is that there is too much of such information emanating from every side with conflicting claims. This does not help to resolve doubts. Rather it adds to the confusion with the overloading of communication channels with contradictory message indiscriminately.

Persuasion : Public Relations communication is aimed at bringing about a change in attitude. But is it ethical to manipulate public opinion? Basically, a Public Relations person is an advocate of a cause, client, company or institution. The individual idea or institution needs the expertise of a skilled advocate. The advocate is essential to make the modern democracy work.

Factors at Work

The term 'Principle' implies either-

(a) the basic general truth of the concept, or

(b) the guidelines within which the concept is supposed to operate.

The principles governing and guiding all Public Relation activity depend on the principles of communication.

Principles : Since the individuals respond differently to the same stimuli and their response to a communication is also very selective, therefore the P.R. professionals need to evolve a set of principles to guide their efforts.

Honest Communication : Increasing literacy rates and growing education has led to an attitude of skepticism towards a kind of communication that seeks to influence, motivate or persuade them. Thus, the first principle ought to be that P.R. communication should be honest and sincere.

Tackling Information Overload : The mass audience suffers from 'information overload' i.e., Communications being targeted by different interest groups from all sides to the same audience. It is necessary, therefore, for the P.R. practitioner to be careful in 'positioning' his P.R. messages. Instead of directly sending persuasive messages, one can adopt a strategy of injecting ideas and information into that broad stream of communication, for e.g., a newspaper that flows incessantly to the target publics.

Use of Intermediates/Opinion Leaders : Berelson, Lazarsfeld and Gandet propounded the two-step flow theory of communication.

"Ideas often flow from radio and print to the 'opinion leaders, and from them to the less active sections of the population. While the concept of the 'opinion leaders' is useful, the problem involved is in locating them as they are not clearly identifiable by position or otherwise. However, there is evidence that some media are far more suited to imparting information and ideas to opinion leaders in the areas they cover than others. Choice of appropriate media, is thus, a crucial task for the P.R. professional. Also, the two-step process is now partially being displaced by audio-visual media like the TV, radio, video and films, which bring the reality directly into the lives of the audiences.

The researchers have identified three separate groups in the "leader" category. These are:

— Vocal Activists who devote themselves to advocating a cause;

— Leaders such as the mass media and key educators;

— Power Leaders like the politicians, bureaucrats, judges and others who have the power to take actions that affect organizations and society.

Among the three most important groups is that of the Power Leaders, who can actually make things happen. The other two groups have access to the power leaders, but have little power themselves. However, the information input that gets to the Power Leaders is much more from the vocal activists and opinion leaders than from the general public and the public organizations. As a result of this disproportionate pattern of input, Power Leaders often tend to assume that the distorted impressions they receive from the small articulate groups are what the public feels. This aspect has to be borne in mind, when the P.R. professionals interact with Power Leaders.

Choice of Tools : The growing visibility of events, through the mass media, has led to higher public reaction levels. Therefore, as a principle the PR professionals need to know all that could be made to capture the imagination by becoming real forces in people's minds.

Ensuring Receptivity : For the PR to be effective, the basic principle that always needs to be kept in mind is that the target public must be in a 'posture of receptivity'. This is of critical importance in PR. It is a recognized fact that the favourable inclination of an individual towards all messages from a given source is the result of his total experience with that source.

Public Attitude : These principles should be further applied to influence public attitude, the basic function of PR. An 'attitude' is the feeling for or against some person, organization, issue or object. It can be defined as the degree of positive or negative effect associated with some psychological object, which may be a symbol, phrase, slogan, idea, towards which people can differ with respect to positive or negative effect. The motives that arouse attitudes in individuals originate in desire for reward, self-defence, expressions of personal values and acquisition of knowledge. Attitudes may be shaped by a desire for reward.

An attitude, once aroused in an individual, may be repressed due to external influence or willpower.

Attitude and Public Opinion : Attitudes become opinions. The basic motives, inducing persons to express their attitudes in the form of opinions, are their desire for comfort and convenience, safety and protection, pride, affection and to escape pain. The opinions of individuals are activated by their attitudes which are motivated by mental and physical forces inducing to express themselves. People are usually not aware of their motives impelling them to express attitude in the form of opinions. It is here that Public Relations steps in. The basic objective of PR is to measure and anlayse the influence of the public opinion, which is shaped by the attitudes of the individuals comprising the public. Therefore, it is important for PR personal to understand-

— the meaning of attitudes,

— why people hold the attitudes they do,

— the role of attitudes in the opinion-forming process,

— the motives that cause people to express their opinions, so that the public relations communications could appeal to the needs and motives of the people.

— The PR practitioners can plan events and try to use these to change attitude and opinions.

Role in Life

The PR is essentially a management function, it is the social philosophy of management expressed in policy decisions and actions resulting from these policies. PR seeks to perform its management function through effective information dissemination which is an aid to management.

Today the organisational management is not only-confined to managing products, material, manpower, money and mobility, but also newer areas like instant communications, multiple forms of transportation, globalisation of markets, computerization, automation, and active trade-unionism. New Management techniques such as management-by-objectives have been developed. All these areas could be assessed and analysed through various management techniques within the enterprise. However, the new challenges thrown up by the 'broad marketplace of ideas' are not only intangible, but also subject to easy manipulation, charting or quantifying with any kind of managerial discipline.

The forces which create difficulties for any management, could be tracked down to one source—the human climate and public attitudes. Recognition of this fact has led to gradual development of approaches towards managing the human climate Public Relations, is one such approach of mailing the human climate for the ultimate benefit of the organization and its publics. This approach can be summarised as incorporating the four primary functions of the PR :

Analysing and Predicting Issues and Opportunities : The political and economic fields are the vast playing fields of public attitudes Fighting for the pros and cons of the public policy.

It is in this arena of public attitudes that the PR functions by analysing issues of importance and relevance to the organization or predicting opportunities that have the potential to benefit the organization. Whether it be issues, crises, emergencies or any such problems, or opportunities of any kind, it is the PR function to see these early, identify their shape and contours long before they actually mature.

Also, in understanding an issue, one should realize that an issue arises when one or more of an organization's publics develop a grievance, or perceive a threat or a fear. Before submitting to the natural reaction and rushing to the defence, it is wise for a PR professional to explore how the grievance, threat or fear arose, before developing plans for dealing with it. Here's seven-point plan to handle a grievance, before it becomes an issue or a problem for the management.

(a) Analyse the reasons for the grievance. Is there something wrong with the activities of the organization-a problem of quality, of explanation, of service? Is there a gap in communication?

(b) Analyse the source of the grievance and the nature of people who make it.

(c) Study all the facts about the subject of the grievance. Review all reports and documentation. Discuss the matter with experts within the organization.

(d) Review outside reports and sources of the grievance, if any.

(e) Make an objective study of the present attitudes of the concerned department, among competitors and comparable organization, among critics and in the public media.

(f) If the climate is unclear, analyse further through informal opinion surveys to gather clues among groups affected by the grievance, even among those that might get involved.

(g) Determine the action plan; coordinate, form a broad coalition, assign responsibilities, and inform the management for policy decision.

Therefore, rather than waiting for the new public goals to emerge into the public policy and reaction, the PR professionals devise a new approach. This is aimed at continuously narrowing the gap between emerging public goals and the goals of the organization. This is known as the 'interactive approach'.

The two pre-requisites for using the interactive approach successfully are-

(a) management's ability to anticipate external change; and

(b) its willingness to adjust the organization's normal operations to minimize the gap between performance and expectations.

Information Gathering and Monitoring Trends : The most important force affecting all organizations today is the opinion of

the people. Public opinion is constantly changing with the time and trends in society. Here, for any PR person, it becomes important to gather information and analyse the same in terms of what goes in the minds of Public (investors, employers, consumers and others). Also, constant monitoring and gathering of information of changes in the present environment is a must.

Information gathering and monitoring have been the fastest growing and the most significant facets of the development of the PR in the last decade. It involves the identification, evaluation and communication inward to the organization of information about the outside world that may be value to the organization in managing its affairs.

Even while keeping track of the changing public attitudes towards an organization or its publics, the PR provides an information base for the.management to act upon. Even in the case of internal information, the PR departments could provide the necessary support by monitoring trends among the different publics of the organization.

Communication Planning and Information Dissemination : Communication planning and information dissemination is another important function of the PR. It involves identifying the target audiences, careful planning of messages aimed at bringing about positive opinion and dispelling misunderstanding if any. It is just not enough to frame a good public policy. The challenge lies in planning and communicating all the good deeds of an organization to its public, both internal and external in a very effective manner.

After gaining understanding of the public opinion about the organization, and thereby, modifying or improving the policy by influencing and counselling the policy makers, the immediate task facing a PR person is the planning of communication activities and campaigns that will explain the company, its products, and services to the publics. After identifying and planning a communication message the immediate task of a PR practitioner is to choose the right media by knowing the intended audience. The media of communication are the vehicles for disseminating messages. These could be external or internal; television, radio, opinion leaders etc. Information dissemination is carried out through press releases, press conferences, video and audio news releases, press rejoinders, letters to editors etc. Information dissemination function of the PR is-a far broader concept than issuing of news releases or press rejoinders. It is the function of 'letting the public know' by using the means appropriate to the situation.

Advisory and Counselling Role of PR : The personnel are the eyes and ears of the policy-makers in an organization. Their success depends on the extent to which they can influence shaping of the management policy. Constant information gathering and processing helps the PR personnel in analysing trends, and in predicting consequences of policy. This gives them enough information to guide and counsel public policy-formation. Today's administrators require the assistance and wise counsel of the skilled PR specialists in reshaping organization's operations and policies, to promote goodwill, and increase productivity.

The advisory role of the PR is not only towards the top management of an organization, but also towards the other departments and divisions in that organization. PR does not customarily establish policies or make basic operating decisions, but it bears a direct responsibility to identify and recommend to the management appropriate decisions and policies to assure the maintenance of a balanced PR perspective. The success of the PR profession's performance of this function that determines the ultimate success of the entire organization. Thus, today's administrations are in need of wise PR counselling for giving shape to an organization's policies or even managing operations.

Communication Process

The essential basis of all public relations work is the communication process. Reduced to the simplest formula communication is the transfer of information from one person to another or more recently to an apparatus which stores or passes on news. This process almost always takes place between four or five factors: the organization or initiator (e.g., a business corporation or trade association), the communicator (e.g., media person or a public relations agency), the message (e.g., a press release or a lecture), the medium (which may be a newspaper or the radio or television or a book or a letter), and finally the addressee (e.g., the newspaper reader or the owner of a telephone or teleprinter, or the viewer of a television programme). The message is transmitted by spoken or written word, or by image, or a combination of these, or other media such as music, colour, mimicry, design, odour and sense of touch.

For satisfactory information in a certain field, the following points must be observed :

(1) The volume of information must be adequate.

(2) The density or frequency of the information must be in accordance with practical experience.

(3) The information must be clear and readily understandable.

(4) The information must be objective.

(5) The information must be up-to-date; it must be presented without unnecessary delay, i.e., immediately or at the most, only a short time after the event.

(6) The information must be aimed at the proper direction and must make use of the proper media to reach the sector of the public for which it is intended.

The Fundamentals

(1) Measures, evaluates and interprets the attitude of various public bodies connected with the organization or establishment.

(2) Assists management in defining objectives for increasing public understanding and acceptance of the organization's plans, policies, programmes, services or products, and personnel.

(3) Equates these objectives with the interests, needs and goals of its various public, and

(4) Develops, executes and evaluates a programme to earn public understanding and acceptance.

Humanizing administration makes it sensitive to public opinion which is the main objective of public relations. The results are:

(1) The purpose of administration is completely reoriented — there is the shift from Rule to Service.

(2) Its functions are enormously increased — in numbers, variety and complexity, and

(3) Its methodology changes from trial and error methods to modern management techniques.

Definition : By "Deliberately planned and sustained effort to establish and maintain mutual understanding between an organization and its *Publics.*"

This is the definition of public relations, the meanings of the vital words in this are:

Deliberate : Because public relations practitioners try to make it clear that the success of their job depends on the premise that nothing should happen by accident. Starting with a set of carefully created objectives, they must ensure that whatever they do after wards will take them accurately and inevitably towards those objectives.

Planned : Because public relations practitioners are always in control of what is being done, nothing is left to chance; so they must work to a plan and on a planned basis. The thought is sufficiently vital for it to demand the double emphasis of 'deliberate' and 'planned'.

Sustained : Because public relations practitioners are always trying to implement a thought or an idea that will remain with the person at whom it has been aimed. The pressure must, therefore, be maintained. Human memories are short. There are many things for people to try and absorb. Sporadic attacks on their consciousness and awareness merely mean that they will tend to forget.

Establish and Maintain : Because it is not difficult to establish a code or policy but not so to maintain its implementation with an undeviating steadiness of purpose.

Understanding : Because of the difficulty in bridging the lawful gap in any process of communication between what the 'sender' means and what the 'receiver' thinks he means — they are not necessarily the same.

Organization : Because no man can work in a vacuum. Everybody works for somebody. A public relations practitioner works for an organization. To put it at its most simple, it is his job to see that the organization is understood and appreciated.

Publics : Because the organization for which the public relations professionals work wants to be understood and appreciated by people around it who affect what it does or are affected by what it does.

Some other Definitions

Edward L. Bernays : "Public Relations is the attempt by information, persuasion and adjustment to engineer public support for an activity, cause, movement or institutions."

John W. Hill : "The management function which gives the same organised and careful attention to the asset of goodwill as is given to any other major asset of business."

Herbert M. Baus : "Public Relations is a combination of philosophy, sociology, economics, language, psychology, journalism, communication and other knowledge into a system of human understanding."

Charles Plackward : "Merely human decency which flows from a good heart."

Robert Heilbroner : "Public relations is Dale Carnegie — winning friends and influencing people-writ large."

***George F. Meredith* (Former President of the American Public Relations Association) :** "Everything involved in achieving a favourable opinion."

***Scot M. Cutlip and Allen H. Center* (Authors of *Effective Public Relations*) :** "The communication and interpretation and the communication and ideas from an institution to its publics and the communication of information, ideas and opinions from those publics to the institution, in a sincere effort to establish a mutuality of interest and this achieves the harmonious adjustment of an institution to its community."

Frank Jefkins(in his book Public Relations in Word Marketing): "Public Relations mean what is says— relations with the public. It aims to create and maintain confidence. It is a system of communication to create goodwill. It produces that intangible quality or asset—goodwill, and earns credit for achievement."

Max K. Adler (One of the most experienced and best known of market researchers) : "Its object is not to sell a product but to produce a favourable image of a company and improve on it, if necessary."

K. R. Balan (Professor of Public Relations) : "The profession which does not make you consent without your consent by highlighting the rewards of 'mutual understanding' and the risks in 'Misunderstanding' between individuals, groups, governments and nations in this restless world of "Man, The Unknown" is considered to be Public Relations."

The International Public Relations Association : "Public Relations is a management function of a continuing and planned character, through which public and private organisations seek to win and retain the understanding, sympathy and support of those with whom they are— or may be—concerned by evaluating public opinion about themselves, in order to correlate, as far as possible their own policies and procedures, to achieve by planned and widespread information more productive cooperation and more efficient fulfilment of this common interest."

The Official Gazette of the French Government : The duties of a public relations practitioner whether he belongs to the staff of a firm or is an independent consultant, are to devise and submit to the firms or organisations employing his service the means of establishing and maintaining good relations, based on mutual confidence, with the public and keeping to be informed of their achievements and, more generally, of all matters relating to their operations. These duties may also be extended to include the relations of firms with their own staff. The public relations practitioner is responsible for implementing the recommended policy and for measuring results...."

The Fine Art of Public Relations : PR is not the job of the Public Relations Officer alone, PR is everybody's business— a privilege if performed, and if not, an opportunity missed.

Public Relations has certainly emerged as one of the most potent and essential tools of modern management. This art is by no means new to India. Three centuries before the birth of Christ, we had Ashoka's inscriptions on the pillars in different parts of his empire in the local scripts, which were essentially to inform the people about his policies and to create goodwill. This was an example of PR, which took into account the need to approach people in their own language.

What is PR? Some half-truths : People seem to have some strange notions about PR men. According to some, the PR men are a breed of people who wangle things for you by most questionable methods. For others, PR men spend time in 'wining and dining' and incur fabulous expenses for their organisations. For some others PR is an effort to cover up the sins of an organisation. In the modern competitive environment, we all know that these notions have no basis in reality and are at best only half-truths.

Advertising, Publicity and Public Relations : PR is sometimes confused with Advertising and Publicity. Advertising is defined as a paid form of non-personal communication, about an organisation and/or its products, that is transmitted to a target audience through a mass medium. The basic objectives are to inform, to persuade, to solicit, to appeal or to remind the market. Publicity, on the other hand, can be defined as "non-personal stimulation of demand for a product, service, or business unit by planting commercially significant news about it in a published medium or obtaining favourable presentation of it upon radio, TV etc., that is not paid for by the sponsor." Since an average reader assumes that the information conveyed emanates not from the commercial communicator but from the staff of the medium itself, the credibility and acceptability of such information is likely to be more than in the case of advertising.

While advertising is, all tongue and no ears (that is, it is a one-way communication) PR is the eyes and ears guiding the tongue since it helps understand expectation, wants, aspirations and diagnose the various causes for complaint, guiding and providing an appropriate response to them.

Publicity is certainly one of the instruments of PR but it would be as wrong to equate publicity with PR as it would be to equate the stethoscope with the practice of modern medicine.

Need for PR : Need for PR is inherent in the very nature of modern society. Society is made up of many groups of people, each with its own interests which are sometimes conflicting. The harmonious functioning of such a society needs the help of PR.

People are conscious of their rights as citizens, as consumers, or as employees. Managements are aware of what Philip Lesley, the famous PR consultant, terms as the 'people factor' in all management decisions and actions. All these call for PR.

Managements realise that it is also their responsibility vigilantly to develop consciousness towards fulfilling legitimate public expectations and to be honest and considerate in all their dealings with various publics.

In PR, the word public is generally used plurally, to denote that there are several identifiable, independent, homogeneous groups with which an organisation has to deal. They are the shareholders, government, central parliament, state legislature, local bodies, customers, competitors, dealers, suppliers, press, the community around, our own employees and so on.

PR for Whom? : It is an approach to problems that is equally valid for all commercial companies/organisations, non-profit academic institutions like Universities. Service Organisations like LIC and Hospitals, Local, State and National Governments, Political Parties, Trade Unions and even Religious Bodies. In fact, PR was first practised by the Army in the First World War.

Communication with Publics : The press is the most powerful medium of communication. If we get a favourable press, half the public relations battle is won.

For an effective consumer PR, an awareness amongst all employees of our organisation about the need to deal with consumers with courtesy, openness and promptitude is primarily needed. Some standing arrangements to handle customer complaints are to be made. Complaints must be immediately acknowledged with a promise to investigate. We must not cover up failures but must get at the truth and work out remedial measures. If we are at fault, there must be no hesitation to apologise and offer remedial steps. Even if the complaints are frivolous or groundless we should send a polite reply explaining the position. A mistake honestly admitted and with promise of corrective action will always have a soothing effect and establish our credibility.

PR involves lobbying and maintaining relations with legislators, government officials and community leaders. We can thus participate in community affairs and contribute to local causes like maintenance of parks, help some school activity or sponsor sports competitions.

Employee Relations : A satisfied work-force is a valuable asset and the overall success of an organisation can be favourably or otherwise affected by its relations with employees. The successful PR of an organisation with its staff depends on factors like pro-active personnel and industrial relations, satisfactory recruitment policies, proper selection, training and development of staff and providing good working conditions and adequate financial rewards etc.

2

Basic Concepts

The first actual use of the phrase 'public relations' was made by President Thomas Jefferson in 1807. While drafting his Seventh Address' to the Congress, he scratched out the words 'state of thought' in one place and wrote 'public relations' instead.

The Origin

Though it would appear that Public Relations owes its origin to President Thomas Jefferson, history points out illuminating examples set by some whose names have gone down its pages. They did not know it was public relations that they were practising. They went about doing good for those who came under their purview. These were recorded in history as an act of doing good to the people by freeing them from oppression and the like.

Queen Elizabeth I of England who came to the throne in 1558 at 25 years of age had no previous administrative experience of any description.

To realize what she was faced with, one has to consider the conditions that existed at the time. The kingdom was torn with dissension—both political and religious. The national sport was violence. The leaders of the different factions were ready to revolt on any pretext. Communications hardly existed. Elizabeth had no police force, no standing army and her subjects had nothing but disdain for women in public life. Society was geared to strong-arm methods.

Yet Elizabeth controlled the country for 45 years. She raised it from a third rate power to a first-rate one. By the time she had completed her reign, she was the most popular monarch that had ever sat on the throne. Possibly many people realize this because it is emphasized only in history books. What is not realized, it seems, that how she accomplished it.

The first thing she did on taking office was to appoint people for their ability, without regard to their background or position. Indeed, this dedicated body of men who, in most cases, have long been forgotten by history, were not only her administrators but also her public relations men. They, in turn, surrounded themselves with men of like dedication whose main object was to explain to the people what the government was trying to do. Elizabeth, herself, spent half the time she was on the throne, travelling up and down the country on appalling roads, listening to complaints of her subjects and explaining what she was trying to do.

The result was that, although many leaders in the country rose in revolt against her during the 45 years of her reign, none succeeded in becoming even a moderate threat. The man in the street would not support them. He believed that the Queen was doing what was right and proper for the country having regard to the then existing conditions.

This was borne out when Spain—the greatest country in the West at that time—declared war on England. The people rose up and armed themselves to defend their country. The Queen appeared in front of her army, dressed in armour, and she said this to them: "Although I am only a woman, I am also your Queen and I have come to lead you. If necessary, I will die with you."

This so inspired these very rough men that they accomplished feats quite beyond their normal capabilities.

When you consider how difficult it was in those days to convey a message to an individual—far more to a whole nation—Elizabeth's career must stand as be of the greatest Public Relations campaigns over carried out. The men who did it have long since been forgotten. But their job was not to make themselves, but to make an individual famous.

The study of the origin of public relations provides a helpful insight into its functions, its strengths and weaknesses. The history is a fascinating story. But a comprehensive history remains to be written. Published histories have been telescoped and oversimplified. There has been an overemphasis on novelty, and on a few of the many colourful personalities. Even a slight probing of history will quickly dull the sheen of novelty often given to public relations.

The effort to deal with the force of opinion and to communicate with others goes back to antiquity. Only the tools, degree of specialisation, breath of knowledge and intensity of effort required today are relatively new. Increased specialisation and emphasis give the delusion of newness.

The span of history has extended over many decades. The factors, including its origin and development, are many and complex. The turbulent stream of history rushes along in a manner that defies neat cataloguing. The history of public relations cannot be told by simply saying that it grew out of press agentry. Nor can it be fully told in terms of the initial influential career of an Ivy Lee. The power of public opinion to control human affairs has been recognized down through the centuries. Although the phrase 'Public Opinion' was not coined until the eighteenth century, the force of peoples' opinion was demonstrated and recognized in ancient times. With recognition of the power of peoples' opinions, there came, in response, practices which we now call 'public relations'. They were of a most rudimentary sort, to be sure. Public opinion played a part in shaping events among the early Greeks and Romans, even though the publics were small in size and number, and channels of expression limited, and the communications crude.

The Greek theorists studied the importance of the public will; even though they did not use specifically the term 'public relations'. The urban culture of ancient Roman Empire gave scope to the opinion process through certain phrases and ideas in the political vocabulary of the Romans and in the writings the medieval period related to modern concepts of public opinion. The Romans inscribed upon their walls the slogan "S.P.Q.R.", "the Senate and the Roman people". Later, the Romans discovered the expression Vox Populi, Vox Dei, 'the Voice of the people is the voice of God.' Machiavelli held that the people must either be caressed or annihilated.

Efforts to communicate information to influence viewpoints or actions likewise can be traced from the earliest civilizations. Archaeologists found a farm bulletin in Iraq which told the farmers of 1800 B.C. how to sow their crops, how to irrigate, how to deal with field mice, how to harvest their crops. This effort was not like today's distribution of farm bulletins by our department of agriculture.

Much of what is known of ancient Egypt, Assyria and Persia, was recorded as efforts to publicise and glorify the rulers of that day. There is nothing strange about it; for, even today we come across State governments run by different political parties vying with each other to buy one, two or even three full-page space from the media to publicise their achievements with the 'chief ministers' pictures in the centre position !

Indian Roots

In the Sanskrit drama, "Shakuntala" written by the great poet Kalidasa, there is a 'scene' in which he has mentioned about a sea-trade merchant who died in a shipwreck. He is said to have died intestate. Having received confirmation about the rich merchant's death, the finance minister in the court of King Dushyanta submitted a "note" to the King informing him of the sad event and recommending that all the properties of the deceased be acquired by the State as he had left no heirs to inherit his properties.

King Dushyanta did not take immediate action on the minister's recommendation. He applied his mind, and then sent for the minister and told him: "The deceased being one of the wealthiest merchants engaged in overseas trade he might have married more than one wife; if so, where are they living, and whether any of them is in fairly way."

On making discreet enquiries, as ordered by the King, the finance minister could find out one of his wives who was, in reality, carrying a baby to be delivered soon. The matter was reported to the King who immediately arranged to issue an'order'that all the properties should devolve on the baby to be born soon ! Thus Public Relations and its concept of practice have been in existence in India from time immemorial, perhaps even before the Westerners had knowledge of its philosophy.

In the 18th century, Shri Adi Sankara, the greatest religious leader, went about from place to place, engaging himself in discussions and disputations with leaders of different creeds and sects with his superb dialectical skill deflating false dogmas and shattering erroneous presumptions. Sankara Bhagwan travelled throughout the length and breadth of the subcontinent as many as four times and established five monasteries, one each at Sringeri and Kanchipuram in the South, Dwarka in the West, Badrinath in the North and Puri in the East.

Similarly, Swami Vivekananda, a disciple of Sri Ramakrishna Paramhamsa, wandered all over India, from the Himayalas to Kanyakumari, to have a firsthand knowledge about his motherland and to offer solutions to the problems of the people. This pilgrimage of Vivekananda was one of the most significant events of his life and is of great value to public relations professionals to enlarge on "mass communication".

What of saints like Thiagaraja, Kabir, Tulsidas, Tukaram, Purandara Dasa, Dyaneswar, Pothana, Chaitanya Mahaprabhu who diffused knowledge through the traditional media of communication in the language which the people easily understood.

How could the great Public Relations personality of the 20th century, Mahatma Gandhi, create such implicit faith among the Indian classes as well as the masses to join hands for achieving political independence ? How could beloved Bapu succeed in his mission of waging a bloodless "war" against the then mighty British Empire? Bapu believed in establishing contact with those in India and abroad. He wrote thousands and thousands of words in his "Young India" and "Harijan"; travelled the length and breadth of India; organized many meetings; spoke and talked tirelessly until be had reasons to believe that the country had understood his mission and what each Indian had to do to strengthen his hands. His pattern of public relations practice (although Bapu did not say he was practising Public Relations) and his communication with his followers was based on the concept of credibility. This credibility over the period of years generated "mutual understanding" between him and his countrymen. ("Mutual understanding" is the core of Public Relations.)

In New Guinea there are many tribes. Among them are Khunghli and Khungha. If a person belonging to Khungha happened to cause' death, wilfully or accidentally, to one of Khungbli, the leaders of both the tribes call for a Panchayat Meeting, and pass a resolution that the Khungha member bear all the expenses connected with the funeral, and on the top of it, convey 72 pigs, 9 parrots, one cow and a bottle of arrack. This is with a view to prevent the growth of animosity between the two tribes arising out of the sad incident.

The first stage of Public Relations begins with the United States of America to which the world owes the modern development of PR. The study of various developments in the USA shows various stages of its gradual development. According to Scott Cutlip, PR began in America in the 16th century when Sir Walter Raleigh persuaded people from various parts of America to settle in rural Virginia in pursuance of his land settlement policy. Then, the first organized effort was made to win and mobilize public opinion with the American Revolution.

The next stage came with the American Constitution. According to Dr. Cutlip, the declaration of Independence is a PR document written out of respect for the opinions of mankind. The American civil war also helped the advancement of PR in the sense that the opposing parties were represented to the public through public relations.

According to Dr. Cutlip, PR began to develop in the 1880's because this was the beginning of American industrialisation. Next 25 years witnessed the advancement of PR due to the advancement in the field of communications. Also, in 1896 Presidential candidates used PR as means to reach the masses.

In 1900, the first PR consultancy known as 'Publicity Bureau' was formed in Boston. In 1915, Ivy Lee made his declaration on truthful recording of facts on behalf of Pennsylvania Rail-road Company for handling the Rail-road accidents. The success he achieved proved important in recognizing the force underlying the PR movement.

The period from 1929 to 1941 was marked by tremendous economic, social and political changes in America and around the world. They were accompanied by propaganda, publicity, and PR on a scale never known before. As a result of the depression (1929-33), PR activities were greatly enlarged. Business now realised the need to explain its contributions to the entire economic system.

As the decade came to a close, Europe was already engaged in the Second World War. In 1941, the armed force? became interested in PR. People had to be formally educated in it and PR journals were Started in 1944. The importance of PR had developed by the fifties.

As in many other countries, PR in India has passed through a number of phases as the profession has developed to meet changing needs. Long before the newspapers and other media came on the scene, great men like Shankara spread their messages throughout the country through the traditional media of communication. Mahatma Gandhi, the greatest communicator of our time, used prayer meetings and "Pada Yatras" as the vehicles to convey his message. As such, public relations is not new to India.

The history of ancient India shows that the kings also felt the need to have good public relations with their public. Rulers were doing something to influence public opinion by appointing Information Officers or PR men.

Although a formal history of PR in India is yet to be written, we can trace the development of PR in India in the following four phases. Each phase represents certain objective needs of the situation.

Modern Era

The first phase covers the period from the nineties of the last century to the beginning of the Second World War when PR was not practised in a deliberate manner, but from a policy of philanthropy or out of sheer necessity to provide information. The notable example in this regard is the House of Tata. Another example of PR in India during that period is provided by the Indian Railways.

The Tata Iron and Steel Company went into production in 1912. From the very beginning, the House of Tata started practising community relations by building Jamshedpur as a model township. They paid attention to the social, cultural and economic development of the society. The establishment of Jamshedpur township with facilities of water, electricity and schools is an outstanding example of good community relations.

During the First World War in order to disseminate information about the war the Government set up the "Central Publicity Board" in 1920. Later this name was changed to "Publicity Bureau" and it was shifted to Simla. It consisted of representatives of Army, Air Force, Navy and foreign political departments with the Ministry of Foreign and External Affairs. In 1921, the government established a body called 'Central Bureau of Information' which gave information other than war information. In 1935, this bureau was merged with the Directorate of Public Instruction. It was changed to Directorate of Information and Broadcasting in 1939. Then, this directorate gradually developed.

When the railways came to India in the 1920's as private enterprise, it was felt necessary to attract people to travel by trains. So, the publicity of railways was started and primary effort was made by the G.I.P Railways. The other railway companies also started organising PR activities by showing films and by extensively advertising in newspapers and journals. All these developments marked the birth of PR activities in India.

After the Second World War, PR in India entered the stage of a conscious activity. This was in response to a number of new factors, such as the emergence of a vocal public opinion for a total war effort. The Indian public was in general, against the war. A Department of Information and Broadcasting was created to carry on systematic campaigns for such measures as recruitment of defence forces, price control and rationing of foodgrains. The Department comprised a number of units such as the War Purposes Exhibition Unit, the Films Division, and the Central Bureau of Public Information.

Simultaneously, certain commercial organizations, which had already been practising public relations in an unconscious manner, began organising their PR activities in a conscious way. For example, the House of Tatas formed a Public Relations Division at their Head Office in Bombay in 1945. Many other organisations, during this period, conducted institutional campaigns in the Press to win public support and sympathy for their efforts.

In Free India

The third phase of PR development is represented by the Post-Independence period. As a result of independence and the emergence of new political, social, economic and cultural institutions, PR activities developed. New programmes were brought out and several media came into existence. The two important factors responsible for the boosting of PR activities in the Post-Independence period were the emergence of institutions of Parliament and State Legislatures and the adoption by the government of the Industrial Policy Resolution and the Industrial (Development and Regulation) Act.

The Government of India felt the need to inform the masses of its policies and programmes in all spheres of national development in order to win public confidence and cooperation. The Ministry of Information and Broadcasting set up different departments like Publications Division, Films Division, etc., for two way communication between people and the government.

With the Industrial Revolution and the expansion of industrial and business activities expansion of PR was necessitated. Business had also realised the necessity to adjust itself to the new situations.

In 1958, PR Society of India (PRSI) was established to promote public relations as a profession and to formulate a Code of Ethics of PR. PRSI has nine chapters in different parts of the country. The Society is recognised as the national PR organization by the International Public Relations Association and is one of the founder members of the PanPacific Public Relations Federation.

Evolution and Development

The next phase saw the formation of professional organizations of public relations practitioners in various parts of the country, notably Bombay and Calcutta. The Public Relations Society of India was formed in Bombay in 1958. A few years later, the Public Relations Circle in Calcutta reorganized itself as the local chapter of PRSI.

Although a few localised courses in PR had previously been run it was not until April 1968 when the first Public Relations Conference was held in Delhi through which an organized effort was made to win national recognition; for, Public Relations Circle in Calcutta reorganised itself as the local chapter of PR as a profession. It was at this conference that a Code of Ethics was adopted and the parameters of the PR profession defined.

The Second Public Relations Conference dwelt on the status of PR practitioners in respective organisations. Judging from the large participation from public sector companies, it was apparent that an awareness had been created, particularly in government, that its public relations force needed to be more effectively and meaningfully utilised.

The next stage in the development of public relations was a proper understanding of the nature of the environment in the country and the changes that constantly take place. It was the topic of the Third Conference.

The theme of the Fourth Public Relations Conference was 'Towards a More Responsible Citizenship', underlining the need for meaningful and purposeful contribution of PR practitioners to the development of a healthier society.

With the rapid growth of the PR profession in India and the entry of an increasingly large number of men and women into the PR field, an urgent need was felt to emphasise professionalism. The Fifth All India Public Relations Conference was devoted to discussions in depth on the ways and means of achieving greater professionalism. 'PR in the Eighties' was the theme of the Sixth All India Public Relation; Conference held in Cochin in January 1978. The very choice of the theme was a measure of the growth and maturity of the profession in India.

The development of PR activities in India is indicative of the acceptance of PR as an important function of management. These activities are engaging attention of all commercial and progressive organisations both in private and public sectors.

Public relations movement in India has travelled a long way since the early days when it was fighting for recognition as a profession. It was then regarded only as a junior partner of publicity and was generally ignored. And now it has come to stay with us.

Today, there are Public Relations 'chapters' in Bombay, Ahmedabad,, New Delhi, Kanpur, Calcutta, Visakhapatnam, Hyderabad, Bangalore, Madras, and Cochin. More 'chapters' are likely to be organised in other areas like Assam. The 'chapters are affiliated to the National Council of Public Relations Society of India. The headquarters of the National Council moves from 'chapter' centres in consonance with the workplace of the 'President' who is elected by the Central Body of the National Council Members, generally once in two years.

That public relations profession has earned the credibility of the government also can be noted from the fact that a 3-year degree course was inaugurated by the University of Madras, way back in 1975. How dedicatedly the "public relations society of India's" senior professionals were involved will be discernible from the Vice-Chancellor's kind remarks in his "Foreword" to this book.

And that India now stands at par with other Western countries in attaining professional excellence is proved by the International Public Relations Association (IPRA) having accepted our invitation to hold the 9th Public Relations World Congress in Bombay.

(The International Public Relations Association (IPRA) was founded in 1955. It is a worldwide and fraternal organization.)

The 1st World Congress was held in Brussels in 1958, the 2nd in Venice in 1961, the 3rd in Montreal in 1964, the 4th in Rio de Janeiro in 1967, the 5th in Tel Aviv in 1970, the 6th in Geneva in 1973, the 7th in Boston in 1976, the 8th in London in 1979, and the 9th in Bombay in 1982, between January 19 and 23.

The 9th World Congress in Bombay was attended by nearly 900 delegates from as many as 36 countries. Some of the overseas delegates were accompanied by their spouses, and there were few Nobel Laureates. These personalities contributed a great deal to cross-fertilize their ideas not only on the problems and prospects relating to public relations and communication profession but also on subjects which concern the world today: science and technology, energy and ecology, education and the like. Thus the theme of the Congress happened to be Interdependent World. Because it was an international 'Congress', such a theme was considered to be appropriate. At the same time, it was in tune with our country's heritage and philosophy on the importance of "interdependence". "Interdependence" in this context means "mutual dependence" aimed at each other's benefit.

Achievements of the 9th Public Relations World Congress

1. Without exception, perhaps, the overseas delegates felt this was one of the best World Congresses on Public Relations. It is appropriate to quote Ms Denny Griswold, Editor of "Public Relations News", published from U.S.A. During her discussion with my good friend, Jolly Mohan Kaul, Editor of "Capital", Calcutta, in February 1982, she told him: "...that this 9th Public Relations. World Congress was one of the best, and that those who would be organizing the next one in Amsterdam in 1985, would have a difficult task to match up to this one."
2. Media and 'management' support was the best accorded to any great event of this nature.
3. The real achievements are that the theme "The Interdependent World" could lift the role of public relations from the hitherto conventional sense in which it was discerned and change the notion that public relations is everything else in the negative sense—but public relations.
4. We could focus the attention of Indian public relations practitioners on the need to enhance their professionalism, and recognize the wider scope of this discipline in our growing country.

Some Benefits

1. We could demonstrate the wealth of talents, communication skills, and the sustained steps taken to spread Public Relations Education and awareness among public and Drivate sectors as well as educational institutions and academies.
2. The involvement of IPRA is sure to give the public relations profession in India tremendous mileage and recognition.
3. All the overseas delegates will be effective spokesmen on India. Thus they would be our effective communicators. Delegates to such International Congresses are always able to create better goodwill abroad for us than the

conventional tourists, and here again, public relations practitioners can be better ambassadors in their own right as communicators.

4. The six 'live case studies' showing the problems that public relations practitioners were confronted with, and how they attempted to tackle them and with what results, were really useful to the other practitioners including those in India. And the Public Relations Exhibition was really educative.

The Perception

The word 'public' which is found in this book throughout refers to any group of people who share a common interest. The employees of a company are an example of a public—good pay, the company's stability and future, and the opportunity for advancement are a few of the common interests of members of a company. Some publics, such as employees, are part of an organization; these are called 'internal public'. Such publics as those who buy the products or service of the company are called 'external public'. The internal and external publics will differ from one kind of organization to another.

The public from whom opinion emanates is a varied creature. It comes in many forms and sizes and has a multitude of wants and desires. For example : Employees always desire for more and more remuneration and other benefits; the employers, in turn, look for corresponding production increase. The Government always expects to collect more taxes to meet the expenditure connected with its aim of rendering social justice ; the citizens desire the taxes to be kept down to the minimum. The politicians desire to cling fast to the office of power until death doth retire them, and the public which voted them to power is interested in their performance. Each of these groups is a public of a sort, and tries to attract a distinct audience.

"Relations" is the outcome of mutual understanding derived from the process of sharing of the "common interest". By integration of these two human dements, *viz.*, "Public" and "Relations" we get "Public Relations", which has been accepted the world over as Management function.

Public Relations furnishes means whereby we, as individuals, groups and nations can reach out to others, extend ourselves, tell our stories, in today's complex, complicated—but still great world. In a world that constantly grows bigger, more streamlined, faster and more complicated, the need for self-expression becomes more difficult to fulfil. Hence tensions and conflicts between nations, groups, classes and economic strata arise. How we, the public relations professionals, are to go about their duties will be quite discernible from the definition.

"Public relations is the deliberate, planned, and sustained effort to establish and maintain mutual understanding between an organization and its publics."

The most vital words which the definition contains are clarified below :

The meaning of the vital words in the definition are :

Deliberate : because public relations practitioners try to make it clear that the success of their job depends on the promise that nothing should happen by accident. Starting with a set of carefully created objectives they must ensure that whatever they do afterwards will take them accurately and inevitably towards those objectives.

Planned : because a public relations practitioner is always in control of what is being done, nothing is left to chance ; so he must work to a plan and on a planned basis. The thought is sufficiently vital for it to demand the double emphasis of "deliberate" and "planned".

Sustained : because a public relations practitioner is always trying to implement a thought or an idea that will remain with the person at whom it has been aimed. The pressure must therefore be maintained. Human memories are short. There are many things for people to try and absorb. Sporadic attacks on their consciousness and awareness merely mean that will tend to forget easily.

Understanding : because of the difficulty in bridging the awful gap in any process of communication between what the 'sender' means and what the 'receiver' thinks he means ; they are not necessarily the same.

Organization : because no man can work in a vacuum. Everybody works for somebody. A public relations practitioner works for an organization—a government, business, charity or any other. To put it at its most simple, it is his job to see that the organization is understood and appreciated.

Publics : because the organization for which the public relations practitioner works wants to be understood and appreciated by the people around it, who affect what it *does* or are affected by what it does.

The integration of the two human elements, 'Public' and 'Relations'; form Public Relations.

Possibly the most important of all the words in the definition is 'understanding. Without it, the public relations man can achieve nothing. At the same time, it is a mistake to try to learn them profession. It is best to try to find alternative words to explain them, to make the meaning clear to the person reading or hearing the definition. Words mean different things to different people. To an antagonist of public relations it is easy to regard the words as baleful and sinister. A protagonist will regard them as sharp and packed with meaning.

The induction of public relations practice in an organization will give us the following definition:

> The management function which evaluates attitudes, identifies the policies and procedures of an organization with the public interest, and executes a programme of action to earn public understanding and acceptance.

It will now be obvious that public relations is an applied social and behavioural science in that it:

1. measures, evaluates, and interprets the attitude of various relevant publics ;
2. assists management in defining objectives for increasing public understanding and acceptance of the organization's products, plans, policies and personnel;
3. equates these objectives with the interests, needs, and goals of the various relevant publics, and
4. develops, executes, and evaluates a programme to earn public understanding and acceptance.

Having regard to the political, economic and social environment in which the product of "mutual understanding" is the means to gain acceptance in the marketplace of "public", public relations as a management and advisory function has to be won, not by words but by deeds of the professional communicators who have proved the value of their work in all walks of life.

The Meaning

The definition accepted by the public relations professionals as defined by the Institute of Public Relations is : "Public Relations is the deliberate, planned ana sustained effort to establish and maintain mutual understanding between an organization and its publics."

Peter Hiddlecombe in his "International Public Relations Encyclopedia" published by Grant Helm gives definitions coined by experts the select ones of which are:

Edward L. Bernays : 'Public Relations is the attempt by information persuasion and adjustment to engineer public support for an activity, cause, movement or institution.

John W. Hill : 'The management function which gives the same organized and careful attention to the asset of goodwill as is given to any other major asset of business.'

Herbert M. Bans : 'Public Relations is a combination of philosophy, sociology, economics, language, psychology, journalism, communication and other knowledges into a system of human understanding.'

Charles Plackard : 'Merely human decency which flows from a good heart.'

Fortune (Magazine): 'Good performance, publicly appreciated because adequately communicated.'

Robert Heilbroner : 'Public Relations is Dale Carnegie—winning friends and influencing people—writ large.

George F. Meredith (Former President of the American Public Relation Association) : 'Everything involved in achieving a favourable opinion.'

The International Public Relations Association, The Hague, May 1960 : 'Public Relations is a management function, of a continuing and planned character, through which public and private organizations seek to win and retain the understanding, sympthy and support of those with whom they are—or may be—concerned by evaluating public opinion about themselves, in order to correlate, as far as possible, their own policies and procedures, to achieve by planned and widespread information more productive cooperation and more efficient fulfilment of their common interests.'

Carl Byoir : (one of the most successful U.S. publicists) : Public Relations is whatever the individual practitioner thinks it is.'

Scot M. Cutlip and Allen H. Center (Authors of "Effective Public Relations") : 'The communication and interpretation and the communication and ideas from an institution to its publics and the communication of information, ideas and opinions from those publics to the institution, is a sincere effort to establish a mutuality of interest and this achieves the harmonious adjustment of an institution to its community.'

Max K. Adler (one of the most experienced and best known of market researchers) : 'Its object is not to sell a product, but to produce a favourable image of a company and improve on it, if necessary.'

Frank Jefkins (in his book 'Public Relations in World Marketing'): P.R. means what it says—relations with the public. It is practically a self-defining term. It aims to create and maintain confidence. It is a system of communication to create goodwill. It produces that intangible quality or asset—goodwill, and earns credit for achievements.'

The Ministry of Information, French Government, Official Text dated October 23, 1964, which appeared in The Journal Official de la Republic Francaise, The Official Gazette of the French Government: 'The duties of a public relations practitioner whether he belongs to the staff of a firm or is an independent consultant, are to devise and submit to the firms or organizations employing his service the means of establishing and maintaining good relations, based on mutual confidence, with the public and keeping it informed of their achievements and, more generally, of all matters relating to their operations. These duties may also be extended to include the relations of firms with their own staff. The public relations practitioner is responsible for implementing the recommended policy and for measuring results.

'The information he supplies about the organization must in all cases carry mention of its source, be strictly objective and be absolutely free of propaganda, commercial publicity or advertising content. The Press Officer carries out the duties defined above as a specialist in relations with the following information media : Press, films, radio and television. The duties of a public relations practitioner and of a Press Officer are compatible with their practising at the same time as a professional journalist or advertising agent. The only remuneration for public relations or Press work shall be the fees of the client or salary of the employer on whose account this work is undertaken.'

This translation by Claude Chapeau appeared in 'Eleven Years of Public Relations', a brochure prepared by Galeries Orleanzises, France, and published in April 1965.

In 1969 the British definition was accepted by a Select Committee of the House of Commons set up to consider the Declaration of Members' Interests, when a deputation of the Institute of Public Relations headed by Herbert Lloyd gave evidence before it.

Lucien Matrat (Public Relations Manager of Union Industrielle de PetrolesUlP and Council Member of the International Public Relations Association) : 'Public relations is a mode of behaviour and a manner of conveying information with the object of establishing and maintaining mutual confidence, based on mutual knowledge and understanding, between an organization—a corporate body carrying out various functions or activities—and the different sections of the public, internal and external, that are affected by some or all of these functions or activities.'

K.R. Balan (Professor of Public Relations) : That profession which does not make you consent without your consent by highlighting the rewards of 'mutual understanding' and the risks in 'misunderstanding between individuals, groups, governments and nations in this restless world of "Man, The Unkown" is considered to be Public Relations.

'The Game of Public Relations Definitions' : It can be deduced from reading through the definitions that the word 'Public Relations' is used in at least three senses. The relationship with those who constitute an organization's publics or constituents, the ways and means to achieve favourable relationships. Thus, the one term is used to label both "means" and "ends" to name a condition and to express the conduct of actions related to that condition.

Although singular in meaning, the term is spelled and spoken as a plural. It is often used interchangeably with Publicity, Advertising, Propaganda, Promotion, Diplomacy, Lobbying and Public Affairs. The term is used as a noun. As an example, "How is your Public Relations" ; as a verb, "They really Public Relationed that situation", and as a modifier, "It was a Public Relations Triumph."

For at least fifty years, practitioners, editors and authors have sought to capture the essence of the function in a phrase, slogan or book title that might catch on popularly and dispel misconceptions. Amongst these are :

> X (the Deed) + Y (the way the Deed is interpreted) = Public Attitude
>
> *Good performance is publicly appreciated.*
>
> PR = Performance and Recognition.
>
> Pathway to public favour.
>
> Crystallizing Public Opinion.
>
> The Engineering of Consent.
>
> The conscience of an organization.
>
> Doing good and getting credit for it.
>
> Deed First, then Words.
>
> Virtue brings its own reward.

Role of Public

For any 'establishment', be it government, business, industry or even religion, there is no such thing as a single public. For most trading corporations the public can be divided into the following sections :

1. Shareholders and potential shareholders of the company ; together with city editors, financial writers, stockbrokers, and others whose opinion on the financial standing of the company is influential.
2. Employees and potential employees of the company, and their families ; appropriate trade unions ; employment officers appointment boards and training officers concerned with advice on careers.
3. Suppliers and potential suppliers of raw materials and other goods or services to the company; any trade associations to which these suppliers belong; subcontractors wherever applicable.

4. Wholesale and retail trade customers and potential customers and any trade associations to which they belong.
5. Consumer customers, actual and potential; a category which may include special classes such as the housewife, the motorist or the sportsman, and also companies which are clients under contract. Under this heading may also be included school children and students (in so far as they eventually become customers) and the teachers who influence them.
6. Other companies in the same industry, and the firm's own trade association.
7. Communities in which the company operates : the authorities and residents of areas who are affected by its physical presence or its activities, in ways other than by purchasing its products. Towns where the company has factories come into this category ; so do places where employment is created or removed in local industry as a result of contracts or subcontracts by the company.

In addition, and running right across the board as it were, is a group covering M.L.As, Members of Parliament, editors, university dons, school teachers, and others who have an importance out of proportion to their numbers because of their power to influence others.

The ways in which the opinions of these groups matter to a company vary in kind and degree, but each can at some time or another become a major factor in its prosperity.

The view taken by investors can make it easy or difficult to raise capital or to succeed in a takeover battle. An impression that the company is "a good firm to work for" can bring it more, better and happier employees. Suppliers who regard the company as "a good firm to do business with" will make their best goods and services available. Potential customers are more likely to buy from a company which is well known, well-spoken of, and whose products or services are recommended. People who find the company behave as a good neighbour will be more interested in sending their sons and daughters to work for it, and in providing the amenities it wants to develop its business. Politicians and leaders of opinion assume particular significance in the case of companies for which monopoly, nationalization or a specific tax are live issues.

A company which tries to use PR for an isolated purpose—to stimulate consumer sales or to spur on recruiting, for instance will find itself disproportionately handicapped compared with the company which looks on its PR as a single, integrated policy, it may also be disappointed with the results, for the reputation of acompany cannot be split in this way. In the long run, for example, it would be foolish to seek acceptance for even a good product while ignoring bad labour relations at the factory.

If general management were doing its job efficiently, should it not be tackling public relations in its stride ? Why should a company employ special staff, whether on its own payroll or as consultants, and allocate a special budget to this work ?

The job of the professional PR man is threefold :

1. To keep management informed of public opinion, and of events and trends likely to affect its reputation.
2. To advise management on the policies and actions it should adopt in order to gain and keep goodwill; and on the likely effects, in terms of public opinion, of any policies and actions dictated by other factors. (Goodwill, leading to cooperation, will be considered in terms of specific objectives in the sector concerned; such as, acceptance of a new product or high standard of recruits.)
3. To apply PR techniques to solve problems in which the company's reputation is at stake (and this can be virtually always), and to maintain a continuing, positive programme of action to secure goodwill, presenting the company in all its aspects to all its audiences by every appropriate medium of communication (good behaviour cannot be appreciated until it is known). This executive side of PR

man's work includes the company's relations with the Press, radio, television; the production of many kinds of printed matter, including company reports, house magazines, wallcharts, brochures and even books; films and filmstrips; exhibitions; the design of company stationery; the way the firm receives its visitors; a watching brief on the way it answers its telephone calls, writes its "letters, handles complaints; its policy on donations to charity; and an infinite variety of items beyond.

3

Public Opinion

A 'public', from the standpoint of public opinion, is a group of people with similar interests who have a common opinion on a controversial subject. A group of workers confronted with the controversial question of whether to strike or not to strike is a public with a similar interest in employment, involved in the process of forming public opinion. On the other hand, the same group of workers standing at a bus stop and unanimously agreeing on the perfect weather is not involved in public opinion formation, as no controversial question confronts the group.

The Definition

'Opinion', according to Webster's Seventh New Collegiate Dictionary, is "a view, judgement, or appraisal formed in the mind about a particular matter." An opinion is stronger than an impression and weaker than positive knowledge. It implies a conclusion thought out, yet open to dispute. A more or less settled opinion is a 'sentiment' and, if held firmly, a 'conviction'. A 'view' is an opinion more or less coloured by bias.

Public opinion is an expression of a belief held in common by members of a group or public on a controversial issue of general importance. The public opinion forming process emanates from the expressed individual opinions of members of a group whose views are subjected to the influences exerted by the group.

Public opinion is usually expressed after controversy, dispute, and debate over some controversial question which concerns the welfare, doctrines, and value system of a group. For public opinion to be aroused, there must exist a contemporary issue or question of some concern about which members of the group are likely to have disagreement. An issue is a situation or occurrence which threatens to disturb the prevailing mores of a group, creating more or less of a crisis and arousing discussion and the expression of public opinion. Civil rights in India, notably after the last 'national emergency', is one such issue which has begun to confront the Indian public. The testing of nuclear materials in the atmosphere is an international issue which causes people throughout the world to take affirmative or negative positions on the question. The visits of Jimmy Carter and James Callaghan to India early in 1978 January, have some relevance to this.

Public opinion is not simply the opinion of the majority of a group. On each issue the interested public will divide itself into two or more differing points of view which will not necessarily be contradictory or mutually exclusive. The number of views that can be differentiated, however, will be a function of the attitudes and previous experiences of the individuals making up the public as well as a function of the complexity of the issue. The opinion must be representative of the group as a whole. Thus, public opinion is the complex of beliefs expressed by a significant number of persons on an issue of general importance.

The Approaches

The basic objective of public relations is to measure, analyse, and influence public opinion, which develops from the attitudes of individuals comprising the public. Therefore, it is important to understand the meaning of attitudes, why people hold the attitudes they do, and their role in the opinion forming process.

Attitudes are the feelings or moods of a person for or against some person, organization, issue, or object. They represent the predisposition of an individual to evaluate controversial questions in a favourable or unfavourable manner. Simply stated, an attitude is a way of looking at situations. An expressed attitude is an opinion.

New Trends

Changes in attitude occur when an existing attitude no longer provides a person with satisfaction or when his aspirations are raised. Changes in attitude are accomplished by communications to create new beliefs or by appealing to the emotions to arouse favourable or unfavourable attitudes. Changes in attitude are also brought about by problems, frustrations, or dissatisfaction of an individual with his cherished beliefs, self-image, economic status, value system, and other circumstances. A worker satisfied with his wages and working conditions may change his attitude toward his employer after listening to a labour-leader describe the need for increased wages and better working conditions. Appeals to the physical, social and economic needs of people are most effective in changing their attitude.

Psychological Phenomenon

Attitudes and their expression in the form of opinions are psychological phenomena of the individual. A group is capable of not forming an opinion. Since a group cannot form an opinion, how is public opinion formulated ?

Public opinion is formed by individuals composing a group, who express their own opinion on a controversial issue. Public opinion is a composite opinion resulting from the interaction of the individual opinions of members of a group. The transformation of individual opinion into public opinion, by group stimuli, is a distinctive characteristic of the public opinion process. This metamorphosis is sometimes referred to as the group mind, in which is combined the opinions of individuals in the group, converted into public opinion.

The "Dictionary of Mass Communications" defines public opinion as the expression of all members of a group who are giving attention in any way to a given issue. The process starts with an interaction of individual attitudes, mind, sets, and beliefs concerning an issue. It is essentially the product of a collective mental life, which, in a democracy, includes the expression of the majority, if there be a minority, and the minority at any given time.

Public opinion involves a transformation of individual opinion into group opinion, brought about by the influence exerted by members of a group on the individual's opinion. The opinions of people in a group are influenced by what they hear from opinion leaders, other members of the group, or persons outside the group; what they read in newspapers, magazines, and books; what they see in life about them or on television. Apart from group pressures, individuals' opinions are influenced by their needs, emotions, experience, heredity, culture, economic status, and education. Out of the interaction of individual attitudes, opinions, and the opinions of the group emerges public opinion.

Group Influences of Individual Opinion : An individual who is a member of a group manifests certain characteristics in his thinking and behaviour which contribute to the formation of public opinion. The thinking of an individual in a group is characterized by identification, conformity, anonymity, sympathy, emotionalism, nobility, oppression, symbolism, and rationalization.

Rational Basis of Public Opinion : While the opinions of elemental groups are influenced by appeals to their emotions, intelligence and comprehension play an important part in formation of public opinion of advanced groups. As a result of education and improved communication, today public opinion is based on rational thinking. More persons are weighing and considering information on controversial questions, suspending their judgements until they have the facts, and evaluating the information they receive from various sources. Individuals are asking themselves : Who says that ? What are his basic interests ? How is he trying to influence my thinking ? What exactly does he mean ? The public is increasingly on guard against pernicious propaganda by questioning information on issues communicated in the Press, over the air, in books, and in conversation.

Factors at Work

The factors of 'culture', 'family', 'religion', 'schools', 'social group', 'economic class', and 'race' interact with the active, direct effects of what people see, hear or read—their 'experience *Our environment and our experience fuse.* These primary factors of opinion formation and change lead to the intense competition for public attention.

Culture : No man lives unto himself alone. From birth to death, a person is influenced by others. The family, play group, school, church, city, state, and nation are organized ways of social relations. They make possible a richer life than could be attained if individuals lived in isolation. To put in short "Man shapes these institutions and, in turn, is shaped by them. " Public relations has its own role in this process.

The family : The family, the germ cell of society, is the first moulder of opinions. Within the family is to be found the germ of all such potentialities that later ripen into love and hate, work and play, obedience and revolt, reverence and agnosticism, patriotism and treason. It is the matrix which moulds the human personality and gives it the initial impetus and direction determining its goal and means to its fulfilment.

Religion : One basic human trait that binds nearly all people together is religion, the belief in a supernatural, universal power. Religion is a vital force. Both believers and non believers are affected by it, and no effort to change public opinion can omit or deny its strong influence.

School : The influence and importance of the school in the public opinion process is powerful in a state that regards an educated, enlightened electorate indispensable to a free society. What is taught by the teachers at school and acquired by the pupils from their fellow pupils is the interaction of forces that shape knowledge beliefs and attitudes.

Economic Class : Sometimes overlooked in exploring the roots of attitudes are *economic associations and status,* the individual's stake in the economy. Although the "economic man" concept is getting demolished, none would deny that economic motivation and influence are strong with most people. A person's status as an unskilled labourer or as a management executive determines, in large measure, the way his attitudes are bent and shaped. Attitudes of the different income groups towards the role of government are proof of this.

Social class : Somewhat related to the influence of economic class is that of *social status.* Certainly one's position as member of, say, Golf Club, Race Club or Freemason Lodge will determine his outlook, sources of information and opinion. Thos who belong to art circles, and travel widely, see events differently from those without these advantages. But it is important not to confuse income with social status. High income may indeed mean high social status, but it may not. Determining factors are family background, education, occupation, home and neighbourhood. *Status influences every phase of one's life.*

Race : Another factor increasingly important in shaping our mental setup in these days of schism and segregation, of black power and white backlash, is one's race as prevalent in the West still. Our People in India also are no exception to it. We read in the print media stones of high caste groups looking down upon the so-called backward classes".

Because what people see, hear or read is recognized as a primary force influencing their opinions, there is an inevitable struggle as to what public shall not see read or hear. This competition for men's minds becomes a battle of communication and censorship waged with slogans, symbols and stereotypes in all media of communication in our schools, plants, stores and offices. Communication and censorship or the lack of them, tend to regulate one's opinion and the rate of change.

Makers of Opinion

The opinions of people in a group are influenced by what they hear from 'opinion leaders', sometimes from other members of the group of persons outside the group.

An individual who is a member of a group manifests certain charactertstics in his thinking and behaviour which contribute to the formation of 'public opinion'. The thinking of an individual in a group is characterized by identification, conformity, anonmity, sympathy, emotionalism, nobility, oppression, symbolism and rationalization.

As a result of education, experience in men and matters, the opinion of the leaders is based more on rational thinking. They weigh and consider information on controversial questions by suspending their judgement until they have facts. They do not evaluate the information they receive from various sources until they are sure of the source from which such information has emanated.

The Research : Public Opinion Research includes image surveys, motivation research, effectiveness surveys, and individual public studies, two or more of which may be used concurrently in determining the character of opinion. Opinion research seeks answers to what people think about a business or non profit organization and why they think as they do, as well as their attitudes toward company principles, practices, and products. In addition to determining the views of the public as a whole, studies are made of opinions of individual publics, such as employees, stockholders, suppliers, dealers, neighbours, and educators. The effectiveness of Public Relation activities in creating favourable opinion of a company or industry is also studied to determine possible improvements in the communication programme or indicated changes in company policy.

Image Surveys : Image surveys determine the institutional profile or corporate image in the public mind by ascertaining the attitudes of the public toward an organization, how well they understand it, and what they like and dislike about it. Image surveys seek to understand how well a company is known, its reputation, and what the public thinks about its products, services, prices, advertising, personnel, and practices.

Motivation Research : Motivation research ascertains why the public looks with favour or disfavour or disapproval upon a company or industry. It seeks to discover, through depth interviews with a representative sample of the population, which motivates the public attitude toward an organization. To understand the motives which influence an individual's opinion, it is necessary to explore the psychological factors which shape his attitudes towards a company. A company's public image may be affected not only by its own policies and actions, but also by the attitude of the , public toward the industry of which the company is a part. Motivation studies are made to discover the underlying emotional factors which influence public opinion of a company or industry.

Effectiveness Surveys : Effectiveness surveys are used to measure the impact on public opinion made by the company's public relation activities. One of the most precise measurements of the change resulting from the impact of communications on public opinion is a before and after study of the attitudes of the public. Prior to the start of the campaign, a representative sample of the public is interviewed to determine public attitudes and the extent of public knowledge of the company or industry. After the campaign, the same people are interviewed to see if there has been any change in their opinions as a result of the public relation messages.

The reliability of this type of survey is questioned by some public relation' researchers, because the "before" interviews focus attention of respondents on the company and issues being discussed in communications. As a consequence, respondents are more conscious of the messages, and their impressions of the campaign are not typical of the public as a whole.

Effectiveness surveys are used to measure the response to company communications by its public; also to measure public opinion of specific events such as open houses, anniversary celebrations, plant closings, strikes, and other activities.

Individual Public Studies : In addition to researchers' views of the general public; studies are also made of the attitudes of individual publics. Numerous corporations abroad, and a few in India, make periodic employee opinion surveys to determine their views of the company, its policies, practices, working conditions, management, and supervision. The attitudes of the families of employees are also surveyed. The most effective technique for conducting employee opinion surveys is to question all employees in groups of 10 to 30, asking them to complete questionnaires on questions related to the company and their work. The employees are assured that their responses will be kept anonymous.

Typical questions asked in employee surveys are:

> How do you think the rules are enforced in this company? (Too though, tough, easy, too easy.)
>
> If employees increased production on their jobs, who do you think would benefit? (Customers, stockholders, employees, management, all of them, no answer.)
>
> Do you think a company should close down a plant which is not making a profit? (No, yes, no answer.)
>
> When two people have identical positions, should the one who does the best job get more pay? (Yes, no, no answer.)
>
> If you were president or plant manager, what would you do to improve this company or plant? (This openend question provides management with information about what employees think of their work, the company, any its problems.)

Opinion surveys are also made of the people in plant communities, including employees. Example of a face-to-face interview to obtain answers is given below:

> How do you feel about this town as a place to live? Would you say it is a good place to live, average, or poor place to live?

In your opinion, does waste material in the river create much of a problem?

Are you bothered by smoke, unpleasant odours, or dirt in the air?

Aside from providing jobs, can you name any other things that this company does for the town? What?

What have you heard or read about this company most recently?

Some questions in the survey are designed for company employees such as:

On the whole, how would you rate this company as a place to work? Would you say it is good, average, or poor place to work?

Most companies have both good and bad points. What are some of the things about this company as a place to work, that are not so good?

Laws and Rules

Hadley Cantril some years ago worked out some laws of Public Opinion on the basis of intensive study of the trends over a decade. Cantril holds that trends, as recorded by the polls, support these generalizations:

1. Opinion is highly sensitive to important events.
2. Events of unusual magnitude are likely to swing public opinion temporarily from one extreme to another. Opinion does not become stabilized until the implications of events are seen with some perspective.
3. Opinion is generally determined more by events than by words— unless those words are themselves interpreted as "events'".
4. Verbal statements and outlines of course of action have maximum importance when opinion is unstructured,

when people are suggestible and seek some interpretation from a reliable source.

5. By and large public opinion does not anticipate emergencies; it only reacts to them.
6. Psychologically, opinion is basically determined by self-interest. Even its words, or any other stimuli, affect opinion only in so far as their relationship to self-interest is apparent.
7. Opinion does not remain aroused for any long period of time unless people feel their self-interest is actually involved or unless opinion—aroused by words—is sustained by events.
8. Once self-interest is involved, opinions are not easily changed.
9. When self-interest is involved, public opinion in a democracy is likely to be ahead of official policy.
10. When an opinion is held by a slight majority or when opinion is not solidly structured, an accomplished fact tends to shift opinion in the direction of acceptance.
11. At critical times, people become more sensitive to the adequacy of their leadership—if they have confidence in it, they are willing to assign more than usual responsibility to it; if they lack confidence in it, they are less tolerant than usual.
12. People are less reluctant to have critical divisions made by their leaders if they feel that somehow they, the people, are taking some part in the decision.
13. People have more opinions and are able to form opinions more easily with respect to goals than with respect to methods necessary to reach these goals.
14. Public opinion, like individual opinion, is coloured by desires. And when opinion is based chiefly on desire rather than on information, it is likely to show sharp shifts with events.

15. By and large people in a democracy are provided educational opportunities and ready access to information. Public opinion reveals a hardheaded common sense. The more enlightened people are to the implications of events and proposals for their own self-interest, the more likely they are to agree with the more objective opinions of realistic experts.

Counsellor Earl Newsom has compressed the relatively little known about public opinion into these principles :

Identification Principle. People will ignore an idea, an opinion, a point of view unless they see clearly that it effects their personal fears or desires, hopes or aspirations—your message must be stated in terms of the interest of your audience.

Action Principle. People do not buy ideas separated from action—either action taken or about to be taken by the sponsor of the ideas or action which people themselves can conveniently take to prove the merit of the idea.

Unless a means of action is provided, people tend to shrug off appeals to do things.

Principle of Familiarity and Trust. We the people buy ideas only from those we trust, we are influenced by, or adopt only those opinions or points of view put forward by individuals or corporations or institutions in whom we have confidence.

Unless the listener has confidence in the speaker, he is not likely to listen or to believe.

Clarity Principle. The situation must be clear to us, not confusing. The thing we observe, read, see or hear, the thing which produces our impressions, must be clear not subject to several interpretations.

4

Aims and Objectives

Public opinion is like an iceberg. We know only the tip of this iceberg, while a large part remains submerged. Hence, simple observations may not suffice. Hence, the importance of fact finding as the starting point of any PR programme. It is a battle for men's minds which can never be considered to have ended. Its aims are:

(1) To convey to the public the policies and programmes of the organisation.

(2) To interpret the external world to the top management and interpret top management's decisions and policies to the external publics.

(3) To change people's attitudes.

(4) To overcome people's prejudices, suspicions and dislikes.

(5) To establish goodwill and understanding between organisation and public.

(6) To bring about an adjustment between the organisation and the socio-economic environment.

(7) To build an image of the organisation as a dynamic forward looking organisation.

Public relations thus serves as a detector, evaluator, interpreter and communicator.

The Channels

The basic tool is communication, to inform and persuade the Public by providing the right kind of information to remove misconceptions, if any, and to promote understanding and to establish the credibility of the organisation.

Press Releases : The publicity department prepares a brief factual account of events like annual accounts, progress made in the year, opening of new offices, launching of new plans, diversification of activities and circulates it to the media.

Press Conferences : The chairman and others give an opportunity to the media people to seek information through questions, thus exposing the institution to critical evaluation. This also indicates the willingness of the management to share the information frankly and freely.

Sponsored Visits : Sponsored visits of media men to offices.

Sponsored Article : Sponsored article by executives of institutions in newspapers and magazines.

Special Drives : Insurance week, claims and deposit clearance campaigns etc., create favourable public opinion.

Significant Elements

Human Relations : It is getting along well with the 'Public,' both internal and external. No man can work in a vacuum. Each person who works in an organisation has to get along with the other; he should be aware of the other and show interest in his progress as he does for his own.

Empathy : Empathy is feeling with the other person. Feeling sorry for him is sympathy. Empathy can be regarded as the primary prerequisite for a satisfying experience in any relationship where a certain degree of depth of understanding is expected.

Persuasion : There are two forms of intercourse between individuals and between groups: force and persuasion. If one party compels another to do something instead of persuading him, this is despotism, it is against the principles of proper conduct, sanctioned by society. A sense of human interest on the person who is being persuaded will understand and appreciate the cause and effect of his action.

Dialogue : It is conversation with a purpose. It is 'reason's only weapon. 'It is not a bargain-basement transaction with haggling and bickering; it is a low form of negotiation.

Dialogue is a reasonable exchange of ideas bringing into being a new form of knowledge: the use of dialogue is for influencing behaviour, selling goods or inspiring ideas.

Conciliation and Compromise

These are generally involved in dialogue. When speaking to an unfavourably disposed group or person, the first talk is to conciliate people and breakdown prejudice. He is a clever person who, under the circumstances, succeeds in bringing a state of urbanity into a gathering that is marked by discussion.

What is 'Public'? : Public is a group of similar individuals, an assortment of persons having the same interests, problems, circumstances, goals. Public is a varied creature and it comes in many forms and sizes. It has a multitude of wants and desires, and has its own likes and dislikes. It is a source of opinion.

Relations : Human wants create the need to establish relations with one another. The respective wants of two individuals will profoundly affect their relationship. To understand any relationship, therefore, one must understand the wants and desires of those involved.

Relationships are of every possible type. We have relationship by rank: superior to inferior: equal to equal. We have relationship which may be neutral. At any rate, it is there, to be accepted, ignored or altered, as desired.

How to Establish Relations? : For this purpose we may classify our universe into three groups of people: Those who know you and like you. Those who know you and do not like you. Those who neither know you nor care for you. The third is usually the large majority.

Now the aim should be to reach a position where those who know you and like you stay that way. Where those who know you and do not like you, change their opinion, and those who neither know you nor care for you, wish they could meet you and do business with you. The techniques to be adopted here can be likened to a fisherman. By selecting the worm as the bait, the fisherman goes by the taste of the fish—not by his own taste.

Thus the interlinking of the two human elements, viz., Public and Relations becomes Public Relations — which has now become a profession, and accepted as an arm of all management functions.

Why Public Relations? : We live in an inter dependent world: developing countries depend on the developed countries for technological, economic and other kinds of assistance. For example, oil-less countries depend on oil-rich countries, and oil-rich countries, in turn, depend on oil- less countries to export their surplus of food and allied items of production. And oil-producing countries have necessarily to depend upon others as they cannot produce in their own lands other items required by them — industry, commerce and business depend upon those who could help run their affairs by employing their skills and knowledge and vice versa. Government depends on the public for men and money as well as public acceptance of their policies and programmes. Politicians depend on the citizenry for money and votes, and the citizenry, in turn, depends on the politicians to represent them in the Parliament and State Assemblies.

What Public Relations can do? : Public Relations can help win friends and gain their goodwill and that of the community at large: help build favourable image of an organisation or individuals; promote products and services: goodwill of employees;

overcome misconceptions and prejudices; forestall attacks by interested groups or individuals; educate the public to a viewpoint; national integration; international understanding.

What Public Relations will not do? : Public Relations is a profession which will not make you consent without your consent. A public relations professional is fundamentally a catalyst. Upon his initiative, management takes action to obtain a favourable consensus from the various publics. The fact remains that what is best for the shareholders may not be best for the society, and conversely, there are situations where what is best for the society may be incompatible to the interests of the company and its shareholders. The skill at resolving such a conflict is really what public relations is all about.

A public relations professional is not a magician nor will he white-wash a spotted image. Nor is he the good-natured fellow who will keep the inquisitive newspaper reporters away from the management. Nor is he the man who churns out the goodwill of the company year after year even if the origin of good does not exist.

Mutual understanding is the core of public relations. There can be no mutual understanding without communication. For, while the number of 'publics' we recognize has increased over the years, the people who make up these groups have also changed in at least two specifics. They are more *sophisticated* and they are more *involved*. Both of these sophistication, and involvement, can be attributed to the present phenomenon known as the commuication or information explosion.

Correlationship with Journalism

Public Relations

Legend : Ultimately recognizing that it is not the be-all and end-all of the constant seareh for wealth only, man's mind eared for something which will bind humankind as a community, and that is Public Relations.

Public Relations is everyone's business: dating back to Adam and Eve. The 'forbidden fruit' would have remained uneaten but for the good PR effort of 'Satan'.

Again, but for sage Narada, the greatest PR personality, gods like Lords Shiva and Vishnu would not have accepted the responsibility of annihilating the evil force in the Asuras and deliver the Devas from their clutches.

(1) Public relations begin when we come in contact with people.

(2) Public relations is based on human relations, a helpful attitude knowledge of one's own subject, ability to generate confidence in one's organization, sticking to the truth, balance in the presentation of controversial issues and fair minded impartiality in dealing with men and matters.

(3) Public relations is a profession which does not make you consent without your consent in that it considers all its 'publics' as relations and all its relations (with the publics) is public.

(4) Public relations highlights the rewards of mutual understanding and the risks in misunderstanding between individuals, groups, governments, by "deliberate, planned and sustained efforts to establish mutual understanding".

(5) The public relations profession demands of the practitioner the skills of a general who knows how to make war. the talents of an advocate who can speak for his clients, the strategy of a politician who knows what strings to pull and the knowledge of a psychiatrist who understands how crazy people are and why craziness is not bad.

(6) What the management defines... public relations refines.

Journalism

Legend : There are two newspapermen, three personages of particular distinction in history: Edmund Burke, the great parliamentarian, flattered the press gallery by pointing to its members and naming them the Fourth Estate, far more important than the other three estates in Parliament.

Thomas Jefferson said that he would prefer newspapers without a government to a government without a newspaper. Incidentally, it is he who struck the words 'state of thought' and wrote 'Public Relation' instead in his 7th Address to the Congress.

Voltaire set a standard for freedom of speech by telling Helvetius, "I disapprove of what you say, but I will defend to the death your right to say."

Against this backdrop what is expected of newspapers and reporters notably in our country:

(1) The produce of their work is vitally important to the readers and the country.

(2) Should justify their freedom to report by writing accurately and interestingly and by interpreting fairly and intelligently the significant happenings and truths of their time.

(3) They must know their public; it will help if the reader knows something of the problems of the reporter and the editor, and they go about solving them.

(4) If a newspaper is published to advance a cause, it is only a house journal, not a newspaper.

(5) A perfect newspaper will be the voice of the lowly and oppressed and forgotten people, champion of the underdog. The chief function is to hold up a mirror to the happenings of the day.

(6) Appraise your report, is it a statement of fact, interpretation, opinion, arguments or special pleadings? In an important report is some one named as authority?

(7) An editorial page which offers genuinely worthwhile fare will not have to worry about lack of readers.

(8) A courageous publisher supported by an inspired, intelligent and dynamic reporting and editorial staff might find his great fulfilment as a newspaperman and as an Indian in making his publication desired by the public outside its present circulation and because of its authentic and well-written reports about national affairs.

(9) To sum up newspapers should consider themselves as tenants of society.

The Interaction

(1) One of the functions of a PR person is to edit a house journal. This is industrial journalism. An editor of a newspaper conforms to the highest standards of journalism— informative, educative, instructive, stimulating, interesting and generally inspiring. The PR executive who edits the house journal also follows standards of the newspaper editor.

(2) The aim of a newspaper is to bring the citizenry and the government closer to each other. Similarly the PR department of a business corporation strives to bring the corporation closer to its related 'Publics'.

(3) If, say a new policy evolved by a company is likely to affect the morale of the employees, the PR executive discusses the pros and cons of the policy with the Board of Directors. Likewise, the editor of a newspaper has a conference with the editorial staff to analyse any measures adopted by the government which are considered not in the interest of the public at large in the long run; then the 'editorial' is framed accordingly.

(4) How Public Relations comes face-to-face with journalism:

(a) When a 'press release' has to be made.

(b) When a press conference is convened.

(c) When open house, plant tours and exhibitions are organized, good relations with the working journalists, feature columnists, editors has to be developed to keep them informed of the significant features of each event pertaining to the company.

(d) As and when Companies, Chambers of Commerce, Trade Associations... organise Seminars relevant to the larger interest of business and with particular significance to the well-being of the nation, e.g., National Integration, 'Ecology and Environment', Export Promotion... public relations plays a dominant role in getting the press persons involved with a view to making them interested in the proceedings so that conclusions/recommendations/ decisions reached will be duly highlighted in the columns of the newspaper and a suitable editorial is also written.

(5) In the following areas of public relations profession, the practitioner has to follow the editors governing;

(a) Dedication to objective and reality

(b) Social responsibility

(c) Professional integrity

(d) Public interest.

Code of Ethics : International Code of Ethics for Public Relations as adopted by the Public Relations Society of India at the 1st All India Public Relations Conference, New Delhi, April 21, 1968.

CONSIDERING that all member-countries of the United Nations Organisation have agreed to abide by its Charter which reaffirms "its faith in fundamental human rights, in the dignity and worth of the human person" and that having regard to the very nature of their profession, Public Relations practitioners in these countries should undertake to ascertain and observe the principles set out in this Chapter.

CONSIDERING that, apart from 'right', human beings have not only physical or material needs but also intellectual, moral and social needs, and that their rights are of real benefits to them only in so far as needs are essentially met.

CONSIDERING that, in the course of their professional duties and depending on how these duties are performed, Public Relations practitioners can substantially help to meet these intellectual, moral and social needs.

And lastly, CONSIDERING that the use of techniques enabling them to come simultaneously into contact with millions of people gives Public Relations practitioners a power that has to be restrained by the observance of strict moral code.

On all these grounds the Public Relations Society of India hereby declares that it accepts, as its moral charter the principles of the following Code of Ethics, and that if, in the light of evidence submitted to the Society, a member of this Society should be found to have infringed this Code in the course of his professional duties, he will be deemed to be guilty of serious misconduct called for an appropriate penalty.

Social Obligations

(1) To contribute to the achievement of the moral and cultural conditions enabling human beings to reach their full stature and enjoy the indefeasible rights to which they are entitled under the "Universal Declaration of Human Rights".

(2) To establish communication patterns and channels which, by fostering the free flow of essential information, will make each member of the group feel that he is being kept informed, and also give him an awareness of his personal involvement and responsibility and of his solidarity with other members.

(3) To conduct himself always and in all circumstances in such a manner as to deserve and secure the confidence of those with whom he comes into contact.

(4) To bear in mind that because of the relationship between his profession and the public, his conduct—even in private—will have an impact on the way in which the profession as a whole is appraised.

(5) To observe, in the course of his professional duties, the moral principles and rules of the "Universal Declaration of Human Rights".

(6) To pay due regard to, and uphold, human dignity, and to recognise the right of each individual to judge for himself.

(7) To establish the moral, psychological and intellectual conditions for dialogue in its true sense, and to recognise the right of the parties involved to state their case and express their views.

(8) To act, in all circumstances in such a manner as to take account of the respective interests of the parties involved; both the interest of the organisation which he serves and the interests of the publics concerned.

(9) To carry out his undertakings and commitments which shall always be so worded as to avoid any misunderstanding, and to show loyalty and integrity in all circumstances so as to keep the confidence of his clients or employees, past or present and of all the publics that are affected by his actions.

(10) Subordinating the truth to other requirements.

(11) Circulating information which is not based on established and ascertainable facts.

(12) Taking part in any venture or undertaking which is unethical or dishonest or capable of impairing human dignity and integrity.

(13) Using any 'manipulative' methods or techniques designed to create subconscious motivations which the individual

cannot control of his own free will and so cannot be held accountable for the action taken on him.

International Code

* I believe in public relations as the determining factor that brings about harmony of understanding between government and government, government and people, group and the public, and individuals and the public.

* I consider the practice of public relations as based on broad general knowledge; logical and objective thinking; discretion; tact; imagination; talent of expression; an active desire to understand and help people; and, above all, absolute integrity.

* I will maintain as essential to the successful practice of public relations a working knowledge of all avenues of approach to the public such as books, pamphlets, magazines, newspapers, trade and employee publications, house organs, annual reports, brochures presentations, letters, speeches, proceedings, lectures, motion pictures, photographs, radio, television, the drama, the school room, and all events that shape and symbolize given activities and by which they are known to the public.

* I shall keep faith with the individuals or activities I represent, with the means of communication with the public, and with the public itself; I will not accept assignments that are antagonistic to each other or those that are anti-social and I will shun activities that deviate from the highest ethical stan dards.

* I shall be alert to public trends, motives, thought, action and reaction so that I shall be a propagandist only in the finest sense of the word.

* I shall collaborate in assuming constructive civic and social responsibilities.

* I shall not obtain any business by means of fraudulent statements or by use of implications unwarranted by fact or reasonable probability and shall comply, both in spirit and letter, with all the rules and regulations prescribed by law and government agencies for the health, safety, and progress of the public.

* I shall not perform, or cause to be performed, any act which would tend to reflect on or bring into disrepute any part of the practice of public relations.

* I believe in public relations as the liaison between the fibre of the nation and the ideas, products, and services that make it strong and I subscribe to these standards as the Code of Public Relations.

Standard Behaviour

Public Relations Society of America : As Members and Associates of the *Public Relations Society of America,* we share a responsibility for the good character and reputation of the public relations profession. Therefore we will adhere to the following principles and standards of practice:

(1) We will keep our objectives in full accord with the public welfare as well as the interests of our clients or employers.

(2) We will be guided in all our activities by the standards of accuracy, truth and good taste.

(3) We will safeguard the confidence of both present and former clients or employers.

(4) We will not engage in any activity in which we are directly or indirectly in competition with a present client or employer without the full knowledge and consent of all concerned.

(5) We will cooperate with fellow practitioners in curbing malpractices.

(6) We will support efforts designed to further the technical proficiency of the profession and encourage the establishment of adequate training and education for the practice of public relations.

To the extent that we live up to these principles and standards of practice, we will be meeting our responsibilities for making the profession in which we are engaged worthy of continued public confidence.

5

Significant Elements

Good human relations is people getting along well together with the 'internal' publics as well as the 'external' publics.

Behind the facade of every 'person' employed in an organization, there is the human element. Each should be aware of the other and show sincere interest in his official and personal progress.

When a collection of good people becomes a well knit team, their capacity for production is astonishingly increased, and this is true even though each is performing an individual task.

People with power and prestige buy a man or woman's time; they can even buy a measured number of skilled and prompt actions per day, but they cannot buy enthusiasm, initiative, loyalty. They have to earn these things by applying more the spirit of the rules and regulations which govern the performance of their duties.

We start, in our thinking and in our idealistic manifestos, with the false assumption that "people are essentially alike." Then, when we find by experience that they are unlike, we confuse the issues and denounce and persecute each other because we are different. We should, instead, try to find out in what way we are different then proceed to learn why. This, in a nutshell, is human relations.

Empathy

Before embarking on PR career, which involves direct or indirect selling your way through life, it is important for the person to get some notion of what *empathy* is and grasp the significance of the role it plays in one's life.

What is Empathy ? : Webster says it is "Imaginative projection of one's own consciousness in another being." In advertising, then it is the Agency representative's—it is seeing matters as others see them. It is the executive causing himself to feel as others feel, and even his feelings for them. The empathic executive treats each client in a considerate manner. His capacity for empathy permits the executive to be sympathetic to the client's experiences and prejudices; perceptive to the client's attitudes and beliefs, sensitive to the client's hopes and fears, receptive to the client's ideas and reactions, and appreciative of the client's objectives and values.

When empathy is operating, the PR executive thinks in terms of his 'publics', not just himself. He gives his client no impression of conceit, superiority, condescension, criticism, irritation or impatience. Instead his sincere question is "How can I help the client get what he wants most?"

Being an empathic executive is an art—it is an ability a PR executive must acquire and master if be is to realize his full potential. This takes time, planned practice, experimentation and experience. A PR executive should want to perfect his skill in this area until his attempts to understand each of his 'publics' are automatic.

Empathy contributes to a PR executive's success in several ways. It helps making client's relationship better. It fosters greater understanding. Empathy tells an executive when he should be firm and when he should be more restrained, when he should talk and when be should remain silent, even whether be should joke or be serious. The empathic PR executive is more accurate than the non empathic competitor in interpreting what a client/buyer says or does.

Empathy encourages the client to be frank and sincere with the PR executive, or reveal instead of conceal. In encourages the client to welcome and even to look forward to subsequent with the PR executive because the client considers him an ally and a friend.

Empathy, as a sage put it, is feeling with the other person—not feeling sorry for him—which is sympathy.

Empathy can be regarded to be the primary prerequisite for a satisfying experience in any relationship where a certain degree of depth of understanding is expected. A PR manager write his experience as follows :-

The day when I was travelling from Bangalore to Madras by road, I decided to try the eating house at Krishnagiri about which my good friend used to talk so often.

Having entered the impoverished dining hall, after a wash, I waited for the leaf to be laid on my table. Presently, an elderly lady appeared to say : "Sir, the cook's assistant has unfortunately toppled the rice pot on the oven. Fresh rice is already in the process of preparation. Within seconds it will be ready. Meantime, if you so please, may I give you a plate of freshly fried homemade 'pappads' and also, if you like, a cup of lime 'rasam' (soup) just taken out of the oven.

Without knowing that it was "empathy", an ingredient of public relations she was demonstrating, the benevolent lady reacted to the situation like a seasoned corporate public relations executive: the lady apparently put herself in the shoes of a member of the public; in her empathy, she anticipated a problem and tried to mitigate it as far as she could. She did not attempt to twist the truth. Her frank explanation dispelled the misunderstanding which would have resulted from a lack of information—as such lack of information is : apt to give rise to a grievance which could be avoided. She knew instinctively that goodwill grows in a spirit of thoughtfulness and blighted by neglectfulness. Unknowingly she applied one of the main principles of corporate responsibility or social obligation, "that when you impinge on the convenience of the public, it is not their problem but yours."

Persuasion

There are two forms of intercourse between individuals and between groups: force and persuasion. If one party compels another to do something instead of persuading him, this is despotism, and it transgresses the principle of proper conduct sanctioned by an intelligently and spiritually refined society. It is usually a mentary discussion, and city views. Even a small public relations department should consider such an intelligence service an essential part of its activities, weakling who runs away from persuasion. He does not want to risk being persuaded against his prejudices. A person with strength of character can listen to persuasion, weigh what is said, and arrive at informed conclusions.

Before engaging in persuasion, take time to settle a few questions in your mind : What do I wish to accomplish ? What are the interests of the people to whom I shall be talking ? What are the facts I wish to tell them ?

When a speaker seeks to bring about a change in belief or conduct, the hearer must not only understand and approve; he must accept. The speaker needs to minimize misunderstandings and difficulties by giving adequate explanations. "Because I say so" is not an acceptable or effective reason to give in dialogue, debate or persuasion when recommending some action. A sense of human interest is a valuable asset to anyone indulging in persuasion. Human interest is what you notice that is of dominant interest in the person to whom you are presenting your case. Consider what will appeal to him. Whatever your objective, you must start with his present state of knowledge and belief.

Here is a skeleton upon which you may erect a structure for persuasion :

(a) show that a problem exists or a situation needs correction;

(b) explain the essential elements of the problem or the various aspects of the situation;

(c) tell about the reasons for failure of previous attempts;

(d) show why your solution is the best one;

(e) picture your solution in operation, including the benefits it will give to others and the satisfaction it will give to those who join in reaching it.

Don't forget to include a specific suggestion in your conclusion. Tell in definite terms the nature, place, time and method of the response you desire from the participants.

Principles of Persuasion : The following are condensed from sources like "Principles of Persuasion" by Wilbur Schram and Donald Roberts, and "Process and Effects of Communication" by Katz and Lazarfeld.

Research in the social sciences has brought, in recent years, some tentative principles of persuasion based on experimental research :

1. To accomplish attitude change, suggestion for change must first be received and accepted. "Acceptance of the message" is a critical factor in persuasive communication.
2. The suggestion is more likely to be accepted if it meets existing personality needs and drives.
3. The suggestion is more likely to be accepted if it is in harmony with group norms and loyalties.
4. The suggestion is more likely to be accepted if the source is perceived as trustworthy or expert.
5. A suggestion in the mass media, coupled with face-to-face reinforcement, is more likely to be accepted than a suggestion earned by either alone or with another, other things being equal.
6. Change in attitude is more likely to occur if the suggestion is accompanied by other factors underlying belief and attitude. This refers to a changed environment which makes acceptance easier.
7. There probably will be more opinion change in the desired direction if the conclusions are explicitly stated than if the audience is left to draw its own conclusions.

8. When the audience is friendly, or when immediate but temporary opinion change is wanted, it is more effective to give only one side of the argument.
9. When the audience disagrees, or when it is probable that it will hear the other side from another source, it is more effective to present both sides of the argument.
10. When equally attractive opposing views are presented one after another, the one presented last will be more effective.
11. Sometimes emotional appeals are more influential; sometimes factual ones are. It depends on the kind of message and kind of audience.
12. A strong threat is generally less effective than a mild threat in inducing desired opinion change.
13. The desired opinion change may be more measurable some time after exposure to the communication that right after exposure.
14. The people you want most in your audience are least likely to be there. This goes back to the censorship of attention that the individual invokes.
15. There is a "sleeper effect" in communications received from sources which the listener regards as having low credibility.

    In some tests time has tended to wash out the distrusted source and leave information behind.

Dialogue

Dialogue is conversation with a purpose. It is reason's only weapon. It is a civilized operation, democratic and constructive, and those who refuse dialogue are playing a game with some serious overtones. There was no dialogue in the primitive medicine man's manipulation of people's passions.

Democratic institutions and political freedom cannot survive without discussion, criticism, and deliberation. Are we too busy enjoying life to engage in a dialogue designed to make possible the continuation of life ? Or too ignorant ? Or too lethargic ? Or too parasitical ? All these entered into the decline of the Roman Empire.

To take useful part in reaching decisions is to seek understanding through consideration of alternatives. In this debate, traditions and dogmas rub each other down. We attain insight and understanding.

A dialogue is not a bargain basement transaction with haggling and bickering, a low form of negotiation. Neither is it a situation in which Mukherjee confronts Murthy in a contest, but a conversation in which each presents facts and each consider the other's facts. It is a reasonable exchange of ideas, bringing into being a new body of knowledge. It takes you out of the doldrums of fiddling with good intentions into the region where you act with knowledge and understanding.

Monopoly of the conversation has no place in dialogue. The ball must be thrown back and forth. There is give and take. Participants expect to find things out by examining ideas and facts from several points of view.

This exercise reveals the true personality of those taking part in it. It dissolves the solemn humbug and punctures the know tall; it unveils the person who speaks in malice or in self-interest. It reduces prejudice and builds up mutual confidence, the hallmark of social intercourse among equals.

Effective Dialogue Lies in Seeing from other Viewpoints : Impartiality in listening to points of view is a great aid to the making of good judgements about what is being discussed, and this requires that we try honestly to see things through the other person's eyes.

Many irritations in management functions are due to the fact that some people do not recognize problems which others think are important. Two cultures may have institutions that look very much alike to the outside observer, and, words in their languages which are so alike as to suggest the same meanings, but the realities are different.

In praiseworthy dialogue we show respect for the other man's opinions, and try to push the right button to pen him up so that we learn his teal thoughts. It is easy and immature to ‑ecognize only the spurious and mistaken in a man's contentions; it requires more effort and intelligence to recognize and admit the excellence of some of his ideas.

There are certain simple rules associated with effective dialogue. Much that passes for dialogue is not that at all, but merely the noise made by contending parties or persons. Shake hands ready gong !"

Good dialogue requires common substance, a topic about which the participants are informed and to which all can make a contribution by original thinking. It requires a large measure of goodwill. It begins in an act of faith : the assumption that those who converse will speak honestly reaching understanding, and with generosity.

A good way to start a dialogue is by asking questions and listening to the answers. When Napoleon noticed that his counsellors were simply echoing whatever he said he was quick to call them to order. "You are not here", he told them, "to agree with me but to express your own views."

It is by comparison of views that we reason our way toward truth. We increase the odds of finding the best solution to a problem by considering alternatives.

Quite a few presiding over business corporations in India have learnt to believe that dialogue may be a more effective setting for honest business building, or management reform, or community relations than is the 'Labour Court'. The heart and soúl of dialogue is this : to realize that there is no once and for all answer to a complicated historical or social problem, but only an answer as of now, based upon knowledge of what is really going on.

People have different ideas even about what is a solution. Some are satisfied with a temporary settlement, and are content to have a continuing dialogue in which every new settlement is a step toward a final solution. Others pursue their purposes with a sense of finality; they want things settled once and for all; they wager for all or nothing.

It seems rational to take the first course to seek a philosophy which is adequate for the circumstances of our time. We must recall that ages are no more infallible than individuals. Every age has held many opinions which subsequent ages have deemed not only false but absurd. The way to progress appears to lie in talking over with one another, exchanging and enlarging our ideas, so that we grow into our future. That is dialogue.

Personal Contact

My "guru" used to tell me, It's who you know, not what you know that counts'. As with most generalisations, this has an element of truth—sufficient only to constitute a serious hazard for those who attempt to live by it. A good PRO must know who, what, why, where, when and how. Otherwise he is working 'in the dark' and this can have disastrous consequences.

Nevertheless, knowing people is a great asset and being known is almost equally important. This should not be construed (as it so often is) as giving a carte blanche for a hefty expense account while wining and dining and getting to know all and sundry. On the contrary, the important contacts are those made day-to-day in the normal course of business—and the most valuable are rarely the most expensive. Among these can be counted local government officers and councillors, neighbours, staff and work-people as well as customers and others more directly concerned with the commercial aspects of your business.

From the point of view of the Mr. Fixit that any PRO has to be, the range of contact is always growing and it should never stop. You can never know too many people. Quite apart from the gentlemen of the Press (to whom many consider their essential range of contact can be limited) the complete PRO must know photographers, process engravers and printers, display and exhibition contractors, caterers, designers and artists, advertising agents and advertisement representatives, translators, technical writers and dozens more specialists tool.

This isn't very hard. Most of these people come to your door—or, at least they write to you—looking for business. Others can be chased out very easily from the pages of local papers, trade journals and other readily available references. The secret is to establish and maintain personal contact. It's amazing how many friends you can make in this way and how many more contacts the initial ones lead to.

The contacts on the other side of the fence are generally more difficult to define and often more difficult to make. However, the difficulty in definition is mainly mine and should not be your. Certainly, you should know the opposition—not too well but well enough for mutual recognition and to pass the time of day. But every business—industrial or commercial enterprise—has its own peculiar range of publics (which may be changing constantly) how can I say who you should know ?

When you have defined your own publics, as a basic PR exercise, you should then be able to start a list of contacts to be made ; beginning with your opposite trade associations and working right through to typical customers or users of the product or service you are promoting. And, as you make these contacts, the list will grow automatically, just as it did with the range of supplier/collaborator contacts.

How do you take them ? Mostly, by just getting on with the job and making a point of meeting people instead of always writing to them. Others, simply by phoning to ask for an appointment. If you have mutual interests that make the contact worthwhile, the other fellow will want to meet you as much as you want to meet him.

Cultural Concept

The practice of public relations in a developing country like India is generally at variance with industrially and socially advanced countries like USA, UK, Japan or Germany. Such is not the case with professions like engineering, technology, accountancy, profession and humanities, the reason being that the experience of an engineer in one part of the world is equally valid for another. But when we talk of behavioural science, the experience of an American, Britisher, Japanese or German will not conform to that of an Indian. For, it is here that environment composed of culture, tradition, customs, manners and the like plays a dominant role. So it is necessary for a public professional to have a glimpse into the cultural concept.

Definition : The pattern of those arrangements, material or behavioural, which has been accepted by a society as the traditional ways of solving the problem of its members. Culture includes all the institutionalized ways and the implicit cultural beliefs, norms, values and premises which govern conduct.

Along with eating and sleeping, one universal habit of our species is forming ourselves into bands, tribes, societies. We then evolve various ways and means for holding the group together and giving it structure.

A society refers to a group of people who have learned to work and live together.

A culture refers to the way of life which the group follows.

Culture is the cement which binds the group together—without it, a group is not a society but a mob, an aggregate, a milling mass. Social scientists divide a culture into three chief parts.

1. Habits, customs, ways of behaving, which a child begins to learn almost as soon as he is born. How to keep clean, how to eat his food properly, how to dress, how to comport himself in church or temple and school. The most important habit of all is how to communicate, including the unique gift of speech. He is born with large speech centres in his brain, but language must always be learned.
2. Belief systems, to give him his ideas of right and wrong. Religion, magic, patriotism, property standards are all the accepted symbols and credos of his society.
3. Artifacts, the tools, utensils, constructions, machines which the society has developed or borrowed from other societies. The catalogue of a large mail order house has given us some idea of the artifacts loose in the American culture

today. In 1800, it is safe to say, such a catalogue would not have been a tenth in size.

Journalists and fiction writers speak of the "unwritten law" by which they must mean the culture of tribe. Culture came ages before formal law. Nature people like the Eskimo have no formal law at all; there are no courts or statutes or jails but the living law or culture may enjoin the death penalty just the same. Unless the formal law is in line with the living law, it cannot be enforced. The Prohibition Law in the United States banning alcoholic beverages was an instructive example. One difficulty in setting up a formal international law today is that there is as yet non-international living law, no planetary culture.

Dwelling together in groups is as characteristic of man as the shape of his teeth or his inclination to laugh, "A Special Organism", said William James, "is what it is because each member proceeds to his own duty with a trust that the other members will simultaneously do theirs. A government, an army, a commercial system, a ship, a college, an athletic team, all exist on this condition without which not only is nothing achieved, but nothing is even attempted."

It is difficult to overemphasise the importance of this observation—yet not many of us understand it. If most people were dishonest, if they failed to do what they promised to do, if they did not take care of the children, help others in crisis, society would fall apart. Most people are good, just as the charge account statistics prove; they pay their bills, they can be trusted. The culture concept makes it plain why this must be so. If any considerable fraction—say more than 5 per cent—could not be trusted to do what was expected of them, there would be no dependable culture, no living, growing society—just a prisoner of war camp, with a polyglot mixture of prisoners. A functioning society must be self-discipline. When we talk about "dictators", "the state", "freedom", we often forget this underlying condition.

In Hemosiderins, society rather than the individual has become the primary unit in the struggle for existence. For centuries in the West, philosophers, theologians, educators, businessmen, have concentred on the individual. They have affirmed that he alone was responsible for his sins, his sufferings, his triumphs and his defeats. Social scientists find that the individual is not that kind of organism and cannot be understood in such a conceptual frame. He is a product of his culture, he is a living part of his group and can be understood only in relation to it. To judge his outside, this matrix is like trying to understand a fish without reference to water.

A comprehension of double role of the individual, observes Linton, a separate person as a unit in society, provides a key to many problems of human behaviour.

"Until the psychologist knows what the norms of behaviour imposed by a particular society are and can discount those as indicators of personality, he will be unable to penetrate behind the facade of social confirmity and cultural uniformity to reach the authentic individual." Dr. William C. Menninger made the same point about mental health, as quoted earlier.

Social scientists are a long way from working out all the relationships between the individual and culture, but they have let the study of man out of a blind alley. They have begun to ask the right questions, and have demonstrated that man is a social animal to a degree hitherto unappreciated. Apparently he has always been one since he came down from trees. Sometimes his group comprises only a few families living under the most primitive conditions. Sometimes it fills a continent, but it is always there.

On this broad base, the science of man begins. A baby snake can fend for itself about as soon as it can squirm. A human baby, without a group behind it, either starves immediately, or if natural food is by some miracle available, comes to resemble a gibbering idiot. Civilized man does more things than the savage because he has the opportunity to learn more things; his culture is richer; it accumulates like compound interest. The innate ability of the savage, however, may be that as great.

The culture concept comes closest to the truth about mankind yet discovered by the scientific method. Truth discovered by other methods do not concern us here. History as customarily written, from Herodotus to the present day, seldom focuses on this truth, but rather on kings, generals, popes, presidents, prime ministers, prophets, the great men who rise out of the group, often to torment it. "While the popular view is that the leader makes the times", says Ogburn, "a realistic view emphasizes the exact opposite."

Formal history, with its Caesars and Napoleons, tends to be a record of the abnormal, the geniuses, sports freaks and misfits, the glandular cases of mankind. It stands the social pyramid on its apex. The culture concept puts it back upon its base. The kings and the warriors are dramatic, true enough, but the real story concerns the society which sheltered its children, accumulated invention and wrung a living from nature down through the ages.

The idea that a group can suddenly be emancipated from its past habits is no more sensible than the idea that a man who flaps his arms rapidly enough can fly. If the group could change as fast as some reformers hope, it would have dashed itself to pieces sometime in the Old Stone Age. The group's main task is survival through reproduction and nourishment. The young can be protected, and a food supply secured, only in the momentum of established procedures.

The saying that if the church has a boy until he is six he will be a good communicant for life, has strong support from social scientists. The demonstration that any healthy infant can adjust to any culture—if he is not discriminated against because of the colour or caste—emphasises the vast importance of the earliest years. Five branches of social science are joining today to drive home this conclusion—the anthropologists, linguists, sociologists, psychologists and psychiatrists.

The anthropologists say that since CrowMagnon days, at least, children of any nation or race have had practically the same inborn equipment. But from birth every experience helps to shape a child to the culture in which he finds himself. Even by the age of three or four he has learned hundreds of habits, and received thousands of impressions, which he will not consciously remember later in life, but which already stamp him as a member of Eskimo or Japanese or American society.

The linguists demonstrate that by the time he is six, a child has absorbed the structure of his language and that this structure will shape his whole system of thought throughout his life.

The sociologists emphasise the institutional and community aspects of the culture. The psychologists study the responses of young children, aided with all manner of laboratory equipment—cameras, sound tracks, oneway windows. They analyse the vital process by which an individual becomes a culture carrier.

The psychiatrists emphasise emotional influences on children, showing how early experiences may mould an individual's character, and perhaps produce a mental breakdown in later years.

Scientists talk more and more about the vital importance of security and affection, the feeling of belonging, in early years. A lack of emotional security in childhood may bring serious results, examples of which can be seen in any mental hospital and in outbreaks of juvenile delinquency.

Optimistic Note : Finally, the culture concept gives us hope that many of our problems can be solved. If people were bad by virtue of their "blood", or their genes, or their innate characters, there would not be much we could do about it. But if people are basically all right, and a given problem lies primarily in an adjustment to culture patterns, a good deal can be done about it.

The laws of culture are something like Boyle's law of gases. An individual person, like a molecule of hydrogen, is unpredictable. But there is a definite pattern which the whole group will follow, and which can statistically described. We know, for instance, how many will be born, how many will marry, how many classrooms will be needed in the years ahead. If an observer charts the pattern, he can predict behaviour with reasonable probability. How to bring up children, why they have to be disciplined—not because they are "naughty", but to prepare them for the environment in which they must live. It has been broadened by ideas about the schools and education, about meetings, participation, democracy. It has given new insight into the importance of symbols and ceremonials, such as weddings, funerals, parades.

Finally, when one becomes aware how one personally is culture bound, by curious paradox one is freed a little from one heads. He can look over the walls. He can for the first time in his life begin to understand people of an alien culture. How strange that science should be the cause of a deep ethical experience!

The Functions

There are many objectives that may be achieved through expert public relations activity. Any one of them, any group of them, or all of them may be the basis for an organization's public relations programme. Professional public relations directs every activity toward reaching a selected objective; extraneous efforts are avoided. Objectives that could be sought include :

1. Prestige or favourable 'image' and its benefits.
2. Promotion of products or services.
3. Goodwill of the employees or members.
4. Presentation and solution of labour problems.
5. Fostering the goodwill of communities in which the organization has units.
6. Goodwill of the stockholders or constituents.
7. Overcoming misconceptions and prejudices.
8. Forestalling attacks.
9. Goodwill of suppliers.
10. Goodwill of the government.
11. Goodwill of the rest of the industry.
12. Goodwill of dealers and attraction of other dealers.
13. Ability to attract the best personnel.
14. Education of the public to use a product or service.
15. Education of the public to a point of view.
16. Investigation of the attitude of various groups towards a company.
17. Goodwill of customers or supporters.
18. Fostering the viability of the society in which the organization functions.
19. Directing the course of change.

6

Role in Crisis Management

Crisis Situations

In the year 1978-79, the tyre prices had to be revised almost four times. It created a certain amount of resentment among the tyre consumers, particularly the truck operators. Unfavourable press comments, questions in Parliament and active demonstration against price increases generated a lot of public criticism against the tyre industry.

To meet these criticisms, public relations of one of the tyre companies took upon themselves to have an in-depth discussion with the press. The Editor of a major financial newspaper was invited for a depth interview which was attended by the Chairman of the particular tyre company. In this interview the Chairman was able to convince that price increases were necessary and unavoidable. The newspaper concerned was supplied with adequate data concerning price behaviour of raw materials and other inputs. It was also suggested that the newspaper should cross-check the information supplied by the tyre company with raw material suppliers, dealers and truck customers.

The interview resulted in a comprehensive newspaper review supported by adequate data of raw material prices, cost of production and industry profitability. Gradually, other newspapers also came out with reports and editorials commenting on tyre price increases, and most of these reports were favourable from the industry's point of view. Newspaper clippings were collected and sent to leading transport organizations, government officials, press correspondents and other opinion leaders. The office bearers of various transport organizations were invited by the tyre company officials to fully explain the causes leading to price increases.

Employee house journal was utilized to explain the situation to the employees so that they could represent the industry viewpoint in their private and public discussions. Similarly, field salesmen were also supplied with newspaper clippings and supporting price data to make their communication to the trade and customers effective and persuasive. Other forums such as Chairman's speech to the shareholders, meeting of transport associations and other form of consumer meetings were utilized to meet their communication objectives. All these efforts were supplemented by an institutional advertising campaign to raise the consumer awareness that the tyre was a petroleum based product.

Throughout this period, public relations played a key role in formulating the communication plan cross-checking the feedback from the consumer and reporting to the management the change in public attitude towards tyre pricing.

Thus public relations had shed its light in the manner St. Mathew in Chapter 5, Verse 16 has said: "Let your light so shine before man that they may see your good work."

"Do not hide your light under a bushel" said an ancient sage. Perhaps it will not be incorrect to aver that public relations is almost a religion founded for the avowed purpose of generating goodwill among mankind.

The light of one match can be seen by a hundred thousand people in a darkened coliseum—if there are no other matches.

With a number of thousand matches burning in the coliseum, a single one makes little impression and may be hard to identify. A flash light may be required to get special attention. And that flashlight is public relations.

One can improve one's public relations overnight by getting firsthand contact with one's public and finding out what one has been overlooking. Those who are fishermen will readily admit that it is not by their own taste, but by the taste of the fish, that they determine the choice of bait!

If we are really eager to improve our public relations, and run up against a problem whose solution does not appear readily, let us analyse it.

Suppose it is a matter affecting Allen and Jones. There are three approaches. We need to set down the answers to these questions:

How does this matter look to Allen ? What significance has it for him personally ? How it looks to Jones ? What is its significance to him ?

How does it look to me, an outsider observer, when I compare the way it looks to Allen with the way it looks to Jones ? And then having judged the matter and reached a decision, act with dignity.

Even the most serious difficulty involving persons, groups, organization or Nations can be solved if we are willing to keep ourselves out of the conflict and avoid angry debate.

Negative Aspects

As the saying goes, one cannot carve a figure out of dead wood. To create exquisite art pieces, the craftsman chooses ivory, rosewood or sandal wood. Only such kinds of wood will respond to the skills of the craftsman. In the same way, if the malady of an organization demands public relations remedy, it has to accept the prescription of its professional. If it is not favourably disposed to giving a free hand to the public relations advice, there can hardly be anything for the professional to do. Unless the organization recognizes the fact that only with public acceptance can it stand, without it, it will fall, any amount of public relations talk will have no effect.

A public relations man is not a magician who will whitewash a spotted image. Nor is he the good natured buffer who will keep inquisitive newspaper reporters away from management. Nor is he a man who churns out goodwill for the organization year after year even if the origins of goodwill do not exist. A public relations person is fundamentally a catalyst. Upon his initiative, management takes action to obtain favourable consensus from, its various publics. The fact remains that what is best for the shareholders may not be best for the society and, conversely, there are situations where what is best for the society may be incompatible to the interests of the organization and its shareholders. The skill at resolving such a conflict is really what Public Relations is all about. Public relations is a hardnosed operation. No creative activity is more demanding. Although, often, the objectives may be specific but the means of achieving them are vague, dispersed and general. Also the modus operandi is individual and custom-made for each company.

You cannot build the reputation of a big company by stunt methods; it has to be built on hard facts: the essential truth about its business. Confidence can be won only if the purity of the means adopted is not sacrificed merely for the sake of gaining certain ends. Here the management has to understand the functions of public relations. The latter's role cannot be other than that of finest brokers—to keep management informed of changes in the opinion of its various publics and to communicate to the latter the policy decisions of the former in as convincing a manner as possible. Indeed, to serve as an effective "bridge" between the two. The essentials about public relations, therefore, are : It is a useful profession provided it is employed in the right way, and that public relations men are basically backroom boys to help an organization and its publics to understand each other. Public relations men and women can maintain their impartiality, efficiency and effectiveness if they do not get lost in the glitter of a showbiz business of dining and wining and what not. The role was once defined by the great BurmahShell people so appropriately of P.R.Os should be neither seen nor heard. They should merely ensure the good quality of what is seen and heard."

Scene in India

The absence of adequate number of trained and skilled public relations professionals had placed the profession in the position of the man who tried to explain the nature of an elephant to six blind men.

The story has its element of humour, to be sure. But it would rot be so humorous to the elephant's public relations person if it had engaged one. Yet the partial knowledge of our organizations and our activities is exactly what confronts us today. And today more than ever in the past, the public relations person must take heed of the saying : little knowledge can be a dangerous thing, especially of the environment. The environment of India is such that it is a land of contrasts :

1. About 75 per cent of the population is dependent on agriculture. And even agriculture is in the main carried on by primitive and age-old method of cultivation resulting in a low level of productivity. However, there are a few pockets where modern techniques of cultivation are followed, and productivity in those areas is high.
2. Organized industry absorbs hardly 2 to 3 per cent of the population. Small-scale and cottage industry and retail trade absorb the rest of the urban population. Productivity in this, *i.e.,* the unorganized sector, is also naturally low.
3. Population has been growing at a very high rate, nearly 2.5 per cent per annum in the last decade.
4. As a natural consequence, living standards are low and more than 50 per cent of the population is living below the poverty line.
5. Nearly 70 per cent of the population is completely illiterate. And of the remaining 30 per cent who are literates, the

percentage of those who have been through Secondary Schools would be hardly 10.

6. There are many languages, many cultures and ethnic groups. Although politically a sense of nationhood has undoubtedly developed and economically the country comprises a single market, culturally instead of a common composite culture emerging, there are at least 15 or 16 distinct cultural groups with their own language, their own way of living. Linguistic and cultural differences are not disappearing but growing sharper.

A common handicap for public relations practitioners in India is that they are not being given the status that they deserve and public relations inputs are not being used in Management Decision Making. On behalf of management, on the other hand, it is often stated that they are not getting the right type of public relations professionals, and hence they do not feel they would benefit by taking their advice. Owing to the limited career opportunities in public relations and the failure on the part of top management in most organizations to give public relations the recognition it deserves, the calibre of the people who are currently seeking admission into public relations is not always of a very high order. Thus, a vicious circle has been created. Management feels that the right type of public relations people are not available. And the right type of young people aspiring for a career in business and industry prefer other management disciplines like Marketing and Sales Management, Advertising and Accountancy profession rather than public relations because of the higher rewards they offer.

The vicious circle can be broken only by a determined effort to educate people in public relations and to ensure that those thus trained are able to make a contribution to management decision-making.

Another problem is that there is a serious lack of educators. Almost the entire burden of imparting education in public relations is borne by the first generation of public relations practitioners assisted by the present-day professionals as and when they have the time to do so.

With all that, the profession; as on date, has made significant progress steadily overcoming the Indian environmental limitations.

Peoples' Participation

Like a herd of cattle without a keeper

Like an army without a general

Like a night without the mood

Like a group of cows without a bull

Such would be the country (people)

Where the King is not "Seen".

[*Valmiki Ramayana—Ayodhyakanda*—XIV : 56-58] In every component of governance—whether the quality of it is good or otherwise, the subjects "see" the 'ruler' in it. A ruler by himself cannot accomplish objectives singly ; he has to seek the cooperation of his council of ministers, and, through them, of his executives to discharge the regal responsibilities which his subjects expect of him.

Thiruvalluvar's "Rural" consisting of 70 chapters throws abundant light on this in one of the chapters. In the need for a professional approach to selection of executives, "Kural" says, "men should be appointed to duties who have the ability needed for their performance and resourcefulness to meet the situation arising therein."

Going back to, say, forty years, departments in industry seemed to operate within fairly watertight compartments : Production people made what "they thought they made; best; the extrovert sales tribe jollied up the customers in order to sell what production was making ; the publicity manager produced advertisements, often without reference to the sales manager, and sent off press releases about new products which excited him but which were rarely in production as yet ; so that potential customers were disarmingly told of a nine-month delay before delivery!

The board of directors were even more insulated from reality. Many of them were members of the founder's family. As long as they could pass a satisfactory dividend once or twice a year all was well. They did not want to know what went on. behind the factory gates. The accountants who supplied the balance sheets which guided the board also lived apart from the daily round of producing and selling. Very often the board were unaware of whether they made a profit or a loss during the year until the balance sheet was produced many months into the new year.

That such a world did exist seems almost unbelievable in the context of phenomenal changes in 1980's. The 'change' that is interesting is that 'business' voluntarily subjected itself to what is called "Social Audit" in the same way as they used financial audit. From this it will be discernible that 'merchants', now, consider themselves as tenants of society.

A Social Audit is a comprehensive evaluation of the way a company discharges its responsibilities to its various stockholders and the community at large. It represents a systematic evaluation of a company's social policies.

Performance in areas such as employee relations, consumer relations, government relations and environmental aspects are being measured and evaluated. Management have now come to realise that without such evaluation, they cannot decide what is possible and what should be corrected, lit has become a part of the strategic and operating planning process. This is found to be helping the companies to recognize strengths and weaknesses, threats and opportunities in policies and practice.

Social Audit, a main component of Corporate Relations, has progressed to such an extent that even public sector undertakings like Bharat Heavy Electricals Ltd. have changed not only the concept of public relations practice but also the designation of the managers from "Public Relations" to "Corporate Relations". Most of us are aware of the mighty success it has achieved in local and overseas markets by BHEL's dedicated application of Corporate Relations.

Adverting to the private sector, close perusal of Indian Tobacco Company Ltd. 'Corporate Journey' of April 1982, and other stories in "ITC News" quarterly of 1982, will reveal how a mere tobacco manufacturing and selling company employing a few hundreds at their limited operational bases some three decades ago are one of the pioneers in diversifying their activities : They have, now, Hotels Division, Paper Mills, Exports, Management Consultancy, Leaf Tobacco Research and Development, Packaging and Printing, Carpet Manufacturing and Marketing mostly in overseas markets.

The Houses of Tata, Mafatlal, Bajaj, Hindustan Lever, Colgate-Palmolive, Indian 'Oxygen, Good-year, Hoechst, DCM, Godrej, TVS, ACC, Mahindra & Mahindra, Birlas, JK Group of Kanpur, to name a few, have contributed a great deal to the economic development of India by faithful implementation of Corporate Relations programmes. Due mainly to the progressive and enlightened programmes and policies of these 'Corporate Citizens' abundant employment opportunities have been generated and sizable foreign exchange monies are also being earned. The following are the elements that are involved in the Corporate (Public) Relations policy and which have helped them to gain the esteem of the various segments of Indian and overseas public :

1. Adapting to the counselling based on an understanding of human behaviour.
2. Analysing future needs and predicting their consequences.
3. Research into public opinion, attitudes and expectations, and advising on necessary action.
4. Establishing and maintaining two-way communication based on truth and full information.
5. Preventing conflict and misunderstandings.
6. Promoting mutual respect and social responsibility.
7. Harmonizing the private and public interests.
8. Promoting goodwill with staff, suppliers and customers.
9. Improving industrial relations.
10. Attracting good personnel and reducing labour turnover.
11. Promotion of products and services.

12. Maximising profitability.
13. Projecting a 'Corporate Identity'.
14. Encouraging an interest in international affairs.
15. Promoting an understanding of democracy.

Now let us analyse how professional public relations plays its catalytic role in almost all spheres of human life :

1. Government—National, State, Local, and International.
2. Business and Industry—small, medium, and trans-national.
3. Community and social affairs.
4. Educational Institutions, Universities, Colleges, etc.
5. Hospitals and Health Care.
6. Charities and good causes.
7. International affairs.

With public acceptance and consequent participation of public only can any government stand ; without it, it will fail. Illuminating examples are the 1982 ASIAD, January 1982 Public Relations 9th World Congress, Non-Aligned Summit of 1983. Without public support and active participation India could not have capitalized on these great events and earned the plaudits of the many distinguished visitors from many parts of the world, and their countrymen and women.

Elections. The remarkable increase in the number of voters who exercised their franchise; even old men and women—some trekking long distances—disabled men and women travelling by ox-carts with their friends or relatives to help them in casting their votes, go to show how our people have begun to actively participate in the democratic functions of government. It is also a matter of great interest to people in other parts of the world, and also in India, how these voters could overthrow the oldest political party and vote to power a party of very recent origin ; similarly, the very same voters unseated the new party inside a period of three years vexed with their scramble for offices of power and brought back the old party, giving another chance to govern the affairs of the country in a way better than in the past.

Family Welfare. It is the acceptance of the public, by and large, that the message of the national government to restrict population growth could carry conviction ; with the result there is steady decrease in the number of births.

Mass Media : All because the masses are keen to know about the day-to-day happenings in the country that might have a direct or indirect impact on their lives, members of the audience to radio, television broadcasts as well as print media show progressive increase.

Community Service

Agriculture : The bulk of the country's population is constituted by villagers whose principal occupation is farming. That we are able to increase our production on agricultural front clearly shows that the participation of the farmers in all the governmental promotion of research and development so as to apply all that has been demonstrated to them into their own farm operations, this way they have almost given up their outmoded or rather traditional method of cultivation and harvesting. Here is a true story to support the abovecited statement: It is styled as "Cocoanut Development Project" launched by the National Service Scheme (NSS) on the 15th August, 1982, in Madras city. Carefully choosing the residential area, 10,000 cocoanut seedlings were supplied at a nominal cost of Rs. 80 each. The distribution depended on the demand of the householders. NSS volunteers who were specially trained for this were deputed to help the homes by demonstrating how to dig the pits, what kind of manure and the quantity to be consumed, how to take care of the plant for 6 years until the sapling reached the stage of dwarf tree, and how by planting 10,000 seedlings the homes could earn, in all, Rs. 10 lakhs after 6 years and thereafter. The writer was invited to see the 'function' at various places in the city. The public participation was enthusiastic.

Social Welfare Agencies : How could Shri Ramakrishna Mission, "Nirmal Hridya", Rotary, Lions, Jaycees, Round Table, Helpage render such yeomen service to the needy members of human kind? Without public acceptance of their aims and goals and the dedicated way they operate their 'missions', participation in various ways would not be there so much as we see.

Social Transformation

We are now in the throes of a social transformation. A new era of fresh urges is coming in. There is anxiety all round about the change through which India should pass. There is a growing, conscious educated elite which is keen to become a catalyst in this transformation.

Therefore, in the present context, public relations cannot be something which relates only to the customer-seller relationship but must fit into the social context of which industrial organization is a part.

Whether with regard to public relations in this broader sense or in the narrower sense, the basic issue is that the public relations man has to bean enlightened man. Unless he is enlightened and has a sense of the future of the society to which he belongs, it will be difficult for him to make a success of his job. Winston Churchill once told a convocation "Young men, attach yourself to a movement with a fight before it. Even if you cannot, see the movement to a successful end, that movement will see to it that you are a successful man."

It is essential to belong to a movement. In a way, we are fortunate to live in an era when society is on the move. We must belong to that era when we are in a society which is undergoing transformation. It is good to be a catalyst and a vital element of that social transformation than to be merely an onlooker.

Challenges of Modernization : The basic thing which confronts public relations practice is that our institutions are still outmoded, in many respects, to meet the challenges posed by the rapid events that are trying to overtake mankind in its process of modernization.

Therefore, every institution whether industrial, commercial or political should fit into this challenge. But let us not forget that modernity is not our aim, because we should ask ourselves such questions like, "Modernity for what"? Modernity for what type of social setup ? Modernity is to give a man, and in this case the Indian, greater social justice.

Whether or not we are in a position to give the people social justice as implied by democracy, it is certainly not possible to allow society to go on as it is any longer. All of us are totally against bloody revolution and we do not want the kind of change which forces through a blood bath. That does not, however, mean that if one does not like revolutions they can be delayed by denial of justice. Revolutions in the sense that they affect social relationships, always come every decade without bloodshed. The choice is ours, and therefore, public relations men must become tools of social information brought about without bloodshed.

Public relations is something which not many can afford. But if you are able to create consciousness of the importance of public relations, the smaller firm should also be able to afford it. In the wider sense, even those who practise in the social and political spheres should also be able to use it.

Responsibility

Management in a modern society is accountable not only to the traditional groups which control it but also to the public at large. In the case of public sector enterprises in a planned economy, the accountability is threefold: (a) to the government; *(b)* to the parliament to which the government is answerable ; (c) the general public which is the ultimate sovereign in the democratic society. Public relations in this context is an integral function of management. The concept of accountability to the general public is not something peculiar to the public sector enterprises. Private enterprises are as much responsible to those who plan as well as to those who provide the finance or buy their goods. Even in a society like that of the United States of America which does not have planning, social forces have created public agencies, not necessarily invested with statutory rights but having substantial public publicity facilities at their disposal to make the industrial world accountable to them. In a society which has an elaborate and complex economy, planned or otherwise, economic activity becomes a matter of public interest and public scrutiny. It being so, managers are not only accountable to the groups to which they were traditionally accountable such as those who provide the finance, but also to others.

Public relations practitioners generally classify this public according to particular aspect in which a section of the public may be interested. This is necessary in order to deal with the public in relation to the matter which engages the attention of the given public. Some of these categories are : labour as a group by itself ; investors as a group by themselves ; consumers ; the "government" and what is termed loosely as the general public.

It is also generally recognized that the accountability to the public is not to be discharged by only a particular set of persons who stand out in the public eye as representing the corporate entity of the enterprise. No manager can say that he does not deal with the public and no manager can ignore the public he has to deal with. Public relations as a management function is the responsibility of every man in the context of his own functioning and in the context of the particular aspect of the enterprise which he represents.

Management Function

Management is a science. "Science" because it deals with behavioural attitude and opinion. Smoothening human behaviour and creating favourable opinion constitute an important component of an organization or industry for its healthy growth.

In an organization—medium or large—it is not possible for the management people to handle this complex and time consuming work. So powers are delegated to the Public Relations department.

Public Relations is a management function because it is directly under the Board of Directors or Management. The PR Head is answerable to the management at the top and to other departments like Finance, Sales, Administrative, Personnel or Production. It is illustrated here :

MADRAS COMPANY, LIMITED

CHAIRMAN

Board of Directors

President or Managing Director

Public Relations

Department

Advertising and Publicity Department	Corporate Sector
	Works—Sector
	Production
	Marketing & Sales
	Personnel
	Finance

Board of Directors is the supreme body of the organization ; its head is designated as Chairman of the Board. The second is the Board of Management ; it is constituted by the Board of Directors selecting or nominating or designating a capable person from each department of importance. This group of persons under a Managing Director discharges the management duties of the organization?

Periodically, weekly or even daily, as the case may be, the Board of Management apprise the Board of Directors about the organization's activities covering profit, sales, production, finance—block and liquid assets, accounts receivable, accounts payable and so on. All data is taken out on computer system, if there is one such, or the "Management Information Department."

The Board of Directors delegate the authorities of different types to different heads of departments and make them more responsible to the Board of Directors. Certain powers to take independent decisions are also given. In the same way, the head of the Public Relations Department is appointed by the Board of Directors or by the Managing Director on their behalf. As such the Public Relations is a management function in that, the head of the department is made responsible to carry out the duties as directed, and that he has to report the result of his departmental affairs and actions to the Board of Directors or the Board of Management.

Another important point as to why the PR is a management function is :

> That all activities of the PR department—whether good or bad—whether inferior or superior—whether directed or indirected—whether intentional or unintentional—whether pre-planned or not will affect the organization's credibility goodwill or reputation, profitability and productivity in proportion to how the related functions are carried out—it may bring down to floor level with irreparable loss.

This way—why—the management must take care and interest in directing the affairs of PR department.

It is dangerous to leave the entire responsibility in the hands of the personnel of PR in any organization—whethersmall, medium or large. Management must share the responsibility with PR Executive, Director or Manager, and guide the destiny of the organization. In point of importance, PRO, 'Manager Executive or/Director should be made a member of the management team, and he should be invited to attend the departmental meetings, decision-making meetings and be allowed to take part in the discussion.

Public Relations being a management function, it calls for expertise and skill coupled with knowledge and experience as to how to handle complex situations. Many organizations prefer to an outside PR Adviser in addition to what their own people offer.

Public Relations Man

The making of a successful public relations professional consists in the following :

1. Should concern himself not with the manipulation of people, but with their continuing enlightenment.
2. Should try to elevate his audience rather than degrade them, and that his communication should be addressed to reason and judgement rather than to emotion and prejudice by :
   (a) insisting on truth and full information;
   (b) keeping the message simple and straightforward;
   (c) not overselling or exaggerating;
   (d) remembering that the audience is composed of women as well;
   (e) looking for 'drama'—not making the communication unnecessarily drab and commonplace;
   (f) packaging the communication appropriately—not overdressing or making it too extravagant;
   (g) taking time to listen to public opinion;
   (h) remembering the vital importance of continuity;
   (i) trying to be positive and constructive in every aspect of communication.
3. Should recognize that sound public relations comprises policies and deeds as well words ; that it must deal in truth rather than in deception ; that it must seek to clarify the issues of our times rather than confuse them.
4. While he may undertake to present one point of view for public consideration, he should believe in the inalienable right of those with opposing viewpoints to present their cases also. For he has to realize that his right to speak can be assured only if the guarantee exists for all, including those whose causes are unpopular.

5. Should believe that the democratic process must prevail in the marketplace of ideas, as well as in political and economic affairs.
6. Should believe that the public interest takes precedence over the interests of those he represents; and he should conceive his function as being to assist in conforming to the interests of those he represents to the interests of the public when the two do not coincide.
7. Should recognize that the consequences of his action are affected in the minds of the men and because the human mind has immeasurable potentials for good and for evil, he must approach his task in reverence and awe for the inviolable right of the individual to make his own judgement.

Professional Knowledge

A 'good' public relations professional should know: It is hard to listen; easy to talk. Hard to agree; easy to argue.

Hard to forgive; easy to nurse a grudge.

Hard to see the whole picture; easy to highlight a small section of it.

Hard to appreciate the detail; easy to generalize. Hard to cooperate with others in an attack of a common problem; easy to attack the others, and thus make the problem worse.

Hard to be steadfast; easy to be stubborn. Hard to speak up, when keeping silent is easy but wrong; easy to shout, when keeping quiet is difficult but right. Hard to give; easy to take. Hard to say 'sorry'; easy to bluster.

Hard to be magnanimous; easy to doubt the motives of others. Hard to negotiate; easy to break off. Hard to be patient; easy to be angry. Hard to understand; easy to ignore. Hard to explain; easy to denounce. Hard to love; easy to hate. Hard to build; easy to destroy.

Blessed are the Public Relations Men.

Professionalism in Public Relations : No aspect of public relations practice attracts so much attention and interest today as the problem of finding and developing the personnel who are to be the officers of tomorrow, and senior executives of the day after. It is a topic of popular discussion at very public relations conference. Yet from the welter of conversation and deliberation there has not yet emerged an agreed body of opinion on the relevant aspect of the problem at all—except its importance. Of that there cannot be the slightest doubt, and the need now is for the penetrating appraisal that can lead to the formulation of a sound and clear-cut line of approach to a constructive programme. This can start only at one point—in the basic analysis of the process of management itself, for therein lies the determining factors of the skills to be identified and developed.

Two major factors underlie the skills required effectively to exercise this process—the one is specific knowledge, and the other an adequate personal makeup on the mental and on the behavioural planes. The two are intervene, and are both complex compositions of several contributing elements, few of which can be thought of as "standard". Some are indeed "ordinary", although they tend to be glamourised in the course of popular discussion. They are in the main intangible elements and factors, not susceptible of measurement, but they can all be identified and can all be assessed, if adequate trouble is taken to construct and use skilfully appropriate media of assessment.

The second personal facet has to do with "behaviour", that is to say, with the officer's personal attitude towards and with his superiors, his colleagues and his subordinates, and it underlies his ability to secure and promote the essential cooperation without which management cannot be effective. The officer is responsible for carrying out a process of which an essential characteristics the attainment of a high degree of mutual cooperation from many people; from those who are under his command, and equally—though in a rather different sense—from colleagues in parallel positions, from specialist advisers at different levels of status, and from or with his own superior.

Without reaching for the moon, tentative analysis of experience with a large number of public relations managers has indicated the following as the basic quality'.; is required in the successful managers in the general sense, not taking into account any question of a need for high commercial acumen or related flair:

(1) Mental ability—a combination of planning sense, foresight, orderliness of mind and judgement, which will result in willingness to think straight, and in thoroughness and promptness of decision.

(2) Ability to see the other person's point of view and to be critical of self as of others; this is the basis of ability to work with other people.

(3) Integrity, in the sense of mental honesty.

(4) A restrained self-confidence, coupled with initiative and resourcefulness.

(5) A balanced temperament—particularly the absence of such traits as emotional instability, marked inferiority sense, forcefulness, self-centered outlook.

(6) A sense of humour or of cheerfulness.

(7) Persistence, but not to the point of obstinacy.

Against this background, the peculiar characteristics of the public relations profession as distinguished from other occupations, we take to be the:

> First. A profession of this nature is an occupation for which the necessary preliminary training is intellectual in character, involving knowledge in general and learning in particular, as distinguished from mere skill.

Second. It is an occupation which is pursued generally for others and not merely for one's self.

Third. It is an occupation in which the amount of financial return alone is not the accepted measure of success. In the present-day environment relative to public relations practice, success in business should mean something very different from mere money making. In business the able man ordinarily earns a larger income than one less able. So does the able man in the recognized profession—in law, medicine or engineering; and even in those professions more remote from money-making, like the ministry, teaching or social work. The world's demand for efficiency is so great and the supply so small, that the type of efficiency is high in every field of human activity.

The recognized professions, not excluding public relations, however, definitely reject the size of the financial return alone as the measure of success. These recognised professions select as a test, excellence or performance in the broadest sense, and include, among other things, advance in the particular occupation and service to the community. These are the basis of all worthy reputations in the recognized professions, and public relations is one such. In them a large income is the ordinary incident of success; but he who exaggerates the value of the incident is apt to fall short of real success.

To the business of today a similar test should be applied. True, in business the earning of profit is something more than an incident of success. It is an essential tradition of success, because the continued absence of profit itself spells failure. But while loss spells failure, large profits do not connote success. Success must be sought in business also in excellence of performance; and in business, excellence of performance manifests itself, among other things, in the advancing of methods and processes; in the improvement of products; in more perfect organization, eliminating friction as well as waste; in bettering the conditions of working men, developing their faculties and promoting their happiness: and in the establishment of right relations with customers and with the community.

In the field of modern business, so rich in opportunity for the exercise of man's finest and most varied mental faculties, and moral qualities, mere money-making cannot be regarded as the legitimate end. Neither can mere growth in bulk or power be admitted as a worthy ambition. Nor can a man nobly mindful of his serious responsibilities to society, view business as a game ; since with the conduct of business human happiness or misery is inextricably interwoven.

Real success in business is to be found in achievements comparable rather with those of the artist, or the scientist, or the inventor, or the statesman. And the joy sought in the profession of business must be like their joys and not the mere vulgar satisfaction which is experienced in the acquisition of money, in the exercise of power or in the frivolous pleasure of mere winning.

The core of professionalism in public relations encompasses a lot of ideas, certainly included are the standard virtues—good judgement, loyalty to the organization, prior planning and a sense of urgency.

Some public relations professionals have a class of public they label "opponents". Their opponents fall into at least four categories:

1. Advocates, who propose new actions or modifications of existing ones;
2. Dissidents, who are inefficiently anti and direct their criticism toward the client's organization;
3. Activists, who push for something to be done—legislation, regulation, boycott or the like;
4. Zealots, who are absorbed with one issue and cannot be reasoned with.

Obviously, no one approach can be effective with all of these, and treating them all alike can create enemies where none existed before. You can deal with a zealot by direct confrontation or argument. You can only wither the support he depends on. Treating a zealot as though he were an advocate is futile; and treating an advocate as though he were a zealot can be disastrous.

All of us in the communication business must realize that we are in this together. Free speech abridgements, wherever and whenever they occur, apply to us all.

The business is a special kind, of people who have their heads in the clouds and their feet in the cash-box!

Too often, human services public relations is self-serving, and self-perpetuating, when what is really needed is a campaign to promote human dignity.

New research might study the influence of most media as a primary case of crowd-like behaviour. Research might help us understand the extent to which an idealistic, rational Indian public may exist despite the mass media.

Public opinion is based on information and belief. If it is wrong, it is wrong because of wrong information and consequent erroneous belief. It is not only the right but the obligation of all individuals or the aggregation of individuals, who came before the public, to see that the public has full and correct information. The only policy that should govern is that whatever is said or told should be absolutely correct, and that no material fact, even if unfavourable but bearing on the subject, shall be held back.

The obligation on the other side of that coin is the proper flow of information in the opposite direction, from the public to the organization—and, where just and fitting, the utilization of the data by public relations is an advocacy role. It should include some views that management would hear, so be it. Bearers of such tidings are not to be underestimated—because we are fully aware that with our enlightened support, they can influence the message they bear, in the public interest and, hence, our own.

The practice of public relations profession is not limited to national borders nor is it restricted to the field of business or any other single activity. Public relations is not mere communication, and certainly not merely a tool of management. The modern concept of public relations practice as understood by the enlightened professionals is that public relations is an integral part of the management of any organization, and its main object should be achieve and to maintain humanization with the environment. Business too often has been silent in its defence of capitalism, when its critics became strident did business publicly state opposition.

In conclusion, it may not be inappropriate to quote Leon Bloy, French novelist: "The worst evil is not committing crimes, but, failing to do good one could do."

Professional Maturity

Public relations people have a general tendency to debate where public relations is a profession, trade, occupation, science or :, which the author thinks is a futile and needless exercise, when their achievements speak well for themselves. There is no such bate over professional charters in other disciplines. If maturity public relations profession is there, then public relations people 11 certainly welcome a definition of responsibilities in their areas operation; they would turn, then, their attention to new communication discoveries, strategies and techniques.

Against this background, it is felt that five major factors have apparently retarded the maturity of public relations as a profession:

1. It has grown rapidly the world over in response to needs, with effective sources of training developing much more slowly. Quite few unqualified persons—often with lack of sound motives—have failed themselves as public relations specialists and offered their services with the help of some diplomas obtained from some private institutions. In a number of cases, they have been able to prosper, though damaging confidence in the field and its practices among many of those they have dealt with.
2. It covers an exceedingly wide scope. People with skills in arranging special events or in editing a company publication, for instance, are public relations practitioners. People who encounter such specialists, however, often do not understand the difference between an ophthalmologist and a sychiatrist—both of whom must have M.D., or allied degrees—and often there is an equal difference between persons who have concentrated on separate aspects of public relations.
3. There have been forces within the field and outside that have created misunderstanding. Because journalists tend

to interpret any thing dealing with communication as a form of journalism, many writers have had a narrow view of public relations. Many articles have been based on the preconceived premise that "public relations" is a pseudo-journalist's snobbish term for trying to "use" the press. As public relations has developed and many of its practitioners have prospered, this prejudice has been tinged, sometimes, with resentment. While treatment of public relations has tended to improve gradually, it is still among the most stubbornly distorted subjects covered by the press in general.

Some practitioners, in turn, have tended to create an aura of mystery about the field, to aggrandize their stature and to glorify talents supposedly only they can provide. This has included sweeping promises to make any business tycoon an international personage; assurances that social and economic tides can be reversed merely through propaganda "magic"; and claims of solving a great industry's problems by forming a committee and holding a conference. Propounding of terms like "engineering of consent" to describe a public relations man's functions, that imply both omnipotence and manipulation of the public, has aroused fear of intellectuals and public officials.

4. The fact that the best public relations service is often intangible and comparatively immeasurable, has often made it easier for the charlatan to obtain an assignment rather than the sound practitioner. The man or organisation that spells out specific promises where none can be made; who finds out what the prospect will buy and then develops his presentation accordingly, rather than on what sound judgement calls for; the periodic report that stresses visible items—selected press clippings and circulation figures, regardless of their relations to the problem and objective—these often appeal to the practical-minded management executive who is not trained to understand the nuances of public relations.

5. Until recently there has been little enforcement of any standards that practitioners are expected to meet.

Practices harmful to respect for public relations have been of two general types: those that result in widespread attention to malpractices, and those that are not exposed but still undermine confidence in the field. This may be said of any field of endeavour, from law and college teaching to operating railways. In the case of public relations, the first group has been far less numerous than the second, but the publicized exposes have been deeply impressed on the minds of many people. (Thanks to the "Code of Ethics and Standards" set by the Public Relations Society of America that the public relations profession is now on a better footing than in the past.)

While public relations goes through its process of maturing, the best means of raising standards and protecting the public interest will continue to be educating users of the service, the press and the public on the true nature of the field. The reputation of the professional or practitioner among companies or clients and the best of his contemporaries is the surest measure of his stature and integrity.

The opportunities in public relations are growing in both intensified specialization and broad overall knowledge and talent. The way ahead for success for the individual can come from either direction.

In a world that at times seems to be tenuously held together by too little understood principles of group attitudes, the challenge and opportunities for the field that specializes in understanding and developing group attitudes still appear to be in their infancy.

7

Technical Aspects

Printing Devices

It is impossible to say printing from blocks and type was practised by the Chinese many centuries before it became known in Europe. The earliest European examples of printing done with movable metal type are ascribed to Johann Gutenberg of Mainz, in Germany, and belong to the year 1454.

Photography : It has quickened and cheapened the illustration of books, magazines and newspapers very greatly. Almost every illustration which one sees now a days has been made from a block in the preparation of which photography played an important part. Most photographic printing blocks are divided into two classes: "line" or "black and white" block and "half-tone" blocks. Line blocks are used for reproducing diagrams and pen and ink drawings as plain black lines or patches on a white ground. Half-tone blocks (almost all the blocks used in 'Pictorial Knowledge' belong to this class) are employed in reproducing direct from photographs, pictures etc. in which there are several different tones intermediate between black and white.

'Line' printing blocks : Suppose that a block has to be made of an ornamental black A on a white ground. First a photograph of the A is taken on a glass plate, which shows a transparent A on a black background. This negative plate is placed in a printing frame touching a zinc plate coated with a sensitive film, and is exposed to light for a certain time. The light passing through the A, the only transparent part of the negative, renders all the film which it reaches insoluble in water. The zinc 'positive' is held under a tape and all the film that the light could not get at dissolves and disappears, leaving the A on the surface of the zinc. After further treatment, which includes varnishing the back, the plate is placed in a dish and flooded with acid, which bites into the metal everywhere except where the A protects it. The 'etching' as this process is called is continued until the A stands up far enough above the rest of the plate to be printed from.

Half-tone printing blocks : If you examine with a magnifying glass a printed illustration made from a photograph, you will see that the black parts are speckled with small white dots; that the dark grey parts are larger white dots surrounded by black; that the light grey parts are large black dots surrounded by white, and that the white parts are white sprinkled over with tiny black dots. You will further notice that the dots are in parallel straight lines crossing one another at right angles. Let us suppose that a half-tone block has to be made from a photographic portrait of a person wearing a black coat, a grey waistcoat, and a white collar. First of all, a negative of the photograph is taken with a camera. Just in front of the plate is fixed a glass screen, consisting of two glass plates rule with parallel black lines a tiny fraction of an inch apart. The screen plates are placed face to face with the lines on one crossing those of the other, and forming a black network enclosing tiny squares of clear glass. Each square acts as a minute lens, and throws a dot of light on to the photographic plate. The size of the dot depends on the intensity of the light. The collar will cast dots so large that they overlap each other almost entirety, enclosing tiny spot of darkness wherever two lines of the screen cross. The waistcoat dots are smaller, and do not cross the shadow meshwork of the screen, while the coat dots are very small indeed. In the developed negative the blacks and whites are, of course, reversed. A print is taken from the negative on to a sensitised copper plate, coated with a film which becomes insoluble in water wherever light reaches it. When this metal 'positive' is swashed, areas of film are left wherever the negative was not blackened. The positive is etched with acid, which eats away the unprotected parts of the plate, and the result is a half-tone block, having small points of metal standing up over the collar area, a projecting meshwork over the waistcoat area and a flat surface pitted with tiny depressions over the coat area. Wherever the metal has been left at its original level it will pick up ink from a roller passed over it. At reading distance the individual dots cannot be distinguished. They blend together, giving a tone which depends on the predominance of black over white, or of white over black, as the case may be.

For Newspapers : Because the type is set up by machines which do the work much more quickly than setting by hand; and because the revolving presses used run at very high speeds, printing the copies on continuous reels of paper. The sheets of a newspaper are cut and assembled in their proper order by ingenious apparatus at the delivery end of the press.

Stereotyping : Making casts from set-up type for printing from. A soft pad of tissue paper and blotting-paper mixed with size is laid over the type and beaten or squeezed hard against it till the under side contains an exact impression of the type. The pad is then dried, lifted from the type and placed in a casting-box for its back to be flooded with molten lead which, when it has hardened, is a plate with an exact duplicate of the original type standing up on one face of it.

Lithography

A process of printing from flat stones. The design of picture to be printed is drawn on the stone in a special ink. A wet roller is then passed over the stone, damping it wherever there is no ink.

Next, an inked roller is applied, and this leaves ink on the non-wetted parts only, that is, on the design. When a piece of paper is pressed hard against the stone it picks up the ink, taking a print of the original. Any number of prints can be taken, but the stone must be wetted and inked for each print. Lithography is now used chiefly for large coloured prints, such as posters.

Meanings of '4to' '8vo' '12mo' and '16mo' printed in book catalogues after the names of books:

> They are abbreviations of 'quarto' 'octavo' 'duodecimo' and 'sextodecimo' indicating that the size of a page of the book is respectively a quarter, an eighth, a twelfth, or a sixteenth of a standard-size sheet of printing paper. The size of the sheet itself is usually indicated by the word 'royal', 'crown', imperial etc.

A book is usually printed sixteen pages to one sheet of paper. When a sheet is folded it forms a section, or 'signature' of the book. The first page of each section is marked with a letter to guide the printer and binder. The letters run alphabetically through the book. Some printers use numbers instead of letters.

Right to Information : The right to information is a right incidental to the constitutionally guaranteed freedom of speech and expression. The international movement to include it in the legal system gained prominence in 1946 when the general assembly of the United Nations declared freedom of information to be a fundamental human right and a touchstone for all other liberties. It culminated in the U.N. Conference on Freedom of information held in Geneva in 1948.

Universal Declaration of Human Rights

"Everyone has the right to freedom of information and expression. This right includes freedom to hold opinions without interference and to seek, receive and impart information and ideas through any media and regardless of frontier."

It may be a coincidence that Article 19 of the Indian Constitution also provides every citizen the right to freedom of speech and expression. However, the word 'information' is conspicuously absent.

India's Role

India was a member of the Commission on Human Rights appointed by the Economic and Social Council of the United Nations which drafted the 1948 Declaration. As such it would have been eminently fit and proper if the right to information was included in the rights enumerated under Article 19 of our Constitution. Article 55 of the U.N. Charter stipulates that the United Nations shall promote respect for and observance of human rights and fundamental freedoms and according to Article 56 "all members pledge themselves to take joint and separate action in cooperation with the Organisation for the achievement of the purposes set forth in Article 55".

Information is essential for acquiring knowledge and skill which are absolutely necessary for the proper and effective exercise and enjoyment of the fundamental right to freedom of speech and expression. Depriving an individual of the right to information will have the deleterious effect of denial to that individual of his fundamental right of freedom of speech and expression. However, problems arise in enforcing this right against the state and public bodies. The executive branch of the government, unlike the other two organs, often tends to cloak its operations in secrecy. It will not be possible for any citizen to play his responsible role of making government institutions accountable unless he is privy to necessary information. Public discussion is a political duty; a discussion can only be on the basis of information: a well-informed citizen is the *sine qua non* for the success of a democracy.

The Information

(1) There is an event, identifiable in Time and Place, called a Decision, which results in the occurrence of derivative events.

(2) Information represents Truth — It's a good thing. The more information you have access to the better. The more

people who have access to an item of information, the better. People have right to Information.

(3) Information should be provided to Decision-makers to aid them.

(4) The more Information brought to bear on a Decision the better is the resultant Decision.

Information is more than mere Data Information has complex attributes : Correctness Timeliness Value Ownership Language

Legal rights and Responsibilities of the Buyer Seller Carrier Public

2. Utility, and hence value, of information derives from its use, in Decision-Making

3. What happens as the number of people have access to Information Increase:

GOOD: Unit cost of Information decreases : Improved Management : Liberation of the Mind : Increased Social Responsibility'.

BAD : Decreased Quality : Loss of Privacy : Vulnerability to Malicious Action : Vulnerability to Accident.

Communication of Uncertainty

(1) Telling the Truth, the Whole Truth and Nothing but the Truth.

(2) But what about the usual situation where

You do not know the Whole Truth?

You do not know how much of the Whole Truth You Do Know ?

You do not know the importance (e.g., Relevance) of What you do not know?

(3) Thus, aside from the substantial difficulty of Communicating

What You Do Not Know, How Do You: Estimate the size of

What You Do Not Know?

Express its relative importance.

Role of Mass Media

In the last decade or so. the network of Mass Media in India has been well established. Considering the size of the country, it is most remarkable to see that AIR now reaches 90% of the population and TV more than 80%. It was the most ambitious programme ever launched and successfully completed in the world. Moreover both these tools are no more the reserves of the elite but have become an important pass time for the poor people. One can see the transistor being used by workers on building sites and TV Antennas sprung over the slums. It is a good sign in a sense that if properly handled, these tools are most effective for mass education and passing on information. Today's youth is getting attracted to these media by attending to popular programmes like movies, *Chhayageet, Mahabharat* and some other serials and sports events. However, there is still a lot of scope in using these media for the youth.

Present Status of Youths : With a growing population, a new generation of youth is facing the problem of unemployment which in turn brings a lot of side effects like unrest, drugs, arson and so on. Further owing to increased competitions, many talented youths find it difficult to get admission for higher education in the field of their choice as the 'Percentage for admission has gone up. This brings frustration to the youth. Horizons for career opportunities are widening, new avenues are opened but many a times, lack of information leads to many deserving youngsters losing an opportunity to join such careers. Mass media could be the best channel to pass on career information to youths as it can reach the maximum number at one time.

Youth Categories : Before studying how this channel could be used, let us see the categories of the youth:

(1) Those in schools during 10-12 standards and before that: This category needs to know the avenues open to choose a career, what are the admission criteria, where are the institutes, what employment or entrepreneurship opportunities are opened if they choose a certain career,

how to get information on various institutes, entrance examination, and what vocational training facilities are available even if they are not able to complete schooling etc.

(2) Graduates: They have completed the basic course of education and they have to know what employment opportunities are open, what facilities are available for higher studies in the same or allied field, within and in outside countries, what supporting courses they can undertake to better the qualifications and so on. Also whether any scope exists for starting their own ventures etc.

(3) Educated/Uneducated unemployed : They should know how they can start their own business, small-scale industrial units, village industries and so on. Also what govt. schemes are available, how they can use bank facilities, how they can take vocational training to better their qualifications etc.

Many a time, such information is available in printed forms but it does not reach all concerned due to various limitations. At present, such information is occasionally given on AIR and TV but there is no specific system established, especially on the national hook-up. Many a time, the time selected is odd when youths are out for sports etc. and hence the desired effects are not achieved.

The Guidelines

1. Such career information should be a regular feature on the national hook-up with prime time allotted. It is to be seen as to what is the most appropriate time when the maximum number of youths can take advantage of this information, and it may be during school or college hours when the target listeners are readily available (like country-wide class rooms).
2. Information on career opportunities should be given with the coverage to institutes, their set-up, their admission

procedure and criteria, involving principals, professors or teachers; or to various professional bodies like doctors, lawyers, engineers and those in other fields.

3. Successful entrepreneurs should be interviewed, with coverage given (especially on TV) about how they have established and how they have struggled to overcome financial and other difficulties.
4. Many a time, career information is given by people who are not involved in the system, hence it becomes bookish. This should be avoided.
5. There should be group discussions, quiz programmes, question and answer sessions where youths are also involved to extract such information.
6. Parents should be involved in such programmes and emphasis laid that parents are equally responsible to shape the career of their children and that they must try to get information on career opportunities from various sources.
7. For the educated employed, the facilities available to start their own business or vocation should be provided. Very often, some good schemes remain underutilised owing to lack of knowledge of the people of such schemes who are going to use them.
8. For competitive examinations, important selection criteria for the entrance examination etc. the mass media should be used to pass on the information. The same is true for information on various opportunities available in the defence services, para military forces and police forces.
9. Many service organisations like Rotary International are doing yeoman work in this field; they could be involved in such programmes.
10. May be information on those who have been failures should also be given so that others will get hints.
11. A study group of experts in various fields may be appointed to go in to various aspects of these suggestions

and to find out how best the mass media could be utilised to shape the career of youths.

The Conclusion

1. Once such programmes are made attractive and at times convenient to youths (perhaps a study has to be conducted to find the most effective time) youths will get to listen and view such programmes and then they will be better informed.
2. A follow-up study about how the information has been used by them could be made to see if any change in the pattern is needed. Parents also will be better informed, and they in turn can be effective in shaping the future of their children.
3. Coverage should be given to those who have used such programmes, effectively to better their career.
4. Schemes will be better utilised.
5. Mass media will be a tool not only for entertainment but also for career development of youths.
6. Results of better informed youths to the nation will be—talented youths will be available in various schemes unemployment will be reduced thereby reducing unrest and other such side effects.
7. If we want to plan for a hundred years, we have to invest in the future and the future of the nation lies in the hands of youth.

   I hope our mass media planners will give serious thought to these proposals.

New Setup

In the famous words of U Thant, "It is no longer resources that limit decisions but it is the decisions that make resources". In today's complex world, decisions depend upon collection, selection, and correlation of 'Information' in the shortest time. The "New Information Order" is poised for the commitment. Like its companion the "New World Economic Order" which calls for redistribution of the international power of the purse. The New Information Order" is a demand for the redress of perceived iniquities. this time over the 'power of the world'. It is "The Free and Balanced Flow of Information": not creating and perpetuating an imbalance in the worlds flow of information under the guise of maintaining freedom, resulting in a vast and insidious cultural imperialism built on the western monopoly of the means of international communication.

The Press, quite literally an informer, must make way for the New Order and its new right of "objectivity of information and balance in its presentation". While upholding its rights as an 'informer', it cannot be silent on its duties and responsibilities towards the informed. The traditional concept of rights in the field of communication can no more be on individualist considerations, to the detriment of collective needs. Freedom of information cannot continue to be a sort of instrument of domination in the hands of the information media. For example, does it contribute to the fulfilment of the aspirations and growth of the 'Third World" countries if the Western journalists, rightly or wrongly, give more prominence to the developing countries' problems such as communal fracas, unemployment, food, population, etc. in their reports? Such reports smack of either ignoring or belittling the efforts of the developing countries towards alleviating their problems, often against seemingly unsurmountable odds. How do such reports on social, economic and political developments in the Third World, in terms of 'right' or "leftward" shifts in government policies, be considered objective? Again, how can land reforms, and measures to encourage the development of national industries to the immediate or potential disadvantage of transnational corporations, contain measures to sober the stronghold of a few indigenous business groups over national economics? Legislation to ensure monitoring and supervision of national banking and trade institutions be considered as portents of a country's slide into the communist or socialist ambit?

To make the 'Information System' work meaningfully, that is the 'haves' helping the 'have-nots,' the following steps call for consideration:

First : Regulation of the right to information by preventing abusive uses of the right to access.

Next : Definition of appropriate criteria to govern truly objective news selection. Then : Establishment of a professional code of ethics, enforced by a tribunal empowered to punish violators who disseminate false or distorted information. Finally : Creation of an international convention defining the right of reply for maligned states.

This would include "A list of precisely defined infringements (of) prestige, culture, and values."

8

Scope and Sphere

Today public relations is accepted by all business organizations and by non-business organizations as well. The main field of public relations will, however, remain with business whether it is government or private.

Business today is on trial in India. On trial, its performance has not been generally as good and well-meaning as the public and economists would like it to be. Till the 1957 elections most people said that business was the best scapegoat of discontent in India. Since 1967 a new class of people has started competing with business for that destination, i.e., a class of politicals. In the last few years politicians have made a tremendous advance as a part of the community that has been looked upon with disfavour. In the near future the scapegoat of public annoyance is expected to be taken over from the business man.

However, not all the charges made against business and politicians can be sustained. Both have yet to succeed in their endeavours to establish a good record! People have begun to be more exacting as proved by the last General Elections. The numbers of good business men and honest politicians are yet to become a majority. But there are expectations.

The relations between Government and business have not been too good in our country, both between the British and our Indian industrialists, and between the Nehru Government and our industrialists. Nevertheless, there is a dialogue between the Government and business as, for example, between the Chamber of Commerce and the Prime Minister, although it is not a very effective one.

However, this is not the kind of thing we need. What we do need is a more genuine concentration of mind without any publicity. *This is trying to understand each other.* Business must stop cringing. What should be the objective of the Indian business and Government today?

Public relations today is business, is a counter-offensive to stop being on the defensive and to 'attack' by honest and sincere means. Another aim should be to stand up and justify the good value of free enterprise and stand by the Government when it is in genuine need of such support. The social obligations of business have also to be accepted. To help business achieve it, it is the Government which needs to create favourable climate.

Some years ago, a declaration of social responsibility was adopted at an influential seminar presided over by our revered and late Loknayak, Jaya Prakash Narayan. The declaration reiterated that "every trust has an overriding responsibility to make the fullest possible use of its resources, both human and material, as an individual. Power carries with it obligations. Some regulation by the State is definitely necessary."

In general, self-regulating is preferable to State legislation. As recommended by a social scientist, a social audit by objective experts every three or five years to see whether we are doing our job in a responsible way, and publishing them in reports, can be given due consideration.

There is plenty of scope to reach out to the student population to help industry and institution building, and the promotion and development of citizenship are vital and should be instilled into the community. According to Dr. Scott Cutlip, industry in America is contributing generously to higher education, which it was not doing some years ago. Industry in the US is now providing educational and instructional materials to schools.

The scope of public relations is to interest itself in issues of national importance, *e.g.,* city improvement, environmental pollution, ecological balance, and the like. There ought to be an identification with national objectives that will enable business to grow and the Government to function effectively toward the good of the common man of the village.

The tools that were available to public relations practitioners in the past were relatively few. The tools that have been perfected and are being developed have tremendous potential. Imagine the potential of satellite communication, which we are going to put to good use. It has the potential of affecting the pattern of life of every citizen in every village of the country. It can revolutionize agriculture and education, bring about greater social consciousness, educate the rural masses in the use of modern technology, help in literacy programmes, make people aware about health, hygiene and sanitation. Development of software for satellite communication is a great challenge for all those who want to communicate. The radio and television are other media of communication which have proved to be of immense influence in developed countries. The spread of literacy has made the written word much more meaningful and widened its scope than before. Jet transport and electronic system take your message to the farthest corner of the world in a matter of hours. All these are powerful tools which, if used properly, can bring about happiness and peace to humankind.

Those involved in public relations are aware of the challenge inherent in the situation. Likewise, political leaders, entrepreneurs, managers, social workers, teachers, students, even religious heads and all the rest of India, it is fervently hoped, will become aware of this challenge.

If there is no 'change', there is no public relations. If we all ate the same food as our forbears, purchased and wore the same fabrics used by them and lived in the same type of houses, there would be a basic automaticity between production and consumption, there would be no need to interpret and improve the relationship of the producing of commercial unit and the consuming public which, in essence, is what this topic deals with.

So far 'measurement of things' has been dealt with. 'Measurement of man' is more important. For, we have seen that public relations refers to all the interactions that occur among people, whether they are conflicts or cooperative behaviours.

Part of Management

The institution of public relations arose out of the phenomenal growth of industry in the Western countries in the nineteenth century and the 'public- be-dammed' attitude of the industrialists which came in for strong criticism at the hands of social workers and political writers. The theory of *laissez faire* which held the field then in most of the advanced countries particularly helped this type of attitude. Business did not care for the people. Consequently, the public became intolerant of Business. In course of time, pressure of public opinion compelled business magnates to try to present an acceptable front to the people about the industries which they were controlling. The institution of public relations arose out of this development. Practically all large industries and commercial institutions in the Western countries and many in our own country have public relations staff now, with specific functions and duties.

In the Government of India, the importance of public relations was realised even in the British days. With the emergence of freedom, the need became urgent as Government took over a large number of nation-building Programmes for which public cooperation in a significant measure was necessary. To explain Government's policies and programmes, to indicate to the people the area of cooperation in developmental activities and to keep people informed of the progress of planning and development, a body of specialists was required.

The institution of public relations has often been misunderstood, not without reason. Instead of considering the public relations staff as a part of an organisation and their function as scientific exposition of the merits and objectives of the institution, instances are not rare when public relations staff have been regarded as the personal appendages of the heads of institutions or Ministers. There are pliable and obliging public relations men, too, who have devoted their talent and energy to build up individuals or promote personal publicity. Almost every country has passed through this phase at some stage or the other so that honest public relations people sometimes got frustrated. Some PR men have sadly confessed in their memoirs that they "did work, they detested for money they didn't earn to buy things they didn't need to impress people they didn't like !"

But this really is an aberration of public relations. Public relations at its best is a highly honourable profession. It has the dual role of explaining and interpreting truthfully the policies and programmes of an institution and secondly to keep the policy-makers informed of the people's reactions. It is wrong to expect that a public relations man will project half truth or untruth. Any employer who thinks that by employing public relations staff he can project before the people a false image of his institution or business or that he can bluff people by putting out inaccurate but pleasantly worded stuff follows an extremely shortsighted policy. If public relations is to be successful, it must not compromise with truth.

Wrong use of public relations has aroused criticism and, in some countries, even suggestions have been made that public relations practice should be made illegal except by registered practitioners. While too much importance should not be attached to this suggestion in the present Indian context when public relations is hardly extensive enough to constitute a problem, the suggestion underlines the delicate nature of the operation of public relations. The actual strength of public relations lies in its looseness, flexibility, its informal approach and the deft use of the contacts that a PRO is able to build up. It is thus 'a troubleshooting profession' and in unscrupulous hands it can do harm. In developing countries, particularly in countries which have emerged into freedom after long periods of static existence under colonial rule and where the concept of democracy has not established its roots firmly, a public relations man who happens to be in the confidence of his Minister or department can exercise influence over the press and other mass media. This influence, can be towards the goods, in the national interest or, if the public relations officer so wishes, in the personal interest of the Minister, and ultimately in his own interest as by pleasing the Minister he furthers his own objective. But such practices cannot continue for long. As soon as the national press of a country assumes its vigilant role, undue influence of the PRO ceases.

Competence Necessary

A public relations officer should be sufficiently competent to be welcomed into the policy-making level of the ministry or the institution which he has been called upon to serve. He should serve as a barometer of public opinion and keep the management informed of public reactions. To discharge these functions effectively, the public relations officer should not merely be highly knowledgeable about his institution or his department but he should also be a man of character with respect for truth; he should have a progressive attitude, sincerity, unfailing courtesy, a sense of responsibility to the public and be fair in projecting the views of the institution or the Government which he serves. These qualities, added to imagination and dynamism, can help significantly.

The job of the PRO to the Government is a specialised one. He is the visible and the immediate link between the Government and the various media. It is he who receives the first shock from the media and it is he who communicates the first reaction of the Government to the various media. Therefore, it is essential that a public relations officer maintains a cool temper and does notate ruffled while dealing with controversial issues; that he does not try to bluff or assume an all knowing air but is helpful in collecting information and providing it; and that he avoids red-tape and is not standoffish or evasive in his answers. The PRO should realise that any obstruction that he places in the way of a reporter in getting an answer to a legitimate question or a story will only make the reporter more curious and make him work harder in getting the information he is seeking. Stories collected through sources other than the official sources of the PRO are likely to contain inaccuracies which can only harm the cause of the institution when they appear in public. It should be possible for a PRO who has been able to establish an understanding with the press correspondents to convince them that they are not being obstructed and that there are justifiable reasons for withholding information on certain matters in the national interest.

A PRO should not always take shelter in anonymity. If he has the confidence of his ministry or institution, he should be quotable. Trying always to play safe and exposing a correspondent to shoulder the entire responsibility of writing up stories based on facts and information given to him by the PRO is not fair to the correspondent. He should try to develop himself as the spokesman of his department. For this purpose, he must gain the confidence of his employer and also build sufficient reputation for himself in the eyes of the press. The PRO should not try to either misuse his position or exploit his friendship with the newspaper staff to gain personal benefits. Nor should he try to play the editorial and the managerial staff of newspapers against one another. The judgement of a newspaper man should be respected and direct complaints against the conduct of a press correspondent to his editor should be avoided as far as possible. If an error is of a minor nature, it is worthwhile ignoring it in the interest of good Public relations. But if the error is major and positive harm is going to be caused by such erroneous publication, it should be contradicted. A still better course, depending on the circumstances, would be to give the correct to the correspondent himself and it is more than likely that he would on his own make the necessary correction in his dispatch without even being asked to do so.

These are just a few hints that a good public relations man can keep in view. Basically, it is a problem of human relations. A helpful attitude, knowledge of one's own subject, ability to generate confidence in one's employer, sticking to the truth, balance in the presentation of controversial issues and fairness and impartiality in dealing with the correspondents are important traits of a PRO's character that are bound to go a long way in making him appreciated by his own ministry or the institution for which he is working as well as by the media people.

Finally, the Government or the institution who maintains public relations men should treat them as integral parts of the organisation, give them work and adequate responsibility, provide them with resources and also give them the credit that is due to them. Sometimes, heads of institutions invite outside public relations experts, ignoring their own people. This practice can be justified only for undertaking special campaigns of a temporary nature for which outside agencies may be specially qualified. Otherwise, it is quite easy to make the public relations staff absolutely ineffective by simply ignoring them. It is hardly possible for any public relations man to prove by means of statistics and data the value of the contribution that he is making to his institution. He is not building a bridge or a factory that he can show something physical and tangible. He is selling ideas, dispelling misconceptions, correcting attitudes and approaches. The results of such efforts are not immediately measurable. The correct course for institutions which keep PROs is to select suitable persons and, having done so, take them into their inner counsels so that the PROs can be of real service to them.

The Organisation

The Chief Executive of an organisation, in approaching the highly-important task of analysing his problems and objectives and planning his programme, must bear in mind the two major areas of concern :

1. What important elements of the public and the government think of the organization, and
2. What these people need to know to help them understand the problems, aspirations and accomplishments of the organization.

To varying degrees, these areas apply as well to associations and institutions, profit and non-profit.

The objective of a PR executive should be to detect and interpret public viewpoints to management and to interpret the company's interests and aims to the various 'publics'.

This may entail close preliminary study, either through opinion research or by staff determination, of many areas of the company's interests. It may be necessary to get clear answers to these questions, among others:

1. What are employee attitudes and the extent of appreciation of the motivation that the company's welfare is their welfare?
2. What are the opinions of stockholders toward the company? — A lively interest in progress and prospects, or a cold 'market' attitude? How well are banks, brokers and financial analysts informed about the company?
3. What about customers and the distributing organization? How much do they know of the company, and what are their opinions?
4. What major, national or local current events or trends present problems or opportunities for the company?
5. What interest and participation does the company take in its community, or communities, and what are the attitudes of people and organizations toward the company?
6. Does the company have legislative problems—State, Local or Central and what kind? Also, does it have problems or objectives where administrative or regulatory government is concerned?
7. How well are supervisors and other key personnel informed about the company, and are they interpreting policies and operations to employees and their neighbours?
8. To what extent does management cooperate with schools and colleges with educators as the moulders of the citizens

of tomorrow, and with youth, to be sure they understand the importance of the company or the industry?

9. How well are the company—and the industry—interests being represented and interpreted by the industry association—local, State and national?
10. Have the company's employees been urged by management to take a lively interest in politics, and has the company made its own position on major issues clear?
11. How are the company's Press relations in all the various categories, and what has been the general attitude of the Press? How well are editors and reporters informed about the background, aims, accomplishments and economic importance of the company?

The answers to these questions can set the stage for orderly and effective orientation of programme to meet the company's problems and advance its interests on a broad front.

Importance of Clear Objectives : The first step in programming is to set out clearly and definitely both the long-range and short-range objectives of the company. This applies just as well for associations or institutions.

Long-range objectives are likely to derive from established policies, shortrange from current events or conditions, or the immediate needs of other departments, whether sales, marketing personnel, research, engineering, manufacturing or any other. Or, in the case of associations, the purposes, problems and accomplishments of other services or committees.

Example : An exceptionally effective job of identifying its objectives and methods of obtaining them has been done by my company where Public Relation Officer served for over 20 years:

> The company not only identifies its policies and its goals for the guidance of management and the PR department, but for all its personnel. In other words, it takes the view that every employee is a potential PR man for the company in his own community and in

his contacts with the company's customers, suppliers, stockholders and others.

This was done by preparation of a 'Public Relations Guidebook' —a thick looseleaf book, indexed and departmentalized for orderly study and ready reference. While it serves a primary purpose of a constant guide for management, supervision and PR, it invites other employees to 'join the team' to serve their own and the company's best interests. In the process it instils in all the company's men and women a better knowledge of the company and a pride in their work.

The looseleaf Public Relations Guidebook is clearly tabbed with 14 major sections—Company Platform, What is PR? Public Relations Policy and the PR Division, The Company, The Tea Industry, Industry Groups, Community Groups, The Press, Corporate Advertising, Special Occasions, Emergencies, Speeches, Printed Materials and Visual Materials.

But while this book provides the basic plan of'marathon'PR, this is not enough. At intervals the PR executive meets with his assistants and his PR counsel to sharpen targets of the current programme, examine the impacts of new trends and events, review and reorient priorities, measure progress and plan new activities.

The wellspring of this successful operation flows from the continuing concern and participation of top management. Because, as many a PR man has found out, if top management is not interested, lower echelons won't concern themselves and the PR staff can't do the job alone.

Employee Communications : Quite naturally, the extent ana character of employee communications—usually Target No. 1 in any PR programme—depends on the size of the payroll and the geographical distribution of employees.

Establishing Priorities : The second step in programming is to establish the relative importance of all objectives, so that urgent or very important targets are hit early and with maximum effect.

This must be done with proper regard to the confines of staff, and to timing.

At this point it is possible to gain some view of the size and scope of the programme. This depends, of course, on the scope of operations and the character of the enterprise, and on the various elements of the public it is desirable to reach.

The first requirement is that an organization must decide which of its many interests are of most concern to the public and itself—to talk about important issues that have some meaning, and about the function of its interest as a whole.

The second is that the audiences to be reached must be carefully selected. No mass appeal, however broad, will ever be completely effective in persuading the entire public. Even the great common denominator subject of human health, cannot guarantee a majority of our 61 crore people as audience.

Selection of Audiences : So, knowing that public opinion can be largely affected by the more informed and articulate elements in society, selection of audiences for various appeals is most important. In the community, are we reaching such groups as elected officials, civic clubs, legislators, teachers and professors, teenagers, the religious society, women's clubs, and most certainly the editor of the local Press?

In financial PR, are we keeping an excellent record before financial analysts, bankers, the financial and business Press and associations and groups of allied industry?

Is our emphasis in stockholder relations on winning Institutional Prize with the Annual Report or being sure that every communications method and opportunity is being used to tell stockholders the company's story, simply and clearly? Are we using dividend stuffers, messages with the 'report', special letters on government regulatory problems harassing our company or industry? Does the chairman's message in the annual report tell stockholders. Where the company is headed in the future competition and frankly set forth the problems that must be met? Are stockholders warmly welcomed into the fold, then kept informed?

How about the company publication? Is it lively, informative, clearly written? Or, more important, is it giving the employees what they really want to know—what is happening to the company and its business, and why?

Study after study shows this up as what employees and stockholders want, but we are contenting ourselves with a liberal mixture of departmental chitchat and photographic monuments to management vanity, in place of the solid information employees want? Let's take a cold hard look and see, because we are delivering no bargain if that pretty four-colour cover hides 24 pages of puff and piffle instead of useful fact.

In government relations, it is important to know and to reach State and local representatives hi 'power' and State and local legislators. It is important to establish channels to important committees and their staffs, to regulators, agencies and to the Press which they customarily read. To sum up:

Look at existing policies. Look at the competition. Dig intomaterials available in your files or at the library—in, magazines, government reports, trade association material. Talk to people from the president down, inside and outside the company.

Seek basic facts about the situation and the company. Seek to involve an appreciation of the attitudes you encounter. Define the company's publics narrowly. Evaluate the communications channels. You then are ready to determine the needs and set the objectives.

So you plan what to do (the programme), when to do it (the timing), how much to spend (the budget) and who will do it (the staff).

Plans must be realistic in terms of management's own objectives. It may not be worth doing at all if the result does not contribute to management's goals.

Establishing a Department

In its broadest sense, company public relations is synonymous with good management. The function is not the exclusive concern of a small staff of experts, it is the concern of every one in the company, from the chairman to the 'chaprassi'. One of the most powerful influences on a company's status and reputation is what its own employees think and say about it. If employees are to be goodwill ambassadors for the company they must be well informed on company activities ; they must enjoy a sense of participation in the progress of the company ; there must be recognition for work well done, opportunities for advancement, and fair reward.

These are the most important factors leading to the general agreement that 'this is a good company to work for', and without this prevailing unity of thought among the company's first and most important public, all the efforts of public relations specialists to project the company as a worthy and desirable member of the community will be of little avail. Sound business ethics, high standards of operation, good quality products, and a desire to serve the public—these are the first requirements of good public relations as well as of commercial success.

This basic public relations policy next needs to be translated into a continuous programme of public relations activity, because, today, being a good business citizen is not enough. A systematic job of telling all sections of the public about the progress, policy, products, and services of the company is necessary through all channels of communication and media of publicity. The flow of information must be continuous and planned. It must be honest, accurate information, presented in the form most suited for the various media.

How does the public relations manager set about the task of organizing the public relations function within an established company management ? He must first define its place within that management. Should the public relations department come under the control of the marketing manager, the advertising manager, or the sales manager? Should it be in the managing director's department, responsible to the chief executive, and acting as a service department to all others ? To some extent these questions will be answered by the existing attitude of management.

If management expects the major role of public relations to be promotion aid to advertising, then the public relations manager is likely to find himself within the marketing, advertising, or sales departments. Such a placing carries with it crippling disadvantages because he is under constant pressure to concentrate on promotional activities to the exclusion of most else. He becomes, in fact, an extension of the sales force.

The right place for the public relations function is within the department of the managing director, the general manager, or whatever the chief executive may be called. The reason is simply that public relations is not a one-sided business. It is concerned with the life of the whole organization. The chief executive is the man at the centre of the company's complex web of activity. He is the ultimate decision-maker, the principal spokesman, and perhaps the public guardian of the company's reputation. He must be deeply concerned with, and closest to, the public attitude towards the company, because in the final analysis his decisions mould the image.

The work of the public relations department must be closely coordinated with top management thinking, and all activities touching on policy, such as institutional advertising, must be fully approved by the chief executive. Obviously, what the public relations man says and writes on behalf of the company cannot be at variance with the views and public statements of the top man.

Obviously, there must be close relationship with the advertising department, not only in prestige publicity, but in the use of joint services. Ideally, the public relations manager and the advertising manager should be separate but equal.

The physical location of the public relations manager should for preference be wherever the department of the chief executive is situated. This is usually the head office of the company, for obvious reasons. If the public relations manager cannot be sited in or near the operational area of top decision (perhaps being at the main plant, when the head office is elsewhere) he has a continuing problem of communication to solve. He cannot afford to rely on formal public relations planning machinery to keep him in touch with changes in top management thinking. He must ensure that his face is seen regularly at head office, and he must arrange informal meetings and discussions with senior executives, so that he is constantly in the picture.

Unless the public relations manager is aware of, and part of, company thinking, he cannot hope to do an effective job. Above all, he must have the raw material to enable him to understand the attitudes, policies, and decisions of his company, and he will only get this through discussion, meetings, and exchange of opinion.

Assuming that the public relations manager has been appointed within the chief executive's department, and is directly responsible to him for advising on, and implementing, the public relations programme in all its varied aspects, he could be responsible for :

1. controlling the public relations department, and presenting and implementing, as agreed, all public relations policies and activities;
2. conveying and interpreting to management, information on public attitudes and views about the company and/or the industry it serves;
3. preparing all policy and financial statements on company affairs to the Press, TV, and radio. Handling day-to-day inquiries from the Press, and the initiation of Press interest in the affairs, services, and production of the company, regularly issuing news material on all company activities;
4. advising on the preparation of prestige publications, institutional advertising, films, exhibitions, shareholder relations, house style, community relations, and other relevant activities;
5. instructing the company's financial advertising agents on all matters relating to financial and annual report, advertising and publicity;
6. liaison with the personnel department on all matters relating to the dissemination of internal-information and the company's employee publications.

Obviously, with such a brief, it is not feasible to set up a one-man-an-secretarydepartment; but neither is a vast number of staff necessary. Specialists within the company must be called upon to undertake certain aspects of the public relations programme. Where no internal departments handling such matters as films, exhibitions, photography, or print exist, the public relations manager must go outside to the specialist agency or consultant of his choice. The public relations manager who tries to service every activity and carry every public relations burden upon his own shoulders will be attempting the impossible. Instead of being the initiator and coordinator of public relations activities, he will be the servant of the function, achieving merely a reputation for trying everything and succeeding in nothing.

Deliberately Small

Unless a company is very large, the public relations department should be kept small as a matter of deliberate policy. It is frankly uneconomic to build up specialist sections for public relations purpose where such departments already exist in the company, or when the services can be obtained efficiently from outside.

Once the public relations manager has received clear terms of reference for his department, his problems start. He has to create the machine which will make the policy effective. The first step may be to set up a public relations committee of policy-making executives, with the chief executive, if possible, acting as chairman. This committee can provide the point of discussion and decision on all policies and programmes affecting the company's public relations. It should meet at least once a month, more frequently when circumstances demand. It should deal with policy, and not dabble in executive detail.

The next step is to see that management is gradually made aware of the existence and requirements of the public relations department. An internal educational job has to be started, and the public relations manager will have to talk to senior, middle, and lower management about public relations, explain why he wants their cooperation; and how they can help, and what he may be able to offer to them in return.

These talks can be given at internal management courses or the public relations manager, with the help of the personnel department, can organize his own meetings—much less effective—or circulate an explanatory leaflet. Whatever else he does, he cannot afford to ignore internal education, and even when he and his department are well established it will still be necessary for him to talk repeatedly to different sections of management on public relations activities.

The primary need of the public relations department is for information on company activities, the raw material of company publicity. To initiate a steady flow of information, covering all major aspects of the company's operations, it is necessary to create official channels of communication between the public relations department and the senior men in charge of various activities.

For instance, in each of the major divisions dealing with say, research, production, sales and finance, an official and free line of communication must be established. An agreed procedure must be adhered to between the department and division covering the collection and issue of material in news form. The public relations department which issues news stories and statements without authority is acting irresponsibly. It is essential that all information issued is authentic and factually accurate ; this is as much a safeguard for the Press as for the company.

In order to ensure a constant provision of information from the divisions, a pattern of procedure should be formulated. No two companies are similar, and therefore, public relations procedures must vary in detail.

Public Interest

The company's public relations policy is based on the fact that the company recognizes the value of public interest in its activities. Because of this, it aims to keep the public fully and accurately informed of its activities so far as this is consistent with reasonable commercial prudence.

So that the public relations department may initiate and carry out this policy, it is necessary for the executives of the department to have free access to the heads of divisions and major departments for the purpose of securing information on every aspect of company operation and procedure. The official channel of communication will be with the director of each division and the head of each major department, or their appointed deputies. It is the responsibility of the public relations department to secure the approval of the director or department head before any information is issued to the Press or the public. The public relations department will approach the following senior executives, dependent upon the subject-matter required:

Company policy	...	managing director and/or company secretary
Sales and marketing	...	sales director
Production	...	production director
Finance	...	finance director

No unauthorized statement should be made at any time to the Press, by any individual, in the name of the company. In the event of emergencies or accidents at any of the company's major plants or works the works manager must notify head office immediately, and cooperate with national and local Press inquiries to the full, while an official account and statement is being prepared. Works and branch managers at all times have authority to deal with the local Press on all matters other than those affecting major company policy.

It should not be assumed that contact between the public relations department and the other divisions and departments can only be at top level. On the contrary, a great deal of contact and exchange of information must go on at all times at executive level.

Since the public relations department has the responsibility of advising the company on what form the public relations programme should take, it must evaluate the attitude of the public to the company's products, activities and known plans. The job of evaluation must be continuous, and may take the form of long-term public opinion surveys conducted by a specialised agency.

In addition, the department will need to provide an intelligence service to management analysing current Press comment, Parliamentary discussion, and city views. Even a small public relations department should consider such an intelligence service an essential part of its activities.

The list of functions performed by corporate public relations departments varies from company to company. However, certain standard functions have emerged as common in most balanced departments. They are listed below in approximate order of prevalence.

Public Relations Policy : Develop and recommend corporate public relations policies; contribute public relations viewpoint in formulation of corporate decisions. Provide not mainly to top management but also to other departments and divisions.

Corporate Publicity : Development and issuance, of announcements of company activities to external communications media ; handling inquiries from the press ; development and placement of promotional publicity about the corporation as a whole or any of its units.

Product Publicity : Announcement of new products through editorial channels of communications media ; development and execution of promotional product publicity campaigns.

Government Relations : Maintain liaison with appropriate governmental units at local, State, and national level ; report trends in government affecting the company ; advise action as needed ; help prepare for and direct corporate appearances before investigating bodies or legislative hearing ; direct programmes designed to promote the company's point of view in legislative or regulatory matters.

Community Relations : Plant community contacts performance and/or coordination of corporate "good neighbour" activities, including compliance with environmental protection standards, fostering equal employment opportunity, and cooperating in urban improvement programmes; development of community understanding of company's problems and needs.

Stockholder Relations : Communications between company and shareholders ; also between company and the investment community in general ; development of acceptance of company among investors via broadening exposure of company's policies and financial results in the investment community ; preparation of annual report, quarterely reports, dividend cheque inserts, etc. ;. planning and staging of annual meetings of stockholders and appearances before meetings of security analysts.

Public Relations Promotion Programmes : Institutional promotion programmes designed to build corporate acceptance among key publics; institutional advertising ; public relations literature; special events.

Corporate Donations : Develop policy for company contributions ; process donations requests : administer company's foundation; conduct of employee solicitations for approved drives.

Employee Publications : Prepare and publish employee magazine, newspaper, bulletins, management communications, etc.

Guest Relations : Plant tours, new plant and/or building dedieacations ; guest reception activities.

Miscellaneous : Speakers' bureau; education relations.

Actual Service

Public Relations today involves complete analysis and understanding of all the factors that influence people's attitudes toward an organization. It usually has seven phases :

1. *Analysing the general climate of altitudes and the relation of the organization to its 'universe'.* Every institution functions within a "universe" or system, and is dependent on everything that happens to this totality. It is vital to understand, as well as possible, the trenr's within this system and how the organization may be affected by them. Included in this is "pulse feeling" of the attitudes towards the organization and towards the field it is in, amongst the various publics it may have relations with.

2. *Determining the attitude of any group toward the organization.* This may be the employees, the customers, the stockholders, or some other segment of the public. When the attitudes are known, it is possible to see where the organization is misunderstood and where its policies and actions are creating unfavourable opinion.

3. *Analysing the state of opinion.* It may be that investigation discloses unrest among a group of employees—unrest that may well break out into very serious uprisings. Or the stockholders may express the desire to know more about the company and its products. Or consumers may not identify products with the manufacturer. . Analysis will aid in making plans to improve the opinion of the various groups about which the company is concerned.

4. *Anticipating potential problems, needs, or opportunities.* From analysis and surveys it sometimes is possible to detect in advance what may develop in the attitudes of various groups. Then plans or actions can be recommended to meet those circumstances at the most advantageous time and under favourable circumstances.

5. *Formulating policy.* Analysis may include that certain policies of the company should be modified to improve the attitude held by certain groups. Often the change involves eliminating causes of misunderstanding and misinterpretation.

6. *Planning means of improving the attitude of a group.* With an understanding of what people think of the organization and a clarification of the organization's policies on matters that affect public opinion, the groqndwork has been laid. Next comes the programming of activities that will explain the company and its products, will overcome misunderstandings, and will promote good will.

7. *Carrying out the planned activities.* The tools of public relations—publicity, institutional, advertising, printed materials, employee activities, stockholder reports, company publications, and other things—are then

employed to do the job. With proper preliminary planning and guidance, these become the most tangible phase of a company's public relations activity.

8. *Feedback, evaluation, and adjustment.* Conditions are changing constantly ; the public relations functions both contribute to this change and are affected by it. So it is important to constantly get readings from the publics that are being approached. These help to assess the results and developments, and to adjust the public relations programme—and often the entire policy of the organization—accordingly.

The scientific approach to an organization's goodwill goes far beyond the familiar publicity releases and hitormiss efforts to please employees or members. It is a task for highly skilled specialization and talent. It demands high-calibre thinking by a number of experts ; experience in the ways of public opinion and the techniques of influencing it; and the facilities to do everything that must be done in a well-planned programme.

Managing and Doing

There is a big difference between managing and doing. How successful are you in your managerial practice lies in how well could you understand 'managing' and 'doing' and go about accordingly ; and that is the core of 'Public Relations in Manager Statesmanship.'

The manager often finds himself in the position of the interplanetary traveller who doesn't know how fast he is going until he knows where he is and can't know where he is until he knows how fast he is keeping pace with his activities. Often the result is that the manager knows that he may have to take reluge in spending most of his time dealing with that which makes him most secure, and administrative problem-solving. In other words, h« relies more on *doing* than *managing*. Not that 'doing' is not important. In fact, a managers's *doing* activities may become more important than his managing activities—especially if he has only a couple of subordinates. But there has to be a point where managing activity gets the attention it needs. Only then can a group of individuals be directed and motivated to make a planned contribution toward achievements of group objectives.

It is not unusual for the employee to see his 'boss' as a 'father figure'. This is normal. But it can produce difficulties if the boss is not aware of it and doesn't know how to handle it.

Meeting of minds followed by unity in common action is the salient feature of public relations in manager statesmanship. The following contain some tips which may prove of use in this respect:

1. When an authority commands, the group obeys ; the result is acquiescence.
2. The manager tells ; the staff follows ; the result is assent.

In both these situations, the person of higher status secures the compliance of those of lower status. How much the result is based on status and how much on reasons or emotional adherence is not always determinable. The manager who has had some insight into public relations knows about the efficacy of using 'order' depending upon situations. Examples are :

1. When to "Command"
   - (a) In case of danger.
   - (b) For the lazy and indifferent worker.
   - (c) To the careless man.
   - (d) When the workman refuses to obey safety order and rules.
   - (e) To the agitator.
   - (f) To the workman who refuses to do work as he is told.
   - (g) To stop waste or delay.
   - (h) To the disobedient worker.
2. When to "Request"
   - (a) To the touchy or sensitive worker.
   - (b) To the untrained worker.

(c) To the nervous, irritable worker.

(d) To get a little more done.

(c) To the man who is interested in his work.

(f) To a person of equal footing.

(g) First time you reprimand or caution a worker.

(h) To avoid making a man sore.

(i) To an older man—in age and service.

(j) To the "hardboiled" man.

(k) To do a difficult job in a particular way.

3. When to "Suggest"—for fully experienced workers.

(a) When improved methods are sought.

(b) To the man who is trying to get ahead.

(c) To the man who is trying to assume responsibility.

(d) Try it out with a new group of experienced workmen.

(e) Use it to develop initiative.

Remember : The greater the distance between the giver and the receiver of an order, the more likelihood of misunderstanding and the greater the chance of the reaction of the receiver.

Saving Authority

Authority, like money, may be saved or squandered. It may be invested for security or for growth. It may be hoarded for its own sake. It may be used up in expendable luxuries. It may produce anything—or nothing.

If an investor of money is satisfied with security and slow growth, he deposits his savings in a guaranteed bank account and lets other people worry about using it profitably. If he wants his savings to grow faster, he must learn to do more than check the figures in a Pass Book. He must study the whole field of investing, and learn the nature of money as well as what it can do. He must make his own judgements, and abide by them. He must keep accounts ; he must know how much he has to invest and where the opportunities for investment are. He must keep close control. Not all his investments are likely *to* be successful ; he must liquidate his poor investments, salvaging what he can, and reinvest the proceeds to recoup his losses. He must keep something in reserve, in order to take advantage of unexpected opportunities, but he must realise that idle reserves produce no gains.

As a manager, whatever your level, you can handle authority in much the same way. You can play it safe, or you can invest for growth. But before you begin to invest authority for rapid returns you must :

(a) Take full account of your authority.

(b) Study the benefits and the risks involved in delegation.

(c) Learn all you can about the ability and the character of each of your subordinates.

(d) Use delegation to motivate your subordinates.

(e) Practise delegation at every opportunity.

(f) Devise sound methods of reporting and control.

Take Full Authority into Account. It is a relatively simple matter to "measure" the authority you hold by virtue of your appointment to the position you now hold. Whether or not the company has given a written description of your position or provided you with a chart of its relationships with other positions in the company, you can quickly determine the areas in which you have complete freedom to decide the course of action.

2. Encouraged by the results achieved by the Indian Railways, certain commercial organizations, like the House of Tatas and Birlas, which had already been practising public relations in an unconscious manner, began organizing since 1945, their public relations activity in a conscious way.

3. The Life Insurance Companies of both Indian and foreign origin were also flourishing well prior to our 'Independence', by their systematic and organized PR campaigns. After the advent of the 'Life Insurance Corporation of India (LIC)' neither the Corporation nor the policy-holders derived the benefit expected though it has been communicating with its relevant public via the mass media and through its own "Agents" and "Development Officers". Reason : the element of real public relations to earn the credibility of its public is missing even now in its activity.

4. The Directorate of Advertising and Visual Publicity of the Government of India was consistently losing money. The 23rd Estimates Committee of Parliament had to point out "its role, as in the past, should only be an advertiser's representative"—advertiser in this instance means the Government of India—"and that it should cease to be an advertising agency because the service can be rendered at a much less expense to the exchequer by private agencies." It was as a sequel to PR influence.

5. Acting on the advice of the "Estimates Committee", the Government did make an attempt to economise its expenses. Unfortunately, no simultaneous effort has been made to make a proper assessment of the staff and to engender efficiency for effecting savings in resources. The economy drives undertaken periodically have been perfunctory and have often touched only peripheral expenses like stationery and telephone bills, use of small cars and the like, thereby giving cause for the erosion of credibility of the public which, of late, has become vocal; it is so critical in voicing its opinion that it touches even

9

Economic Aspects

Business corporations, voluntary agencies, religious institutions, and even individuals are increasingly alive to the benefits of Public Relations.

1. During British rule in India, the G.I.P. Railway Co., Ltd. carried on in England publicity and public relations campaign, as far back as 1921, to prompt passenger traffic. Use of media, giant-size posters and informative pamphlets were the public relations adjuncts of the campaign.

Inside India, the Publicity Bureau of the G.I.P. Railway introduced travelling cinema which held open air shows of films at national fairs and festivals. Subsequently, these Public Relations measures were adopted by its counterparts like the Bombay, Baroda & Central India Railway, East Indian Railway, Assam Bengal Railway, Bengal Nagpur Railway, Madras and Southern Maratha Railway, and South Indian Railway, encouraged by the increased earnings of the Great Indian Peninsular Railway (GIPR).

The Railway Board set up Publicity Bureaus in London and New York which undertook extensive advertising in newspapers and journals. These bureaus also participated in exhibitions abroad to popularize the Indian Railways and promote tourist traffic.

the exalted office of our revered President of India : "could not the Government arrange his travel to London to participate in the Royal Wedding in July 1981, in such a way that the expenses of about 50 lakhs of rupees spent on chartering a special plane be reduced to save the public money of a developing country" ?

6. In Western countries there is more awareness of Public Relations. Even small countries like Monaco, Sri Lanka, Bahamas earn considerable amount of foreign exchange—thanks to their public relations professionals whose services the Government do not hesitate to avail of when it is a question of earning money of their exchequer.

No doubt the Leather Goods Manufacturing Industries, Handloom and Garment Goods, and even our Cultural Delegations, to name a few, have done well in earning foreign exchange for us by their participation in International Trade Fairs and Exhibitions. But the fly in the ointment is the lack of expert public relations direction in the matter of sustaining the quality of goods and of making critical study of the real needs and wants of the overseas markets, as well as the way those have to be projected abroad.

7. The nationally to pranking companies like Tatas and Birlas, and Multinationals like Hindustan Lever and Larsen & Toubro have Public Relations departments manned by those who know what is PR and how it could be used to project not only the sale of their goods and services but also of the 'image' in India and abroad.

8. Some rich men, who are also politicians, in Gujarat and Madhya Pradesh availed the services of some of our country's PR professionals' services during the last General Election. They won their Parliament seats by a clear margin, and their election expenses were less by over 35 per cent than those incurred by their "Agents" in the past.

9. From the foregoing discussion it will be quite obvious how time and money could be economised considerably

in various departments of Government and. 'business' activities if only we would choose the advice of such public relations counsellors who possess the expertise as well as the right tools and techniques of reaching different segments of Indian public, and who are also alive to the importance of adapting the same in consonance with our social and cultural environment.

A Particular Case

The illustration relates to the true story of a new type of glucose which was introduced in the London market some years ago.

Glucose in powder form had been accepted as a strength-builder for invalids or those recovering from illness and for children. It was not regarded as a necessity for everyday life. Only a limited amount of money was available for this promotion and the manufacturer wished to obtain a wide sale among athlete and sportsmen as well as among those with more sedentary occupations who used their energy in other ways. Two things had to be established :

(i) Glucose was a good cure for fatigue, faintness and immediate hunger.

(ii) Glucose was a good preventive for all the above and was therefore an immediate source of energy.

To assist in the initial launch of this product, public relations professionals undertook to gain public notice for the glucose tablets on a public occasion where circumstances would be favourable to the objectives to be achieved.

(a) Glucose as a curative for fatigue, faintness and hunger was achieved by using the tablets strategically during the celebration for the Coronation of Queen Elizabeth II. Permission was obtained from the British Red Cross and St. John Ambulance Brigade to supply all their stations set up along the route with cases of tablets. Free supplies of the tablets were sent, with the compliments of the manufacturer, to a number of well-known people who were to be present in the Abbey during the long ceremony. The supply of tablets to the Red Cross stations was widely publicised through the press, and subsequent reports confirmed that the tablets were much used and stood up to the reputation which was being established for them.

(b) The second stage of establishing the "staying factor" of the tablets was carried out by staging a colourful "endurance" test requiring a man to ride on horseback nonstop from Plymouth to London, eating nothing but glucose tablets and drinking only water. This took thirty nine hours and was covered by the press, radio, newsreel and Pathe Pictorial cameramen along the whole route. It was effective in two ways. It illustrated the power of the tablets in warding off fatigue and hunger; and also showed them use in a "manly" context. From this the campaign widened to cover Wimbledon and other sporting activities where it became a normal matter for performers to take glucose tablets instead of sugar, and naturally obtained considerable press coverage. Glucose tablets became accepted by the public as an easy, harmless method of achieving an immediate "dose" of energy.

Problem Solving Process

Public relations is essentially a problem-solving process of four basic steps :

1. Research—Listening : This involves probing the opinions, attitudes, and reactions of those concerned with acts and policies of an organization, then evaluating the inflow. This task also requires determining facts regarding the organization: "What's our problem"?
2. Planning—Decision-making : This involves bringing these attitudes, opinions, ideas and reactions to bear on the policies and programmes of the organization. It will enable the organization to chart a course in the interests of all concerned ; "Here's What We Can Do".

3. Communication—Action : This involves explaining and dramatising the chosen course to all those who may be affected and whose support is essential : "Here's What We Did and Why".
4. Evaluation. This involves evaluating the results of the programme and the effectiveness of techniques used : "How Did We Do" ?

Each one of these steps is as important as the others. Each one is vital to an effective programme. Emphasis on fact-finding and planning is what distinguishes public relations from publicity. The process of mustering information and applying it in Decision-making must be geared to the goals and policies of the organization; otherwise, the four steps add up to meaningless wheel-spinning.

The Effectiveness

The effectiveness of programming rests heavily on the validity of the planning. Prudent long-range planning, anticipating conceivable developments, is more likely to result in:

1. An integrated programme in which the total efforts result in definite accomplishments toward specific goals.
2. Increased management participation and support.
3. A programme emphasis that needs to be positive rather than defensive.
4. Unhurried deliberation on choice of themes, timing and tactics.

Even though the values of planned programming are evident and acknowledged, there is too little emphasis on this second step in the process. These appear to be the main obstacles :

1. Failure of employer? to include the practitioners in deliberations that lead to policies and programmes.
2. Lack of clearly agreed upon objectives for implementing public relations programme.
3. Lack of time, because of pressures of meeting daily problem.

4. The frustration and delays that practitioners encounter in the endless task of internal clearance and coordination with other departments.

A Procedure for Planning

1. A searching look backward.
2. A wide look around.
3. A deep look inside.
4. A long, long look ahead.

Communicating

Choosing the appropriate tools and techniques suited to the relevant 'public' is summarised as under :

I. Internal Communication

Employees : This public can be reached by person-to-person contact over intercom or public address system; by house journals; newsletters; bulletin boards; special letters; circulars; sometimes individually addressed letters to certain cadre of staff of a demo-official or even personal style.

II. External Communication

Shareholders : Welcome letters to new 'shareholders'; the Annual Report.

Government : Central, State and Local : By special memorandum through Chambers of Commerce, Trade Association or through the Chief Executive's authorized official with a memorandum to be submitted to the relative official of the concerned department; personal visit to gauge the attitude of the official toward the purpose for which help is sought.

Press : Inviting Press people and releasing stories over Press Get-togethers or Conferences.

Customer : External House Journal dealing with all that would cover the business activities and special events taking place in their families; sales progress; customer complaints.

Introduction of a New Product: Making an event of it.

Sponsored programmes on radio or television

Community Relations : Participating in the activities of the local community where one's plant is situated.

Fiscal Aspects

There are different approaches for PR budgeting. However, there are only two basic budgeting methods:

(i) the percentage of sales method, and

(ii) the task method.

All others are simply variations (or combinations of variations) of these.

The 'percentage of sales method' consists of arbitrarily taking a percentage of past or future gross or net sales as the budget. The 'task method' sets goals to be accomplished. Then the estimates as to how much it will cost to reach them is made. The approved estimate becomes the outside limit of the budget.

With a percentage method, budgets are more quickly determined since sales figures can be readily obtained from company records or can be forecast by the sales department. The only question to be resolved here is what percentage to use'? Chief disadvantage is that budgets are not necessarily related to actual needs. For, budgets provided for departments with good sales records may be higher than budgets for departments with poor records. Inflexibility can also become a problem. In many companies it is difficult to change an approved budget.

The task method of budgeting offers greater flexibility but requires more careful planning and forecasting. If advance studies are accurate, the budget will be adequate. This method involves many intangibles and undue optimism or pessimism will seriously impair budgetary control.

Whichever method is used, an effort should be made to relate the PR budget to corporate requirements. There are companies of comparable size within the same industry whose PR needs (and budgets) are entirely different. Also, a company's needs are likely to change from year to year.

Whether a company uses people on its own staff or hires outside counsel, roughly two-thirds of the PR budget will be spent on "people time." Activities like sales promotion, advertising should have separate budgets. When there is an understanding of what PR encompasses, budgeting will be less of a problem than if there is no clear line of demarcation.

Given below are guidelines on the different headings under which expenses coming under PR budgeting have to be charged for:

Departmental :	Manpower—including overtime, overheads like heat, light, rents, rates and so on, expressed as a percentage of the manpower estimate, Communications—postage, travel and subsistence; telephones, cables, entertainment, and sundries.
Supplies :	Print, photographic materials, film, visual aids, tapes, and so on, stationery, samples.
Outside Service :	consultancy, creative (copy, art, photographic, film) research, advertising, exhibitions, duplicating and mailing, press conference, temporary help.

The PR budget must be kept flexible because no one can predict with accuracy what the PR programme will require, say, six or nine months later. Emergencies can develop, or unforeseen opportunities arise. Management may change the emphasis and direction of public relations activity. In PR, good budgeting policy dictates that contingency funds be set aside so they will be available if a need arises.

Public Relations and Publicity Budgets : There can be no rule of thumb, no yardstick that establishes budgetary formulas. The PR effort can almost always be tailored specifically to suit a predetermined budget. Therefore, costs will vary with the objectives, scope and work involved in a programme.

The Assessment

With business and other organizations moving toward using computers and other quantifying techniques to "get answers" and "organize" efficiently, there has been some kind of pressure to apply the same methods to public relations. Since this field deals with the most intangible factors, managers must cope with— human attitudes—the discomfort it can evoke in a man trained to be entirely practical and fact oriented is understandable.

However, there is danger that the more effort that is made to apply standards of prediction and measurement to public relations, the more emphasis will be placed on the superficial and the more difficult it will be to make progress against the real problems.

There are several reasons for this:

1. The greatest resource of public relations is human intellect and creativeness. The very ability to perceive why people do not follow the expected patterns and how they might be reached with messages not projected previously is the greatest value an organization or business can receive.

To the degree that direct measurements are attempted against these attributes, there is danger that the unremarkable and the undistinguished—what has been done before and therefore can be measured—will be emphasized at the expense of the unique and the excellent. If managements expect to be able to predict and measure quantitatively in public relations, public relations people will be inclined to confine themselves to things that are predictable and measurable, and the best thinking and creativity will be lost.

2. Public relations must deal with changes in attitude. It must lead its target, not follow it. The greatest source of problems and needs is change. If too much weight is

given to what surveys show attitudes were, it is less likely that public relations programme will have an effect on what they will be.

3. In obtaining data for quantified judgements, it is necessary to probe into the minds of people. The human mind is murky and its ramifications multitudinous. And all the mental resources of a person are arrayed in defence of his private thoughts and feelings. It is not sound to assume that effective measurement of some attitude sindicates the possibility of accurately measuring all others. In any survey, interviews' reactions are meaningful only when the subject is really meaningful to them: a major election, for instance. When queried about something less meaningful—such as acceptable profit margins of metal companies—they may answer, but the validity and stability of their answers—especially numerically and over a period of time—are dubious.

Tangible Goals : While in cases where a very tangible goal of public relations work is involved the measurements can be more specific, it is extremely limiting and harmful to public relations to permit managements to feel that the tangible goal programme is the essence of public relations.

In every public relations programme some sort of evaluation is called for. Usually it is a judgement by the concerned organization and the public relations officer as to what progress is being made toward the objectives that have been clearly established. Aside from this, the differences are far greater than the similarities. No two programmes should even be thought to be alike; it is individual differences and the relationships of human attitudes that make good public relations necessary and meaningful. To apply patterns from other programmes is like using IBM cards to substitute for human relationships on a college campus or in a company's personnel programme

Analysis

This process is to seek, through research, answers to the questions: "How did we do: Would we have been better off if we had tried something else? What did we learn?"' Evaluation leads logically back into fact-finding and feedback—the first step. In a continuing programme, the two aspects of research are hard to separate.

Extensive feedback is essential to an effective communications programme. The obstacles are, obviously, limitations of time, money losses, and lack of knowledge in the ways of research.

This step of evaluation must be viewed as more than surveys or post audits. Evaluation is an ongoing process that enables executives to make up the corrective adjustments required to guide an organization safely through the tides and winds of turbulent seas of opinion. Evaluation must be accepted as a management tool to be used on a consistent continuing basis upon which an operational base of information can be built.

Some basic steps in the evaluation process are:

1. *Select the rationale*: What is the guiding philosophy or model? Is the evaluation to be conducted by internal or external evaluations? Who is the major client?
2. *Specify objectives*: Define and state objectives of evaluation, objectives of all overall institutional mission, objectives of specific elements of public relations programme.
3. *Develop measures:* For example, measures of resources, finances, beneficiary groups, target groups, activities and outcomes.
4. *Administer the measures and collect the data:* Data can be collected in many ways—by observation, questionnaire, monthly reports, interviews and other techniques.
5. *Analyse the data* : Allot sufficient time to assure summarization, synthesis and interpretation.
6. *Report the results*: Findings should be translated into recommendations and shared with others.
7. *Apply the results to decisions*: Recommendations must be expressed in operational statements to assure follow-through.

Evaluation research will forcefully remind the communicator that dissemination does not equal communication.

Generally the audit begins inside the organization and it involves four steps:

1. *Finding out what "We" think:* This means talking to key persons in top and middle management to :
   (a) Assess the organization's strength and weaknesses,
   (b) Identify key publics,
   (c) Determine what areas the external phase of the audit should cover audiences, topics, etc.
2. *Finding out what "They" think*: Talking to important publics to find out how closely their view of the organization matches its executives' perceptions in key areas.
3. *Evaluating the disparity between the two points of view* : Should any such exist, how to arrive at a public relations balance sheet?
4. *Recommendations* aimed at closing the gap.

Measuring Impact : Four-dimensional ways of measuring the effectiveness of a specific programme:

1. *Audience Coverage:* To produce results you must first reach the audience. How large an audience is reached? What are they like? What proportion of the desired audience do they respond?
2. *Audience Response*: How do members of the audience respond. Does the contents of the message strike them favourably or unfavourably? Does it arouse their interest? Does it bore them? Do they understand it?
3. *Communications Impact:* After an appraisal of these immediate reactions, you must consider the impact which a message has on its audience. What are the lasting discernible effects upon people exposed to a message?
4. *Process of influence*: What is the process by which a communication operates to influence its target audience?

Through what channels of influence and mechanisms of persuasion does the message finally affect the individual? How effective is the programme in setting into motion the social progress necessary to influence the opinions behaviour of its target audience?

Measurement of Results : The real test of a communications programme is its results. Did it pay off at the box office, the sales counter, the voting booth? Did the programme bring about the desired reaction and action? Did your message result in the desired modification of a group's attitudes? Actual results offer a sure test. They deserve to be studied and analysed. In addition to observation of results *apparently* obtained, there are other ways of getting at the impact:

1. *The focussed interview* : This involves interviewing recipients of communications and getting them to relate their experience to various parts of a programme.
2. *Impact analysis:* This involves studies to determine short-term and long-term effects on individuals and on groups and subgroups. There are differences in impact to be studied in terms of time span and in terms of individual and group reactions.
3. *Experimental studies:* The ideal way to measure the impact of a programme is by comparing two groups that are alike except for the fact that one group has been exposed to a programme whereas the other has not. The critical feature is in matching the two groups. In such experiments, it is essential to control extraneous influences. Results are obtained by surveys and by panel studies.

Review of Programme

(a) *Organization*: Are related public relations functions organized as a single unit, or scattered throughout various departments? Does the public relations director have adequate management backing to see that public relations responsibilities are considered throughout the company? ... Is size and training of staff adequate to achieve desired public relations objectives?

(b) *Objectives*: Are they clearly stated and understood throughout the Company? Are there areas in which agreement on goals is needed?

(c) *Content*: Do your programmes and activities give adequate consideration to all segments of the public—customers, employees, stockholders, and financial community, government groups, civic, educational and community organizations, the Press, and suppliers?

(d) *Measurement of Results:* Do you have adequate staff, budget and management backing to gauge results of your work? How do these activities compare with those of others in your industry and in other industries? Have you considered an outside specialist to review your public relations programme?

(e) *Control*: What steps have you taken to improve future public relations activities in the light of audit findings? What steps need to be taken during coming years?

The research tools and techniques described above are helpful, but they measure only the bits and pieces and not the overall programme. The total effort must be kept in view. An important step is to periodically review the total programme and measure its results against the assigned objectives. Several "report cards" designed for the purpose go with it.

Public Relations Counselling : It is not the PR professional's job to tell management how to run the business. His role can be defined as "working to assess and evaluate opinions held by one or more of the client's publics, and interpreting findings for management." The consultant then assists management in formulating plans to change or improve public opinion. PR counsellor is but a partner to management—never a substitute.

The extent and nature of counselling will vary with the individual situation. In some cases, a consultant will give his counsel and will also execute a complete action programme. In others, his role is more limited. Essentially, PR counsel makes contribution to management by bringing his experience and specialization in terms of skills and techniques to the task of communication. In other words, PR consultants are one of many voices in the formation of a decision. They never tell a client what he must do. They offer their advice. Naturally it may be taken in full or in part or may not be taken for the time being.

A company can obtain PR assistance in several different ways: One is to create its own PR Department. Another is to employ outside counsel. A third is to combine both internal and outside PR Consultancy Service.

Any of these choices may be right for a particular company. None is instrinsically better than the others. It all depends on the company's needs and the capabilities of the PR staff.

The prime value of using an external counsel is the objectivity he brings. As an "outsider", such a counsellor is less influenced by the pressures of company organization and hierarchy than is an employee.

Is an internal department less expensive? Here again it depends on circumstances. Internal departments can become involved in assignments only vaguely related to PR. External counsel can fritter away expensive time on routine activities. Peak demands or special requirements may make it undesirable to maintain a staff on a full-time, year-round basis.

For many firms, neither an all "outside" nor an all "inside' organization is best. The best programmes seem to result from a combination of both. When internal and external efforts are combined, both working together can usually deliver more than twice the results of either working alone.

Internal Counsel vis-a-vis External Counsel : A company's own PR Department, of necessity, may be limited to specific areas related to the company. An external counsel can usually offer a wider range of skills and specialized abilities than are available within the company. This is especially useful in creative planning or in solving a particular problem. Another advantage often gained from an "outsider" is continuous media contact. An up-to-date knowledge of publicity opportunities and special editorial requirements is essential to the counsellor's successful operation, and this undertaking of media is automatically made available to the clients. Also the consultant deliberately places himself in the position of having to perform a valuable service in order to earn his compensation and the goodwill of the company, and will therefore spark-plug a campaign.

How the Counsel Works : Generally the counsel will begin the service to a new client by exploring the health of the relationships between the client and those publics on whom the client depends. This is sometimes called "Public Relations Audit." When it is completed, after a period of, say, a few months, one of three things are expected to happen:

1. The counsellor tells the client that he finds no problem or threat of harm in communication of a magnitude to require outside assistance;
2. He tells him the problem disclosed by research is in a realm other than that of his field; or
3. He tells him that there are problems that can be solved through the application of public relations techniques.

In the last case, the counsel usually arranges to make a presentation of his findings. In this presentation are exposed:

* The central core of the difficulty.
* Its current status in terms of harm to the organization.
* Related difficulties that must be considered.
* Ultimate alternatives to be faced.
* Desirable objectives.
* A long-range plan towards the objectives.
* An immediate programme of action involving anything pertinent, even if it involves the removal of a senior official, or an aggressive published response to an allegation.

When an organization has its own Public Relations Department, a staff practitioner has four factors working favourably for him and the department:

1. Team membership.
2. Knowledge of the organization.
3. Economy to the organization.
4. Availability to associates.

Choose PR Consultancies : The marketing director who wants to pay for at least some of hit sins while still on Earth can go a little way towards meeting hit objective by engaging in a full scale search for a public relations consultancy.

Picking an ad agency is not the easiest job in the world, but above the line there are a few more maps and sign-posts to guide the client.

For a start, agencies produce a tangible product in the form of their ads, which the advertiser can judge and assess, even if only on the basis of his personal taste. Second, whatever the market, the purpose is much the same—to increase sales or brand awareness and approval—and all agencies go about it in much the same way. Finally, the commission system, however imperfect, provides an open and easily checked system of payment which relates agency remuneration to media expenditure on the basis of a simple scale.

The PR consultancy, however, is offering a service rather than a product, and this makes it even more difficult to assess the effectiveness of a particular campaign. Since the targets for PR activity are many and various, the business now demands specialist skills, and practitioners tend to concentrate on one of several areas, such as financial, corporate, parliamentary or consumer marketing PR. Even the large agencies split these activities into separate divisions. Payment for PR services can vary from one aloin fee or retainer to a system based on man hours, and there are many confusing and arbitrary variants in between.

Extension of the Job

This is not really the fault of the consultancies themselves. The job is by nature nebulous and its extension into many different fields is the result of a growing realisation in commerce of the important role that PR plays. But it means that the client has to sit down and decide exactly what his aims are and what he is looking for before he goes anywhere near a PR firm.

Defining objectives is the first crucial task for the marketing man. He needs to decide what he wants to accomplish, and then break that overall objective down into its component parts. What audience does he want to reach—consumers, trade customers, employees, financiers and shareholders, or local or national government ? What does the message refer to—products, services, working conditions and rewards, business performance or external influences?

He also has to decide : what facilities he requires from the consultancy, how much will be done in-house, and, crucially, the cost of the problem and the value of the operation to his organisation. Once these criteria are established, he can start his search.

While on this, let me make a diversion. The overall practice of PR is undergoing a crucial move towards professionalism, based on sound principles of managing, PR ethical conduct, and greater accountability. The traditional PRO is changing ; he is today not just an expert communicator but also an adviser to his organisation and management.

In this changing status and role of the PR profession, PROs are having to know and understand the changes taking place in the economic, political, social and cultural areas in the country and which affect an organisation's operations. We, as professionals, have to be in the forefront, understanding and interpreting these changes, for those who turn to us for guidance. We must know what are the conditions that can be influenced by PR communications.

The development of PR consultancies in Europe and, now, in India, too, is a further step in the direction of professionalism. In the UK alone, there are about 15 independent and well-known consultancies. In India, at one time, it was "Consilium" only.

Today we have Roger Pereira's firm and, more recently. Good Relations India, among the well-known ones.

A parallel development is that advertising agencies are setting up PR cells. In India we have cells at Mudra, OBM, Trikaya, HTA and will soon have one at Lintas. In fact, earlier on, PR services and advice at agencies for their clients was free. Now, because PR is becoming more and more important and a specialised function they have professional specialists working for them, and thus they are charging for professional PR advice and services.

Before deciding on the choice of selecting a PR consultancy service it is advisable to prepare an outline brief covering your operations, needs, objectives and proposed level of expenditure. Following this, there should be an initial meeting to discuss and develop the brief.

At the meeting the client will be able to find out more about the background and experience of the consultancy, its knowledge of the client's market, its existing range of clients and track record, and its business controls and procedures. The consultancy may subsequently submit an outline proposal based on the client's needs and the activity required, together with an indication of probable costs.

At this stage the client should be down to a short-list of no more than three, and he will then visit the consultancies to conduct more detailed discussions. These will be of a more subjective nature —is he comfortable with the executives, do they speak his language, do they really understand his needs ? He will also investigate the proposed fee structures and budgets. He should by now be ready to make a decision.

So much for the bare bones of the process. These are the formal steps that a careful client, particularly one new to the PR world will take to make sure that be has all the information needed to make a decision. But just as much will depend on his judgement of the people and their work. In this area, as in so many others, recommendations from other contacts, either clients' or people in the media, are important.

Female Presence

The most significant and welcome psychological readjustment we now see is the emergence of women as having equality with men in the performance of political, social and economic roles. Liberation from many concepts of "a woman's place is home" is now a reaiity in India as well.

"The hand that rocked the cradle" has become the "hand" that more and more "mans" even the police force! It is the hand that is clasped warmly by those with goods and services to sell, nation 'image' to promote and its affairs to govern.

The current decade has witnessed a growing influx of women into management. While, initially, they settled for professions like medicine and teaching, it is only now that they have entered the corporate sector, essentially a male dominated system at the senior levels. With more women in their fold, organisations need to understand their aspirations and expectations, their problems and needs, attitudes of men, etc., if they wish to harness their potential optimally. It may be appropriate to examine this issue with International Women's Day having been celebrated on March 8, 1987.

Organisations differ in their work culture, policies, practices and style in relation to recruitment, induction and career growth for women managers'. Some companies, as a policy, do not employ women ; in others, they are employed mainly in staff functions ; and yet in some others where there is marginal representation in the policy and Decision-making levels. Though formal treatment meted out to women may seem on a par with men there is invariably some bias.

Women may be employed for only certain jobs which may not necessarily put them in the mainstream for career growth, or where existence of invisible barriers might prevent movement beyond a particular level. Perceptions that they are not as serious and committed as men are and apprehensions about possible interruptions in their careers prevent organisations from giving serious thought to women as managers. There seems to be a lack of appreciation of the positive role women are capable of playing, which may no result in the not getting groomed for wider job responsibilities.

In the corporate sector, the Sixties heralded the entry of women into managerial positions mainly in the area of public relations and labour welfare. In the mainline functions of marketing or finance there were very few.

In the Seventies, areas of market research and human resources development saw the entry of women. Banks have also been recruiting them, though women managers constitute only seven to eight per cent in sharp contrast to employees being 30 to 3 5 per cent of the work-force. The early Eighties have witnessed an increasing number of women chartered accountants and their induction, for the first time, into the thorny function of industrial relations.

It has only been recently realised that this function can be better handled by women since they have a greater understanding of the emotions of the human being and sensitivity to people. Recently, there was a case of a young woman personnel officer who helped to ease the storm that developed between the agrosuppliers to a food processing firm, who were threatening to turn violent when told that their goods would not be accepted by the firm, due to inconsistency in the quality of supplies.

President Ronald Reagan's appointing Sandra Day O'Conor as the first woman to serve on the Supreme Court of the United States of America is a magnificent example of the "most significant and welcome psychological re-adjustment".

With the steady growth in the activities of the National Council of Public Relations Society of India senior mambars have opportunities to meet with a number of women working as public relations professionals in the Central and State Governments, 'Media' and business corporations. The writer with his senior colleagues work closely with women some of whom are 'Chairpersons' and Honorary Secretaries of P.R.S.I. Chapters in India. Our general impressions are:

1. Such a happy situation where our women are placed, does portend a change for the better. Handled sincerely, more could be obtained from women in a motherly way. To achieve it one needs a different psychology of handling women, in that the profession of public relations does demand such "mothering" from the men professionals.
2. Samples of the talks between us and the PR women professionals quoted from memory are:

   (a) A number of working women have had grounding in some advertising agency and or 'media" to know the people, the jargon, the procedure and the attitudes towards the management executives.

   (b) Many did not appear to have chosen PR career only for the sake of material reward.

   (c) To the question as to their philosophy of the profession, they quipped: "Do the best we can for our employers. If anyone feels ill at ease, they must get out. If we stay, we do not forget who is paying us and why for. But on the other hand, we do not let our employers make us betray our sense of right and wrong." "We seek for responsibility." "We have also learned to put on an angry face without meaning offence where occasions demand. At times of exhaustion resulting in mental strain or when our boss has pointed out some lapse on our part, we try and bear with the situation without 'weeping', either internally or externally."

   "Generally, we do not take ourselves or our job too seriously. But it does not mean that we are not serious bout our responsibilities. If women really want to succeed, they need to be ambitious themselves in the same sense as men are. Being ambitious is in no way wrong and it does not lessen one's womanness; it does not also mean that we try to compete with men to achieve professional excellence at all costs.

   (d) "Our advice to those women choosing this career is: Do not forget the rest of your 'life'.

3. People in service industries like hotels, tourism, travel corporations and the like aver "the more smart women we employ, the more money the industries tend to make."
4. Women respond to courtesy; men respond better to public acknowledgment.
5. Women expect personal appreciation; men in the same position expect plaudits.
6. A man would generally respond more quickly to the game spirit; his love of sport is inherent and if you can appeal to that, you are more likely to win his cooperation than not.
7. Many men might sacrifice comfort for pay, and many women might sacrifice pay for comfort and congenial surroundings.
8. You can appeal more to man's ambition than to the average woman's.
9. A man likes titles more than women. Men generally respond to sense of justice but a woman sometimes tends to settle her viewpoint according to her prejudice:
10. Women have more nimble fingers and are capable of doing artistic work.

Round Up : There is no question of deciding "how equal" are women to men; if such a question were to be posed (under Indian social environment) it will be as much a Human relations problem as any in the organization.

10

The Copy Right

It is hereby announced for the information of the general public that the Government of India have rectified the Universal Copyright Convention and Protocols 1 and 2 thereto and acceded to protocol 3 of the Convention.

The Instrument of Ratification was deposited with UNESCO on 21st October, 1957, and the Convention would come into force in respect of India, with effect from January 21, 1958.

India has been a party to the Berne Convention for the protection of Literary and Artistic Works ever since 1887.

A number of countries from Europe, Asia and America have joined this Convention but the United States of America and certain other American countries have not been members of the Berne Convention as those countries had a copyright system which could not fit into some of the important provisions of the Berne Convention.

The position, therefore, was that though the Berne countries were bound to one another by the Berne Convention, they were required to enter into separate agreements with non-Berne countries in regard to copyright matters.

This position was obviously unsatisfactory and unceasing efforts were made for many years to bring the various countries following divergent systems under a common umbrella in the matter of international copyright.

For this purpose, an inter-Governmental conference was convened under the auspices of UNESCO, at which delegations of Governments of about 50 countries including India were present. This Conference adopted a convention called the "Universal Copyright Convention", along with three Protocols, for regulating copyright relations amongst the countries ratifying or acceding to the Convention.

Universal Copy Right Convention

The Universal Copyright Convention does not, however, supersede the Berne Convention. In fact, the Berne Convention continues to regulate the copyright relationship amongst the Berne countries (vide Article XVII and the Declaration annexed thereto).

The Universal Copyright Convention only established relationships between the Berne countries and the non-Berne countries; it serves as a bridge between the Berne countries and the non-Berne countries. Berne countries ratifying the Universal Copyright Convention will no longer need to enter into separate arrangements with non-Berne countries ratifying the Convention and the copyright relations between such countries will be regulated by the provisions of the Universal Copyright Convention. Likewise, the non-Berne countries which are signatories to the Universal Copyright Convention will claim protection under that Convention in the Berne countries which are signatories to the Universal Copyright Convention, without any further special arrangements.

Basic Principle : The basic principle adopted in the Universal Copyright Convention is of 'National treatment'. It is expressed in Article II of the Convention in the following words:

"1. Published works of nationals of any Contracting State and works first published in that State shall enjoy in each other Contracting State the same protection as that other

State accords to works of its nationals first published in its own territory."

"2. Unpublished works of nationals of each Contracting State shall enjoy in each other Contracting State the same protection as that other State accords to unpublished works of its own national."

Accordingly Indian works and works of Indian nationals can, by virtue of this provision, claim in every non-Berne Universal Copyright Convention country the same protection which is enjoyed by the national of that country in respect of his works published in that country.

Many countries require under their domestic law compliance with certain formalities (e.g., registration, deposit of copies, notice, etc.), for acquisition of copyright within their territory.

The Universal Copyright Convention dispenses with this requirements and provides that it shall be deemed to have been satisfied if all copies of a work bear at a prominent place merely the symbol (C) (the letter C in a Circle) accompanied by the name of the Copyright proprietor and the year of first publication (Article III); Indian works have thus not now to comply with the formalities prescribed in the laws of the non-Berne Universal Copyright Convention countries and will secure copyright protection by reason of the aforesaid symbol.

The Universal Copyright Convention also permits translation of published writings under certain conditions (Article V).

The following non-Berne countries have so far ratified the Universal Copyright Convention:

> Andorra, Argentine Republic, Cambodia, Chile, Costa Rica, Cuba, Ecuador, Germany, Guatemala, Haiti, Ireland, Laos, Liberia, Mexico, Nicaragua, Republic of El Salvador, Republic of Honduras, Republic of San Marino, Uruguay and the United States of America.

It is necessary that the Indian law of copyright should enable India to give effect to the terms of the Universal Copyright Convention. Parliament has passed the Copyright Act, 1957, and is proposed to bring the Act into force and make a suitable order under Sections 40 and 41 thereof for the purpose before January21, 1958.

Text of Declaration

(Geneva, 6 September, 1952)

The Contracting States moved by the desire to assure in all countries copyright protection of literary, scientific and artistic works.

Convinced that a system of copyright protection appropriate to all nations of the world and expressed in a universal convention, additional to, and without impairing international systems already in force, will ensure respect for the rights of the individual and encourage the development of literature, the sciences and the arts.

Persuaded that such a universal copyright system will facilitate a wider dissemination of works of the human mind and increase international understanding.

Have agreed as follows :

Article I

Each Contracting State undertakes to provide for the adequate effective protection of the right of authors and other copyright proprietors in literary, scientific and artistic works, including writings, musical, dramatic and cinematographic works, and paintings, engravings and sculpture.

Article II

1. Published works or nationals of any Contracting State and works first published in that State shall enjoy in each other Contracting State the same protection as that other State accords to works of its nationals first published in its own territory.
2. Unpublished works of nationals of each Contracting State shall enjoy in each other Contracting State the same protection as that other State accords to unpublished works of its own nationals.

3. For the purpose of this Convention any Contracting State may by domestic legislation, assimilate to its own nationals any person domiciled in that State.

Article III

1. Any Contracting State which, under its domestic law, requires as a condition of copyright, compliance with formalities such as deposit registration, notice, notarial certificates, payment of fees or manufacture or publication in that Contracting State, shall regard these requirements as satisfied with respect to all works protected in accordance with this Convention and first published outside its territory and the author of which is not one of its nationals, if from the time of the first publication all the copies of the work published with the authority of the author or other copyright proprietor bear the symbol © accompanied by the name of the copyright proprietor and the year of first publication placed in such manner and location as to give reasonable notice of claim of copyright.
2. The provision of paragraph 1 of this article shall not preclude any Contracting State from requiring formalities or other conditions for the acquisition and enjoyment of copyright in respect of works first published in its territory or works of its nationals wherever published.
3. The provisions of paragraph 1 of this article shall not preclude any Contracting State from providing that a person seeking judicial relief must, in bringing the action, comply with procedural requirements, such as that the complainant must appear through domestic counsel or that the complainant must deposit with Court or an administrative office, or both, a copy of the work involved in the litigation: provided that failure to comply with such requirements shall not affect the validity of the copyright, nor shall any such requirement be imposed upon a national of another Contracting State if such requirement is not imposed on nationals of the State in which protection is claimed.

4. In each Contracting State there shall be legal means of protecting without formalities the unpublished works of nationals of other Contracting States.

5. If a Contracting State grants protection for more than one term of copyright and the first term is for a period longer than one of the minimum periods prescribed in Articles IV, such State shall not be required to comply with the provisions of paragraph 1 of this Article III in respect of the second or any subsequent term of copyright.

Article IV

1. The duration of protection of a work shall be governed, in accordance with the provisions of Article II and this Article, by the law of the Contracting State in which protection is claimed.

2. The term of protection for works protected under this Convention shall not be less than the life of the author and twenty-five years after his death.

However, any Contracting State which, on the effective date of this Convention in that State, has limited this term for certain classes of works to a period computed from the first publication of the work, shall be entitled to maintain these exceptions and to extend them to other classes of works. For all these classes the term of protection shall not be less than twenty-five years from the date of first publication.

Any Contracting State which, upon the effective date of this Convention in that State, does not compute the term of protection upon the basis of the life of the author, shall be entitled to compute the terms of protection from the date of the first publication of the work or from its registration prior to publication, as the case may be, provided the term of protection shall not be less than twenty-five years from the date of first publication or from its registration prior to publication, as the case may be.

If the legislation of a Contracting State grants two or more successive terms of protection, the duration of the first term shall not be less than one of the minimum periods specified above.

3. The provisions of paragraph 2 of this Article shall not apply to photographic works or to works of applied art; provided, however, that the term of protection in those Contracting States which protect photographic works, or works of applied art in so far as they are protected as artistic works, shall not be less than ten years for year of said classes of works.

4. No Contracting State shall be obliged to grant protection to a work for a period longer than that fixed for the class of works to which the work in question belongs, in the case of unpublished works by the law of the Contracting State of which the author is a national, and in the case of published works by the law of the Contracting State in which the work has been first published.

For the purposes of the application of the preceding provisions, if the law of any Contracting State grants two or more successive terms of protection, the period of protecting of that State shall be considered to be the aggregate of those terms. However, if a specified work is not protected by such State during the second or any subsequent term for any reason, the other Contracting States shall not be obliged to protect it during the second or any subsequent term.

5. For the purposes of the application of paragraph 4 of this Article, the work of a national of a Contracting State, first published in a non-Contracting State, shall be treated as though first published in the Contracting State of which the author is a national.

6. For the purposes of the application of paragraph 4 of this Article, in case of simultaneous publication in two or more Contracting States, the work shall be treated as though first published in the State which affords the shortest term; any work published in two or more Contracting States within thirty days of its first publication shall be considered as having been published simultaneously in said Contracting States.

Article V

1. Copyright shall include the exclusive right of the author to make, publish, and authorize the making and publication of translations of works protected under this Convention.
2. However, any Contracting State may, by its domestic legislation, restrict the right of translation of writings, but only subject to the following provisions:

If, after the expiration of a period of seven years from the date of the first publication of a writing, a translation of such writing has not been published in the national language or languages, as the case may be, of the Contracting State, by the owner of the right of translation or with his authorization, any national of such Contracting State may obtain a non-exclusive licence, from the competent authority thereof to translate the work and publish the work so translated in any of the national languages in which it has not been published; provided that such national, in accordance with the procedure of the State concerned, establishes either that he has requested, and been denied, authorization by the proprietor of the right to make and publish the translation, or that, after due diligence on his part, he was unable to find the owner of the right. A licence may also be granted on the same conditions if all previous editions of a translation in such language are our of print.

If the owner of the right of translation cannot be found, then the applicant for a licence shall send copies of his application to the publisher whose name appears on the work and, if the nationality of the owner of the right of translation is known, to the diplomatic or consular representative of the State of which such owner is a national, or to the organisation which may have been designated by the Government of that State. The licence shall not be granted before the expiration of a period of two months from the date of the dispatch of the copies of the application.

Due provision shall be made by domestic legislation to assure to the owner of the right of translation a compensation which is just and conforms to international standards, to assure payment transmittal of such compensations, and to assure a correct translation of the work.

The original title and the name of the author of the work shall be printed on all copies of the published translation. The licence shall be valid only for application of the translation in the territory of the Contracting State where it has been applied for. Copies so published may be imported and sold in another Contracting State if one of the national languages of such other State is the same language as that into which the work has been so translated, and if the domestic law in such other State makes provision for such licences and does not prohibit such importation and sale, where the foregoing conditions do not exist, the importation and sale of such copies inn Contracting State shall be governed by its domestic law and its agreements. The licence shall not be transferred by the licensee.

The licence shall not be granted when the author has withdrawn from circulation all copies of the work.

Article VI

"Publication", as used in this Convention, means the reproduction tangible form and the general distribution to the publication copies of a work from which it can be read or otherwise visually perceived.

Article VII

This Convention shall not apply to works or rights in works which, at the effective date of the Convention in a Contracting State where protection is claimed, are permanently in the public domain of the said Contracting State.

Article VIII

1. This Convention, which shall bear the date of September 6, 1952, shall be deposited with the Director General of the United Nations Educational, Scientific and Cultural Organisation and shall remain open for signature by all States for a period of 120 days after that date. It shall be subject to ratification or acceptance by the signatory States.

2. Any Stele which has not signed this Convention may accede thereto.

3. Ratification, acceptance or accession shall be effected by the deposit of an instrument to that effect with the Director-General of the United Nations Educational, Scientific and Cultural Organisation.

Article IX

1. This Convention shall come into force three months after the deposit of twelve instruments of ratification, acceptance of accession, among which there shall be those of four States which are not members of the International Union for the Protection of Literary and Artistic Works.

2. Subsequently, this Convention shall come into force in respect of each State three months after that State has deposited its instrument of ratification, acceptance or accession.

Article X

1. Each State party to this Convention undertakes to adopt, in accordance with its Constitution, such measures as are necessary to ensure the application of this Convention.

2. It is understood, however, that at the time an instrument of ratification, acceptance or accession is deposited on behalf of any State. Such State must be in a position under its domestic law to give effect to the terms of this Convention.

Article XI

1. An Inter-governmental Committee is hereby established with the following duties:

   (a) to study the problems concerning the application and operation of this Convention,

   (b) to make preparation for periodic revisions of this Convention,

   (c) to study any other problems concerning the international protection of copyright, in cooperation with the various interested international organisations, such as the United Nations Educational, Scientific and Cultural Organisations, the International Union for the protection of Literary and Artistic Works and the Organization of American States and

(d) to inform the Contracting States as to its activities.

2. The Committee shall consist of the representatives of twelve Contracting States to be selected with due consideration to fair geographical representation and in conformity with the Resolution relating to this article, annexed to the Convention.

The Director-General of the United Nations Educational, Scientific and Cultural Organization, the Director of the Bureau of the International Union for the protection of Literary and Artistic Works and the Secretary-General of the Organization of American States, or their representives, may attend meetings of the Committee in an advisory capacity.

Article XII

The Inter-governmental Committee shall convene a conference for revision of this Convention whenever it deems necessary or at request of at least ten Contracting States, or of a majority of the Contracting States if there are less than twenty Contacting States.

Article XIII

Any Contracting State may at the time of deposit of its instrument of ratification, acceptance or accession, or at any time thereafter, declare by notification addressed to the Director-General of the United Nations Educational, Scientific and Cultural Organization that this Convention shall apply to all or any of the countries or territories for the international relations of which it is responsible and this Convention shall thereupon apply to the countries or territories named in such notification after the expiration of the term of three months provided for in Article IX. In the absence of such notification this Convention shall not apply to any such country or territory.

Article XIV

1. Any Contracting State may denounce this Convention in its own name or on behalf of all or any of the countries or territories as to which a notification has been given under Article XIII. The denunciation shall be made by notification addressed to the Director-General of the United Nations Educational, Scientific and Cultural Organization.
2. Such denunciation shall operate only in respect of the State or of the country or territory on whose behalf it was made and shall not take effect until twelve months after the date of receipt of the notification.

Article XV

A dispute between two or more Contracting States concerning the interpretation or application of this Convention, not settled by negotiation, shall, unless the States concerned agree on some other method of settlement, be brought before the International Court of Justice for determination by it.

Article XVI

1. This Convention shall be established in English, French and Spanish. The three texts shall be signed and shall be equally authoritative.
2. Official texts of this Convention shall be established in German, Italian and Portuguese.

Any Contracting State or group of Contracting States shall be entitled to have established by the Director-General of the United Nations Educational, Scientific and Cultural Organization other texts in the language of its choice by arrangement with the Director-General.

All such texts shall be annexed to the signed texts of this Convention.

Article XVII

1. This Convention shall not in any way affect the provisions of the Berne Convention for the Protection of Literary and

Artistic Works or membership in the Union created by that Convention.

2. In application of the foregoing paragraph, a Declaration has been annexed to the present article. This Declaration is an integral part of this Convention for the States bound by the Berne Convention on January 1, 1951, or which have or may become bound to it at a later date. The signature of this Convention by such States shall also constitute signature of the said Declaration, and ratification, acceptance or accession by such States shall include the Declaration as well as the Convention.

Article XVIII

This Convention shall not abrogate multilateral or bilateral copyright conventions or arrangements that are or may be in effect exclusively between two or more American Republics. In the event of any difference either between the provisions of such existing conventions or arrangements and the provisions of this Convention, or between the provisions of this Convention and those of any new convention or arrangement which may be formulated between two or more American Republics after this Convention comes into force, the convention or arrangement most recently formulated shall prevail between the parties thereto. Rights in works acquired in any Contracting State under existing conventions or arrangements before the date this Convention comes into force in such State shall not be affected.

Article XIX

This Convention shall not abrogate multilateral or bilateral conventions or arrangements in effect between two or more Contracting States. In the event of any difference between the provisions of such existing conventions or arrangements and the provisions of this Convention, the provisions of this Convention shall prevail. Rights in works acquired in any Contracting State under existing conventions or arrangements before the date on which this convention comes into force in such State shall not be affected. Nothing in this article shall affect the provisions of Articles XVII and XVIII of this Convention.

Article XX

Reservations to this Convention shall not be permitted.

Article XXI

The Director-General of the United Nations Educational, Scientific and Cultural Organization shall send duly certified copies of this Convention to the States interested, to the Swiss Federal Council and to the Secretary-General of the United Nations for registration by him.

He shall also inform all interested States of the ratification, acceptances and accessions which have been deposited, the date on which this Convention comes into force, the notifications under Article XIII of this Convention and denunciations under Article XIV.

Appendix Declaration Relating to Article XVII : The States which are members of the International Union for the Protection of Literacy and Artistic Works, and which are signatories to the Universal Copyright Convention.

Desiring to reinforce their mutual relations on the basis of said Union and to avoid any conflict which might result from the co-existence of the Convention of Berne and the Universal Convention.

Have by common agreement, accepted the terms of the following declaration.

(a) Works which, according to the Berne Convention, have as their country of origin a country which has withdrawn from the International Union created by the said Convention, after January 1, 1951, shall not be protected by the Universal Copyright Convention in the countries of the Berne Union.

(b) The Universal Copyright Convention shall not be applicable to the relationships among countries of the Berne Union in so far as it relates to the protection of works having as their country of origin, within the meaning of the Berne Convention, a country of the international Union created by the said Convention.

Resolution Concerning Article XXI The Inter-governmental Copyright Conference : Having considered the problems relating to the Inter-Governmental Committee provided for in Article XI of the Universal Copyright Convention, resolves:

1. The first members of the Committee shall be representatives of the following twelve States, each of those States designating one representative and an alternate. Argentine. Brazil. France, Germany, India, Italy, Japan, Mexico, Spain, Switzerland, United Kingdom and United States of America.
2. The Committee shall be constituted as soon as the Convention comes into force in accordance with Article XI of this Convention.
3. The Committee shall elect its Chairman and one Vice-Chairman. It shall establish its rules of procedure having regard to the following principles:
   (a) the normal duration of the office of the representatives shall be six years; with one-third retiring every two years;
   (b) before the expiration of the term of office of any members, the Committee shall decide which States shall cease to be represented on it and which States shall be called upon to designate representatives; the representatives of those States which have not ratified, accepted or acceded shall be the first to retire;
   (c) the different parts of the world shall be fairly represented; and expresses the wish that the United Nations Educational, Scientific and Cultural Organisation provide its Secretariat.

In faith whereof the undersigned, having deposited their respective full powers, have signed this Convention.

Protocol 1 annexed to the Universal Copyright Convention concerning the application of that Convention to the works of Stateless Persons and Refugees.

The States parties hereto, being also parties to the Universal Copyright Convention (hereinafter referred to as 'the Convention') have accepted the following provisions:

1. Stateless persons and refugees who have their habitual residence in a State party to this Protocol shall, for the purposes of the Convention, assimilated to the nationals of that State.

2. (a) This Protocol shall be signed and shall be subject to ratification or acceptance, or may be acceded to, as if the provisions of Article VIII of the Convention applied hereto.

   (b) This Protocol shall enter into force in respect of each State, on the date of deposit of the instrument or ratification acceptance or accession of the State concerned or on the date of entry into force of the Convention with respect to such State, whichever is the later.

In faith whereof the undersigned, being duly authorised thereto, have signed this Protocol.

Done at Geneva, this sixth day of September, 1952, in the English, French and Spanish languages, the three texts being equally authoritative, in a single copy which shall be deposited with the Director-General of UNESCO. The Director-General shall send certified copies to the signatory States, to the Swiss Federal Council and to the Secretary-General of the United Nations for registration.

Protocol 2 annexed to the Universal Copyright Convention concerning the application of that Convention to the works of certain International Organisations.

The States parties hereto, being also parties to the Universal Copyright Convention (hereinafter referred to as 'the Convention').

Have accepted the following provisions :

1. (a) The protection provided for in Article II (l)of the Convention shall apply to works published for the

first time by the United Nations, by the.specialized Agencies in relationship therewith, or by the Organization of American States.

(b) Similarly, Article II (2) of the Convention shall apply to the said organisation or agencies.

2. (a) This Protocol shall be signed and shall be subject to ratification or acceptance, or may be acceded to, as if the provisions of Article VIII of the Convention applied hereto.

(b) This Protocol shall enter into force for each State on the date of deposit of the instrument of ratification acceptance or accession of the State concerned or on the date of entry into force of the Convention with respect to such State, whichever is the later.

In faith whereof the undersigned, being duly authorised thereto, have signed this Protocol.

Done at Geneva, this sixth day of September, 1952, in the English, Franch and Spanish languages, the three texts being equally authoritative, in a single copy which shall be deposited with the Director-General of UNESCO.

The Director-General shall send certified copies to the signatory States, to the Swiss Federal Council, and to the Secretary-General of the United Nations for registration.

Protocol 3 annexed to the Universal Copyright Convention concerning in the effective date of instruments or Ratification or Acceptance of or Accession to that Convention.

States parties hereto,

Recognizing that the application of the Universal Copyright Convention (hereinafter referred to as 'the Convention') to States participating in all the international copyright systems already in force will contribute greatly to the value of the Convention;

Have agreed as follows:

1. Any State party hereto may, on depositing its instrument or ratification or aceptance of or accession to the

Convention, notify the Director-General of the United Nations Educational, Scientific and Cultural Organisation (hereinafter referred to as 'Director-General) that instrument shall not take effect for the purposes of Article IX of the Convention until any other State named in such notification shall have deposited its instrument.

2. The notification referred to in paragraph 1 above shall accompany the instrument to which it relates.
3. The Director-General shall inform all States signatory or which have then acceded to the Convention of any notifications received in accordance with this Protocol.
4. This Protocol shall bear the same date and shall remain open for signature for the same period as the Convention.
5. It shall be subject to ratification or acceptance by the signatory States. Any State which has not signed this Protocol may accede thereto.
6. (a) Ratification or acceptance or accession shall be effected by the deposit of an instrument to that effect with the Director-General.

   (b) This Protocol shall enter into force on the date of deposit of not less than four instruments of ratification or acceptance or accession. The Director-General shall inform all interested States of this date. Instruments deposited after such date shall take effect on the date of their deposit.

In faith whereof the undersigned, being duly authorised thereto, have signed this Protocol.

Done at Geneva, this sixth day of September, 1952, in the English, French and the Spanish languages, the three texts being equally authoritative, in a single copy of which shall be annexed to the original copy of the Convention. The Director-General shall send certified copies to the signatory States, to the Swiss Federal Council, and to the Secretary-General of the United Nations for registration.

11

Two Way Process

The role of Public Relations in communication bridg's the gap between what the 'sender' means, and what the receiver thinks he means both being not necessarily the same.

Communication being a "two-way" process, the sender cannot possibly put across his ideas unless he knows what ideas are already in the mind of the receiver as between Arjuna and Bhagvan Krishna.

In the context of the complex conditions to which we human beings have to accommodate ourselves, and the number of conflicting ideas from which we are compelled to choose, any effort to rush us into decisions would naturally antagonise us and rouse our opposition.

That is why successful communication for good Public Relations is essentially the outcome of a complicated interplay of the principles of communication and virtues of public relations.

All Solutions

There can be no 'mutual understanding' without communication; and 'mutual understanding' is the core of 'public relations'.

There are few problems in life that real communication cannot resolve. If that notion sounds far fetched, perhaps that is because what we normally call communication isn't. We generally think of communication in terms of exchanging information, public speaking, expressing our feelings honestly or being sincere or persuasive. So we think effective communication depends on having special talent, a good vocabulary, the 'right' circumstances, and especially on the receptivity of other people. Effective and true communication does not depend on any of these things; but rather on uncovering within ourselves the ability to communicate.

Real communication is experience of being totally understood by another person.

Real communication is a profound understanding, not merely of the words being said, but of the experience and the meaning behind the words.

Real communication produces results. In relationships, real communication produces harmony, resolves problems, and dissolve feelings of separateness. It is mutual experience of being "known" and results in partnership and a sense of well-being.

In families, when communication occurs, gaps are bridged; misunderstandings, conflicts and resentments disappear. In organizations, effective communication transforms a group into a team. It reduces effort, fatigue and struggle. Work is accomplished more accurately, and efficiently as conflict and tension give way to cooperation and camaraderie.

For most of us, experiences of real communication seem to "happen", without our knowing how or why. Regardless of what we do, it often seems difficult, and sometimes impossible, to really communicate.

While we may not always know how to make real communication happen, we know how we feel when it does occur.

In sum, True communication is creation.

It generates experience in others.

It moves people

It not only delivers information to others; it actually forms their ability to hear.

True communication tranforms both the speaker and the listener. The benefits of such communication are:

(a) A better understanding of co-worker and customer behaviour.

(b) Increased recognition and ability to change ineffective communication styles.

(c) New skills for resolving interpersonal conflicts.

(d) Higher performance standards established through mutual alignment of management and employees.

(e) Increased productivity even under adverse conditions.

(f) Improved interviewing and consulting techniques.

(g) The ability to create an organizational climate of support and trust.

(h) The flexibility to understand co-workers from different cultures.

(i) Active, accurate listening habits.

(j) The enthusiasm to create teamspirit, company pride and goal congruence.

(k) The versatility to communicate across information boundaries as between, say, R & D and marketing departments.

(l) Enhanced powers of interpersonal motivation.

The great value in such communication:

1. A willingness to participate in group activities.
2. A greater ease and clarity in writing.
3. Confidence in presenting briefings.
4. Improving the effectiveness of committees and groups to accomplish tasks.

5. To speak effectively before people and to face people with confidence.

The cabinet of ministers, the board of directors or the governing body of an institution which has responsibility for national, and international, corporate or institutional 'reputation' must learn how to improve its communication techniques if it is to create a suitable environment in which the reputation may flourish. The government will have to learn how to improve communications with its States and as also its overseas friends; the board will have to improve communications with its customers, and with the staff, and also improve communication within the staff structure itself; similarly, the 'institution' should improve its communications with its own members and others who stand by it.

The speaker does not control communication—it is the listener. The speaker can mouth words all day and every day, as all our politicians do. Obviously no one *listens* though one hears him or *hears him speak.* So no communication has taken place.

Recognising the Person

If we are to improve our communication, we must try to learn what it is that makes the person with whom we wish to communicate, listen. If *you* want to tell *him* something, he will listen only if what you say *interests* him, is relevant to him and *means* something to him.

This is the basic premise of any communication activity. "What is in it for the listener?" It is absolutely no use making a statement or a speech, or writing a notice or even a book if you do not take notice of what is in it for the listener or the reader.

What I want to say is not important. What *he* wants to hear is all important. If you want some action to result from your communication, if you want the recipient to do something, then the communication will stimulate the desired action only if it is couched in a language which can be understood and which gives some benefit or satisfaction. If it does not take note of these two simple factors, then the communication will fail.

Make the Recipient Understand it was Important to Him

It is no good blaming the other man if he does not understand your message. The onus is on you to make sure that he does understand.

Managers talking to workers, trade union leaders talking to management, politicians talking to voters, journalists talking to readers, students trying to communicate with the rest of us and advertisers talking to customers; it is up to the speaker to make sure that the listener understands, accepts and perceives the importance of the message. The Key To Communication is Perception.

It is by appreciating the limits of the listener's perception that communication can be improved: He sees what he wants to see He hears what he wants to hear He does what he wants to do.

What he sees, what he hears and what he does are limited by degree of perception, by his experiences, his educational background, his environmental background and his way of life. Underlie stand his situation, couch the message in a way he can perceive, and your communication skills will improve. Think only of what you want to say, use language that you can understand, do only what you want to do, and your ability to communicate will be non-existent.

The Five Principles of Improved Communication

(i) The onus is on the speaker or writer to communicate,

(ii) The speaker must use words which the listener understands.

(iii) What the speaker says must be of interest to the listener.

To be of interest to the listener, it must give some kind of benefit.

(iv) The listener must be favourably disposed towards the speaker.

(v) The environment within which communication takes place must be convenient to both listener and speaker.

Note: A person's behaviour in any situation is determined by two factors:

(i) The environment as he perceives it.

(ii) His particular attitude and disposition at the time.

Techniques of Communication

(a) Tailor the information you give on the basis of the recipient's perception skills.

(b) Transmit information in small units.

(c) Provide an opportunity for feedback.

(d) Provide an opportunity for participation.

If we attempt to communicate in order to change another person's mind, or if we attempt to communicate in order to get action from another person, we must be keenly aware of the fact that he will tend to distrust what does not accord with his emotions and attitudes—so much so that he is quite likely to overlook what is said or to modify what is said in terms of his own experience. We must, therefore, base our communication not only on what we have to say but on *what the listener wants to hear.*

We must try to learn not to show how clever we are by using words that the other man does not understand, because if he does riot understand, he just switches off—thinking you are being clever at his expense he does not bother to listen. Avoid jargon or abbreviations or complex technical phrases.

Procedure and Practice

The communication process itself is very simple. It needs:

A message; a sender; a receiver; a motivating climate.

The last point is probably the most important of all. The receiver must have confidence in the sender, but the sender, upon whom the main onus of the communication process lies, must keep in mind always the fact that to get an idea across you must talk about something that interests the receiver. **Relate** it to his personal benefit, otherwise he **will not listen** at all.

Various Methods

These are also simple to state. They are a combination of:

Sight, Sound, Touch, Smell, and Taste. So easy to say, so difficult to manipulate.

The secret of improving communication is understanding the ability of the other man to perceive the data which is being transmitted. This is presented here under five simple headings:

(i) What he knows (awareness).

(ii) To whom he talks, what media he reads, listens or watches (input).

(iii) What he sees as his future (goal seeking),

(iv) His standards for accepting or rejecting data or the data source (integration),

(v) Value that he relates to the idea and accepts as being true without question (commitment).

Communication by Symbols : *Words* are the most familiar tool or type of symbol employed by communicators. *Words* have power only to the extent the people know their meanings.

Words have flesh, weight, sound and appearance. Words exist for their meanings. Words have to be employed as the means, not as the end. Words are like leaves : Where they most abound, much fruit of sense beneath is rarely found. Words should be used not only to balance a sentence but to balance an idea.

Spoken words are influenced by the quality and volume of voice, tone, pitch, speed of delivery and timing of pauses. When the speaker can be seen, his facial expressions, gestures, movement, manner, and appearance are elements of his communicating. In the use of writing words, choice of words and composition of phrases and sentences are important.

Illustrations are used to communicate. Everyone has heard the old claim that "one picture is worth thousand words."

Numbers are a third type of symbol communicators use. Just about all numbers are clear and finite, they are commonly used to denote sizes and prices, quantities and values.

Forms and shapes can communicate. They can be abstract or they can be the well-known triangle, star, circle, spiral and rectangle.

Finally, *sound, sound effects,* even *silence* are communication symbols.

Why Good Communication is so Important?

Communication, like birth, death, breathing and wanting to be loved, is part of life itself; it is a common experience as well. We all have communicated; we all are communicating; we all will communicate. It might even be said that communication is what distinguishes man from the rest of creation. 'Man', the only animal who can express himself, has the power to express in words. So, he can be identified as a 'communicating animal'!

It would be hard to find the president of a nation, the chief executive of a corporate body, a manager, a supervisor, a salesman, a scientist, a technician or anyone else in a business or in any other agency who isn't at least concerned with the problem of communication in his organization. Even in the case of husband-wife, teacher-taught, parent-child, government public, communications are not that easy as they used to be in the past.

The problems of communication are really the problems of understanding people. Words are tools for achieving effective exchange of information, attitudes and understanding. The problem is that a person is likely to listen through filters. He tends to hear what he wants to hear and disregards what he considers trivial or unimportant.

The snag is that what appears to be trivial to one man may seem positively earth-shattering to another. Another snag is that unless he is very unusual, a man listens defensively, explaining away or justifying what he should understand, if he is to increase his own capacity for being effective.

Very often, if the person receiving communication does listen to the message, he may find reasons for disregarding what is being said as unimportant or incorrect.

Man perceives as a rule what he expects to perceive; he sees largely what he expects to see and hears largely what he expects to hear. The unexpected is usually not received at all: it is neither seen or heard, but is ignored or misunderstood.

Communicator's Objectives : The purposes of communicators are numerous and varied.

Here are some examples :

To Buy	To Teach	To Clarify	To Compliment
To Sell	To Learn	To Confuse	To Criticise
To Inform	To Send Information To Buyers	To Cause	
To Misinform	To Get Information From Buyers	To Prevent	
To Reveal	To Affirm	To Feature Sellers	
To Conceal	To Deny	To Feature Buyers	

To Influence, Persuade, Motivate, or Actuate.

Communication Components : Communication involves :

(a) Transmitter, (b) Message, (c) Media, and (d) Receiver.

Forms of Communication : By just giving a glance to the prevailing system of communication practised by individuals, business corporations, governments, the techniques of communication may be generalized as :

(a) written communication,

(b) oral communication,

(c) visual communication, and

(d) audio-visual communication.

Media of Communication

(A) Written Communication

(a) Letters

(b) Circulars

(c) Orders

(d) Notes and explanation

(e) Memorandum

(f) Leaflets, handbills, brochures, pamphlets.

(g) Reports

(h) Forms and Questionnaire

(i) Manuals, etc.

(j) House Journal

(k) Newsletters, Bulletin Boards.

(B) Oral Communication

(a) Telephone, Dictaphone

(b) Record and Radio

(c) Meeting and Conference

(C) Visual Communication

(a) Slides, Neon and Hoardings without Neon.

(b) Printed pictures, Posters, Banners, Product Display.

(c) Traditional Media, Songs, Folkarts, Bommalattam, Dramas.

(D) Audiovisual Communication

(a) Television

(b) Short films and Documentaries.

Steps in Communication

(a) There must be a source of information—the initiator of the communication

(b) The initiator must put the information into symbols (words, etc.)

(c) The symbols (words, etc.) must be conveyed or transmitted.

(d) The symbols (words, etc.) must be received.

(e) The symbols (words, etc.) must be understood by the receiver.

Factors in Communication

Attention

Interest

Comprehension

Believability

Motivation

In communication, the *symbols* we call *words* have power only to the extent the people know their meanings.

Information Explosion

The so-called "communication gap" within institutions and between groups in society, and even between one country and another has been widening steadily to the point where it threatens to become an unbridgeable gulf of total misunderstanding.

In the meantime there is an information explosion. Every professional and every executive suddenly has access to an inexhaustible supply of data; an abundance which changes the communication problem and makes it both more urgent and even less tractable.

It will be correct to aver that the four fundamentals of communication have been learned mostly through doing the wrong things. That communication is perception, that communication is expectation, that communication is involvement, and that communication is not information. Perception is not logic; it is experience and always part of a total picture. The gestures, the tone of voice, the whole environment, not to mention the cultural and social relations, cannot be dissociated from the spoken language.

The same words (for example, "Nice to have met you, and I enjoyed meeting you") will be received in many different ways. They may be heard as being said with warmth or with coldness, as an endearment or a rejection depending upon the tone of voice, or the action. By themselves, without being part of the total configuration, the words have no meaning at all.

Man perceives, as already mentioned, what he expects to perceive, sees largely what he expects to see and hears largely what he expects to hear. So before we can communicate, therefore, we must know whether communication can utilize his expectation.

Communication always makes demands. It always demands that the recipient becomes somebody, does something, believes something. It always appeals to motivation. If communication fits in with the aspirations, the values, the purpose of the recipient it is powerful. If it goes against his aspirations, the values, his motivations, it is unlikely to be received at all, or at best it will be resisted.

Mutual Understanding

One of the people whose whole livelihood depends upon improving communication is the salesman, and he has learned that in order to get the customer open up, to reveal himself, he asks questions

How? What? When? Who? Where?

Questions which require a straight 'yes' or 'no' should be avoided. If questions are not asked, the other man's problems will never be known.

The important thing when asking questions is to listen carefully to the answers because we all tend to select information with which we already agree. The questioner must be sure that he does not listen only to the things with which he agrees and does not listen to the things with which he does not agree, because these are the very points that it is necessary to understand in order to improve communication.

Hearing Correctly

Listening is a very difficult thing to do. A cardinal mistake is to be so anxious to say what we want to say, that we are not really listening to what is being said. Very often when we are speaking to someone, we notice that he is not really listening. He is just waiting for us to finish so that he can say his piece. If neither person is listening to the other, there is a complete breakdown in communication. '*We* hear ourselves say something, the other person *heard* us say something, but interpreted what he heard in the light of *his* own experience and what we said in the light of *our* experience."

There is a very simple test of effective communication. When a serious impasse is reached in a dispute or an argument, the opponents in the argument should pause and then each in turn should try and repeat *exactly* the point of view of the other person.

It will soon be discovered where the breakdown of communication really is.

If a Company wishes to communicate with its public, staff, customers, shareholders, government, and the public at large, it must create an acceptable attitude in the mind of its public by planning and creating a favourable reputation. A favourable reputation will help establish an acceptable environment in which acceptable communication can take place.

The Principles

1. Perceive your power as a 'listener'.
2. A poor listener can destroy the speaker's desire to talk or his confidence in his ability to communicate.
3. An interested listener can sway the direction of the talk.
4. Ask questions: do not ask questions just to be polite but rather to clarify what is going on.
5. Reflect feelings: that will show you understand what is spoken.

6. Do not by swayed be personal attitudes. Some of the biggest barriers to effective listening are the personal attitudes and prejudices that distort what we hear.
7. Do not react subjectively. When you hear of government offices, you may immediately think of bureaucratic inefficiencies, for example. It is a subjective reaction that clouds the issue and damages the power of an otherwise perceptive listener.
8. "Listen, or thy tongue will keep thee deaf."

And finally a simple example :

Ram : "Shyam, is the message clear ?

Shyam : "Yes, Mr. Ram, the message was clear but I couldn't fully comprehend."

Ram : "Shyam, you said 'the message was clear,' and in the same breath 'couldn't fully comprehend'. That means you have been only 'hearing' but not 'listening'."

"I shall now repeat the exercise .... "

"Please appreciate that the time I have used up to communicate, and you to 'listen', has not

achieved the expected result."

Guide to Good Listening face-to-face

1.	Put the speaker at ease	By your attitude, help the speaker become relaxed and aware of a willing listener. Be not only seen to listen, but felt to listen. And use eye contact.
2.	Listen patiently	The speaker is entitled to be heard, even if you feel his approach is wrong.
3.	Avoid premature arguments	Don't interrupt to question or argue about facts. "That's not so...", "prove it..." and other such interjections only serve to abort the discussion.

4. Stay objective	Try to avoid emotional involvement. Simply try to understand the feelings, or "point of view" of the speaker. Do your evaluating later.
5. Avoid mental rebuttals	Too much time is spent mentally preparing a rebuttal or counter argument, instead of listening. Let the speaker finish before you reach a decision.
6. Remove distractions	Don't doodle or play with papers, pencils or anything else. What about shutting a door or window to eliminate extraneous sound, or turning off the radio?
7. Indicate acceptance	An occasional "yes" or "I see" or even a nod of the head, indicates attention. It can also' acknowledge what is being said (not necessarily agreement).
8. Hold your temper	An angry person almost inevitably gets wrong meanings from words. Anyway, any fool can lose his/her temper. It takes a real person to keep it.
9. Respect pauses or silence	It is all too common for us to "jump in" when the speaker pauses. Silence is an embarrassment for too many people. Don't fall victim to this fault.
10. Redirect a direct question	With few exceptions this helps a great deal. If the speaker asks, for example, "What do you think I should do ?" the reply might be "What do you think you should do ?" Be on guard against too much of this, that might be frustrating.

11. **Be honest with answer**	When faced with a genuine request for your opinion, give it honestly (if you have enough information to do so).
12. **Listen between**	What is not said is important. Be alert to this. Attitudes, moods, feelings often convey far more than words. It calls for a strong feeling of empathy on the part of the listener. Try to find the right "wavelength"

12

Good Communication

As a manager of any organisation, your prime responsibility is to get things done through people. However sound your ideas or well-reasoned your decisions, they become effective only as they are transmitted to others and achieve the desired action—or reaction. Communication, therefore, is your most vital management tool. On the job you not only communicate with words but your apparent attitudes and your actions. For communication encompasses all human behaviour that results in an exchange of meaning. How well you manage depends upon how well you communicate in this broad sense. These ten commandments are designed to help you improve your skills as a manager by improving your skills of communication—with superiors, subordinates and associates.

Ten Commandments

Seek to Clarify your Ideas before Communicating

The more systematically we analyse the problem or idea to be communicated, the clearer it becomes. This is the first step towards effective communication. Many communications fail because of inadequate planning. Good planning must consider the goals and attitudes of those who will receive the communication and those who will be affected by it.

Examine the True purpose of each Communication

Before you communicate, ask yourself what you really want to accomplish with your message—to obtain information, to initiate action, to change another person's attitude ? Identify your most important goal and then adapt your language, tone and total approach to serve that specific objective. Don't try to accomplish too much with each communication. The sharper the focus of your message, the greater its chances of success.

Consider the total Physical and Human Setting whenever you Communicate

Meaning and intent are conveyed by more than words alone. Many other factors influence the overall impact of a communication, and the manager must be sensitive to the total setting in which he communicates. Consider, for example, your sense of timing—i.e., the circumstances under which you make an announcement or render a decision ; the physical setting—whether you communicate in private, for example, or otherwise the social climate that pervades work relationships within the company or a department and sets the tone of its communications ; custom and past practice tie degree to which your communication conforms to, or departs from, the expectations of your audience. Be constantly aware of the total setting in which you communicate. Like all living things, communication must be capable of adapting to its environment.

Consult with others, where Appropriate, in Planning Communi cations

Frequently it is desirable or necessary ,to seek the participation of others in planning a communication or developing the facts on which to base it. Such consultation often helps to lend additional insight and objectivity to your message. Moreover, those who have helped you plan your communication will give it their active support.

B Mindful, while you Communicate, of the Overtones as well as the basic Content of your Message

Your tone of voice, jour expression, your apparent receptiveness to the responses of others—all have tremendous impact on those you wish to reach. Frequently overlooked, these subtleties of communication often affect a listener's reaction to a message even more than its basic content. Similarly, your choice of language—particularly your awareness of the fine shades of meaning and emotion in the words you use—predetermines in large part the reactions of your listeners.

Take the Opportunity, when it Arises, to Convey something of help or Value to the Receiver

Consideration of the other person's interests and needs—the habit of trying to look at things from his point of view—will frequently point up opportunities to convey something of immediate benefit or long-range value to him. People on the job are most responsive to the manager whose messages take their own interests into account.

Follow up your Communication

Our best efforts at communication may be wasted, and we may never know whether we have succeeded in expressing our true meaning and intent, if we do not follow up to see how well we have put our message across. This you can do by asking questions, by encouraging the receiver to express his reactions, by follow-up cantacts, by subsequent review of performance. Make certain that every important communication has a "feedback" so that complete understanding and appropriate action result.

Communicate for Tomorrow as well as Today

While communications may primarily be aimed at meeting the demands of an immediate situation, they must be planned with the past in mind if they are to maintain consistency in the receiver's view ; but most important of all, they must be consistent with long-range interests and goals. For example, it is not easy to communicate frankly on such matters as poor performance or the shortcomings of a loyal subordinate—but postponing disagreeable communications make them more difficult in the long run and is actually unfair to your subordinates and your company.

Be Sure your Actions Support your Communications

In the final analysis, the most persuasive kind of communication is not what you say but what you do. When a man's actions or attitudes contradict his words, we tend to discount what he has said. For every manager this means that good supervisory practices—such as clear assignment of responsibility and authority, fair rewards for effort, and sound policy enforcement—serve to communicate more than all the gifts of oratory.

Last, but by no Means least: Seek not only to be Understood but to Understand. Be a good Listener

When we start talking we often cease to listen—in that larger sense of being attuned to the other person's unspoken reactions and attitudes. Even more serious is the fact that we are all guilty, at times, of inattentiveness when others are attempting to communicate to us. Listening is one of the most important, most difficult—and most neglected—skills in communication. It demands that we concentrate not only on the explicit meanings another person is expressing but on the implicit meanings, unspoken words, and undertones that may be far more significant. Thus we must learn with the inner ear if we are to know the inner man.

The Exaggeration

Exaggeration is an intoxication of words. Language temporarily loses its self-control; it veers around the room making drunken passes at reality, biting its ear, whispering hyperbole, even drooling a little :

> "Bhagwan rajneesh, the speaking god on earth'" "spell binding... magnificent.. a washday mira applied public relations and communication , whiter than white is 'desal's detergent cake" "rajayogi's 'kayakalpa' has restored sexual vitality to even eighty year old men"

> "this is the greatest week in the history of the world since the creation" declared richard nixon when the apollo astronauts returned from the moon. "Ours is the only political party wedded to the gospel of 'ahimsa' of mahatma gandhi" shout, from housetops, congress, congress (o), congress (i), congress (s), congresses (x, y, z.), janta (s) etc., Most excesses do not display the exaggerator's all in its best light: They are merely blurbs. In more complex usage, exaggeration does dynamic and suggestive work ; it can be used to frighten or threaten, to reassure (oneself or others), to glorify or debunk, and, above all, to relieve the tedium of life, to entertain. Exaggeration is one of the methods of all myth—from "panchatantra" king vikramadiya and the ghoul, the parables of ramakrishna Paramhansa...

A child exaggerates his parents' powers to the point of moth; heroes and ideals arise from this distortion toward larger than life.

All caricature, of course, is based on the artist's method of exaggerating one feature in proportion to the others.

The great difficulty with all exaggerations is that while most of the audience may understand that excess and embellishment are in the air, and may automatically do a mental calculation discounting the rhetoric; the fact is that different auditors discount at different rates. It is often difficult to know just how much exaggeration is involved, and how much truth. If, say, a section of those in Punjab, of those in Maharashtra's Vidarbha, of those in Tamilnadu fists in the air describe our Union Government as their Enemy No. 1, how much of that is homicidal hostility, how much is merely political gimmicks ?

In simplest definition, exaggeration is a form of lying. Is it therefore bad, an instrument of untruth ? It depends. Sometimes the artful exaggeration is a way of evoking, of discovering, an essential truth lying below the prosaic surface of things. The very idea of exaggeration presupposes some discoverable, objective reality ; the task of the human eye and scientific intelligence, in this classic view, would be to describe that reality as dispassionately and accurately as possible. The world has its being, outside the fanciful brain of the exaggerator, a romantic whose business it is to distort reality. Still, in the late 20th century, where reality is not stable, where it is instead erratic, skittish, apocalyptic, discontinuous, monstrously surprising (the Holocaust) for example, was an event far beyond the vocabularies of exaggeration, then it is hard to know what is an overstatement and what is not.

But distinctions must be made. There are times when exaggerations are highly useful ; there are times when they may be fatal. Here are a few guidelines :

Do not exaggerate

1. When the sick breadwinner of a large family asks candidly about the prospects of his recovery.
2. When writing military dispatches (before the battle).
3. During your interview in connexion with a responsible post (if you are clumsy and may get caught).
4. When the top management has confided in you to diagnose the ills affecting the organization.
5. When you are holding a dialogue with the Union leaders over some "demands" from the employees.
6. When the district of which you are in charge is faced with serious flood situation owing to the rivers getting flooded hour by hour.

Exaggeration may be helpful

1. When your organization is faced with some troublemakers who are instigating many of the loyal employees to "strike".
2. When your patient does not follow your medical advice on his diet regulation.
3 When one's country is threatened by "War Talks" by the neighbouring country.
4. When one's moral character is deteriorating.
5. When a child plays truant by not attending school regularly or reading his lessons properly.

6. When writing military dispatches (after the battle).
7. When making political speeches.
8. When acknowledging your gratitude for the great favour done to you by some.

Books—A Living Force of Communication

A book demands three collaborators

1. The author who gives it his philosophy, his accumulated knowledge, his soaring words ;
2. The printer who employs all the skills of his craft to make the writing readable ; and
3. The third, perhaps the most important third person, the Reader.

   Only these three functioning together complete the cycle of communication that makes the Book A Living Force.

Powerful Medium of Communication

Music : for the harmony of the Universe—Why not ?

Music : for a wholesome life—Why not ?

Music : as a powerful medium of communication—Why not? What does it matter so long as all living beings on Earth continue to respond to Music ?

While the famous Emperor Aurangazeb, it's said, wanted to bury the sounds of music five fathoms deep, it is still a familiar sight in Indian towns and villages where the vagrant snake charmer makes our common cobra stand spell bound and motionless, with its expanded hood, charmed by the melody from the swift-moving pipe of the charmer.

In September 1972, it was demonstrated at a garden in Virur, near Nagpur, the belief of the owner that plants too could hear soft music. Recorded or live music was played to the plants through a public address system. A retired radio singer has been playing live guitar music followed by rendering of "ghazals" in a husky romantic voice. Sometime in early July 1972 a team of scientists from the Indian Council of Agricultural Research visited the garden to see and assess for themselves the value of the work of the garden owner.

Treatise on "Vedas" throws ample light on how the Ravana of Ramayan epic could acquire enormous power from Lord Shiva whom he could please by playing "Sama Veda" songs on his Veena—instrument.

Saints like Sant Thiagaraja, Tulsidas, Kabir, Chaitanya Mahaprabhu, and a host of such god men and women like Meerabai could most successfully spread "bhakti"—devotion to God—and elevate humankind by employing their musical compositions as medium for communication with the masses.

The early part of this century witnessed the emergence of Mahakavi—Poet Laurate—Subrahmania Bharati, and one of the greatest freedom fighters. Though a fiery speaker, he did not choose the spoken word but sung extempore to revolt against alien exploitation which the people in Southern India did in various ways. So powerful were Bharati's songs that even women and children were drawn to him, and his works are translated in some of the countries in the world.

Even today Indian mothers sing lullaby in Raga 'Nilamburi' to put their babies to sleep. We sing while we plough, while we harvest and dragging a heavy load, obviously to shed the strain involved in the process. And we sing while we pray. Even those who beg on the streets know the efficacy of songs !

There is a song for the occasion when a child is born, in Raga 'Sahana'; while naming the child Raga 'Yadhukulakambodhi' is sung ; on wedding occasions Raga 'Darbar', 'Bhoopala', 'Bhilahari' and the kindred Ragas ; even at death the wailings embrace Raga 'Muhari'. Thus, music as the soul of communication occupies an important place in home, and school, in temples, churches, theatres, in procession and on pilgrimages Music occupied an important place in Mahabharata military affairs. Music was played when the army marched : it heralded the beginning of the battle ; it announced the fall of a chief or knight. Music used to arouse the spirit of compatriots, invoking God's gift and wishing victory, and used to terrorise the opponent. There is a reference that the sound of Arjuna's conchshell made the enemy soldiers still for some while.

The history of war music goes back to the days of Rig Veda, the Atharva Veda which contains beautiful verses eulogising the music to invoke the spirit to fight. The importance of music was appreciated by Marshall de Saxe, who said, "make them march to music." Music still enjoys importance in Armed Forces. Each Regiment has its own band party, which precedes all ceremonial marches including victory parades.

When we listen to the sublime and mournful sonatas of Beethoven, when we listen to the tender melodies of Bellini, to the Shahanai of Bismilla Khan, Sitar by Pandit Ravi Shankar, Violin by Yehudhi Menuhin, Flute by T.R. Mabalingam, we fall into a trance ; the brain burns and swells ; its doors fly open ; the mind sweeps forth into an unknown world where all is dim, dusky, unutterably vast; gigantic ideas pass before us ; we attempt to seize them, make them our own, but they vanish like shadows in our arms. And then, as the music becomes soft and low, the mind returns and nestles to the heart; the senses are steeped in languor; the eyes filled with tears ; the memories of the past take form, and a voluptuous sadness permeates the soul—sweet as the sorrow of romantic youth when the real bitterness of life was yet unknown.

What, then, is the secret of this power in music? And why should certain sounds from wood and wire thus touch the heartstrings to their tune ? It's the voice of nature which the great compositors combine into harmony and melody.

Music rises from the human heart when the human heart is touched by the external world. When touched by the external world, the heart is moved, and therefore finds its expression in sounds. These sounds echo, or combine with one another and produce a rich variety, and when the various sounds become regular, then we have rhythm. The arrangement of tone for our enjoyment in combination with the military dance, with shields and hatchets, and the civil dance, with long feathers and pennants of ox-tails, is called music.

Music is the form wherein tones are produced because it takes its rise from the human heart when the heart is touched by the external world.' Therefore when the heart's chord of sorrow is touched, the sounds produced are sombre and forlorn ; when the heart chord of satisfaction is set, the sounds produced are languorous and slow, when the chord of joy is touched, the sounds produced are glowing and expansive ; when the chord of anger is touched, the sounds produced are harsh and strong; when the chord of piety is touched, the sounds produced are simple and pure ; and when the chord of love is touched, the sounds produced are sweet and gentle. These six kinds of emotion are not spontaneous, but are moods produced by impact from the external world.

Therefore the ancient kings of China were ever careful about things that affected the human heart. They tried therefore to guide the people's ideals and aspirations by means of Mi' (Chinese word meaning decorum), establish harmony in sounds by means of music, regulate conduct by means of government, and prevent Immorality by means of punishment, music, punishments and governments have a common goal, which is to bring about unity in the people's hearts and carry out the principles of political order. The ancient kings did not institute rituals and music for the mere purpose of satisfying the desires of our senses ("the mouth, the stomach, the ear and the eye"), but rather for teaching the people the right taste and the return to normality.

The nature of man is usually quiet, but when it is affected by the external world, it begins to have desires. With the thinking mind becoming conscious of the impact of the material world, we begin to have likes and dislikes. When the likes and dislikes are not properly controlled and our conscious minds are distracted by the material world, we lose our true selves and the principle of reason in Nature is destroyed. When man is constantly exposed to the things of the material world which affect him and does not control his likes and dislikes, then he becomes overwhelmed by the material reality and becomes dehumanized or materialistic. When a man becomes dehumanized or materialistic, then the principle of reason in Nature is destroyed and man is submerged in his own desires. From this arise rebellion, disobedience, cunning and deceit, and general immorality. We have then a picture of the strong bullying the weak, the majority persecuting the minority, the clever ones deceiving the simple-minded, the physically strong going for violence, the sick and crippled not being taken care of, and the aged and the young and helpless not cared for. This is the way of chaos.

Music unites, while rituals differentiate. Through union the people come to be friendly toward one another, and through differentiation the people core to learn respect for one another. If music predominates, the social structure becomes too amorphous, and if rituals predominate, social life becomes too cold.

Music expresses the harmony of the universe, while rituals express the order of the universe. Through harmony all things are influenced, and through order all things have a proper place.

When you see the type of a nation's dance, you know its character...

Man is gifted with blood and breath and a conscious mind, but his feelings of sorrow and happiness and joy and anger depend on circumstances. His definite desires arise from reactions toward the material world. Therefore, when a sombre and depressing type of music prevails, we know the people are distressed and sorrowful. When a languorous, easy type of music with many long drawn-out airs prevails, we know that the people are peaceful and happy. When a strong and forceful type of music prevails, beginning and ending with a full display of sounds, we know that the people are hearty and strong. When a pure, pious and majestic type of music prevails, we know that the people are pious. When a gentle, lucid and quietly progressing type of music prevails, we know that the people are kind and affectionate. When loud, exciting and upsetting music prevails, we know that the people are immoral.

Character is the backbone of our human nature, and music is the flowering of character. The metal, stone, string and bamboo instruments are the instruments of music. The poem gives expression to our heart, the song gives expression to our voice, and the dance gives expression to our movements. These three arts take their rise from the human soul, and then are given further expression by means of the musical instruments. Therefore, from the depth of sentiment comes the clarity of form and from the strength of the mood comes the spirituality of its atmosphere. This harmony of spirit springs forth from the soul and finds expression or blossoms forth in the form of music.

The peasants of all countries sing in their talk, and savages resemble the opera. Their conversation is of a "libretto" character: it glitters with hyperbole and metaphor, and they frequently speak in recitative chanting or intoning, and ending every sentence in a musically sounded, "O" ! Often also, if a man happens to become excited in the midst of a conversation, he will sing instead of speaking what he has to say. The other person also replies in song, while the company around, as if touched by a musical wave, murmur in chorus in perfect unison, clapping their hands, undulating their bodies, all perhaps breaking forth into dance !

Just as the articulate or conventional speech has been developed into rich and varied tongues, by means of which abstract ideas and delicate emotions can be expressed in appropriate forms or terms, so the inarticulate or musical speech—the true, the primitive language of our race—has been developed with the aid of instruments also into a rich and varied language of sound in which poems and songs can be composed. Examples : the lute, "Veena", "Sitar", Violin, "Nagaswaram" and Flute.

Science of Music

There is a science of music but music is not a science. Nor is it an imitative art. It is a language. Words at first were rather sung then spoken and sentences were rhythmical. The human language of songs bears the same relation of the civilized dog to its sonorous howl. There seems little in common between the lady who plays "Veena" or the man at the piano and the dog who chimes in with jaws opened and nose upraised, yet each is making use of the primitive language of its race : the wild dog can only howl, the wild woman can only sing.

Music being the voice of Nature, the great composers combine it into harmony and melody. Let us follow it downwards and downwards in her (Nature's) bosom, and there we discover music, the speech of passion, of sentiment, of emotion, and of love ; there we discover the divine language in its elements—the sigh, the gasp, the melancholy moan, the plaintive note of supplication, the caresting murmur of maternal love, the cry of challenge or of triumph, the song of the lover as he serenades his mate all of which are the varied ingredients contained in the whole shell of total communication.

Electronics Media

To communicate with one another is a compulsive urge of human beings. Civilisations and cultures progress to the extent communications have made them possible. Speech (unaided for its propagation) has a limited distance range. Communication within the family and very closely living families helped the primitive communities. As movement also was limited, there could have been thousands of languages as despaired in the expression 'babel of tongues'. After speech, the next important development was writing. It helped preservation of ideas, of thoughts, of agreements and their transmission from generation to generation. Until paper and printing were invented, even writing could help only to a limited extent for communication between farflung communities and societies. Printing helped the multiplication of information and knowledge and their easy availability to tens of thousands of people. Even though paper and printing extended the range of communication, they could not influence the rapidity of transmission .

It was only from the middle of the last century that rapid transmission of communications by electrical means became possible. Telegraphy helped the transmission of written messages, almost instantaneously, and telephony from 1876 onwards facilitated the transmission of speech, enabling the dissemination of information and knowledge very rapidly. Telegraphy and telephony are, however, means of communication from one individual to another, from any to any and could be said to be private means of communication. What is transmitted by telegraph or telephone could be known to millions only when it was printed and distributed through newspapers or otherwise.

The next quantum jump occurred with the invention of the radio and its utilisation for broadcasting of information from a central source to any and everywhere equipped with a radio receiving device. This is communication from one to many.

By the beginning of the 1930s, almost all over the world radio broadcasting for information transmission over wide communities and areas had been established. From then onwards we could say that the information was becoming more and more electronics based In the 1950s began the transmission of picture along with voice for broadcasting. Television increasingly caught on. The black and white pictures were themselves a wonder, but Televisions became an arresting marvel with colour transmission. It has become increasingly affordable by more and more people because the transistors and the integrated circuits made the mass-produced radios as well as the Television sets cheaper every decade. The invention and increased availability of portable recording and replaying devices enabled the capture of events as they were taking place and their near instantaneous broadcasting throughout the world. Communication satellites with the capability or telephony and telex and television helped the worldwide instantaneous transmission of news and views of events. Before the invention of the telegraph, it took weeks and months for news in one country to be known in other countries and continents. But with the radio and the television, both carried over satellites, distance and time have been so shrunk that information from one continent to another can be transmitted and known in as little time as it takes within a village. In other words, our globe itself has been reduced to a village.

Audio and video cassette recording and their multiplication in millions is enabling the spread of instruction and training and entertainment and education. One illustration of how an electronic involving education spreading system has come up could be useful; India is having the largest unlettered population, at over 500 million. This school-going population is also of the order of hundreds of millions. If all of them are, in the traditional fashion, to be sent to schools, the amount of expenditure over buildings, text books and transportation will be enormous. On the other hand, if all the educational programmes can be recorded on video cassettes and broadcast over countrywide or region-wide media through the satellite, we can have very economically and replan propagated education. What is called 'Projection Television' is a versatile aid. Pictures are reproduced on a very large screen attached to the television monitor, enabling scores of viewers to be instructed with the least expense. Also, instead of libraries of books if there is a library of video cassettes containing text and illustrated and explained by the best teachers, and if these cassettes can be circulated among the schools, the quality of instruction in the village-level schools; which now are poorly staffed, can be fantastically improved.

Electronics, computers and telecommunication media are enabling the simultaneous printing of newspapers from several centres. Electronic book publishing is another rapidly growing activity. Personal Computers, access data bases over telecom media and print out a mass of information in whatever format it is wanted. They are a great aid for information storage, retrieval and processing.

In modern times, because of the industrial revolution and intensive and economic exploitation of resources and increasing consumption of goods and services, huge companies or corporations and organisations are a necessity. They are also economically efficient. It is very necessary that all these companies and organisations explain to the masses of money-providers and consumers why and how they are performing and how best their services could be utilised by the consumers. This is one of the most important aspects of public information and relations that every corporate organisation has to undertake. While newspapers could be useful only for a fraction of the 30% of the lettered people in India, mass communication media like radio and television are the most effective and economic means of mass information. Huge organisations become powerful because of their size, and hence become more and more impersonal and bureaucratised. Customers and may be even the workers will find themselves helpless in understanding or reacting with these organisations. Various communication media, audio and video cassettes and electronic reproduction methods enable a public instructional and information programme to be carried out easily. They are the means by which minds can be informed and influenced for the achievement of an organisation's goals and for the transformation of society.

A Poser to the Modern Communicator

1. Does the communicator recognize that technologists and scientists must come to grips with certain concrete problems the solutions for which would permit the lean 'Third World Countries' 'peopled look near 'fat cats' in rich countries?
2. Can the 'New Information Order' check more effectively the sources (of information) which feed the 'Third World Countries' so that they can get only such 'information' as will help the growth in the long run?
3. What can be done against the bottleneck that is developing between the unlimited information capacity of modern communication system and the limited reception and assimilation rate of individuals?
4. Can communicators help in encountering the danger of overpopulation?
5. Can communicators arrest the dangerous tendency toward over-urbanization?
6. What can be done to educate children, adolescents and adults to be fit citizens in a materially stationary civilization on a high culture?
7. Can communicators create awareness among the people of 'developing countries' that, except who are physically and mentally unfit to work, the rest of them must give their shoulders to the government?
8. What can be done about "Information Pollution"? Some of the elements which contribute to Information Pollution are : political lies, political scandal, character assassination, rigging the elections, interference in judicial administration, pornography, violence and sex via audio-visual media, and many similar or other pollutants.

13

Information Culture

In the famous words of U. Thant, "It is no longer resources that limit decisions but it is the decisions that make resources. In today's complex world, decisions depend upon collection, selection, and correlation of "information" in shortest time. The "New Information Order" is poised for the commitment. Like its companion "New World Economic Order" which calls for redistribution of the international power of the purse, "The New Information Order" is a demand for redress of perceived inequities, this time over the 'Power of The Word'. It is "The Free and Balanced Flow of Information" : not creating and perpetuating an imbalance in the world's flow of information under the guise of maintaining freedom, resulting in a vast and insidious cultural imperialism built on Western monopoly of the means of international communication.

Purposeful Communication

The Press, quite literally an informer, must make way for the New Order and its new right of "objectivity of information and balance in its presentation." While upholding its rights as an "informer", it cannot be silent on its duties and responsibilities towards the 'informed'. The traditional concept of rights in the field of communication can no more be on individualist considerations, to the detriment of collective needs. Freedom of information cannot continue to be as a sort of instrument of domination in the hands of the information media. For example, does it contribute to the fulfilment of the aspirations and growth of the "Third World" countries if the Western journalists, rightly of wrongly, give more prominence to the developing countries' problems such as communal fracas, unemployment, food, population, etc., in their reports. Such reports smack of either ignoring or belittling the efforts of the developing countries towards alleviating their problems, often against seemingly unsurmountable odds. How do such reports on social, economic and political developments in the Third World in terms of 'right' or 'leftward' shifts in government policies can be considered objective ? Again, how Land Reforms, measures to encourage the development of national industries to the immediate or potential disadvantage of transnational corporations, measures to sober the stronghold of a few indigenous business groups over national economies, and legislation to ensure monitoring and suppression of national banking and trade institutions can be considered as portents of a country's slide into the communist or socialist ambit ?

To make the 'Information System' work meaningfully, that is the "haves" helping the "have-nots", the following steps call for consideration :

FIRST : Regulation of the right to information by preventing abusive uses of the right to access.

NEXT : Definition of appropriate criteria to govern truly objective news selection.

THEN : Establishment of a professional code of ethics, enforced by a tribunal empowered to punish violators who disseminate false or distorted information.

FINALLY : Creation of an international convention defining the right of reply for maligned States.

This would include "A list of precisely defined infringements (of) prestige, culture, and vaiues."

Shape and Content of Meeting

The shape and content of a meeting differ from a debating society. Debate is different from discussion. Where healthy discussions take place the "knowhow" knowledge of dealing with men and matters is generated. Then it becomes a meeting with an objective. Where the interests of individuals dominate, then it tends to become a debating society ; and no worthwhile decision towards the progress of an organization comes out. Where the members of the "board" do not create a situation where it assumes a sort of "Board Room Battle", then "do-how" decisions are generated.

1. No one person can be expert in everything : so to make good decisions you need the participation of more and more executives who may be anxious to contribute to the form and content of the meetings.
2. As the number of Central, State and even Local Governments come out with 'regulations', now and then—unlike in the past—so too the number of occasions for meeting tend to increase in order to find out correct ways and means of compliance.
3. We cannot ignore some murmurings in the corridors of executive chambers, "the core problem with meetings is not so much the amount of time they absorb as the amount of time they waste !" More precisely, many executives may agree that what messes up so many meetings is the inability of a few to perform effectively and efficiently before the audience. No executive can be too smart if he hasn't learned to communicate.
4. Once people start arguing and committing themselves to specific policies and actions, you have used up the creativity of the group.
5. A meeting is really a peer level review. It is very revealing. You see how someone thinks on his feet, how he answers a difficult question, and whether he is an orderly thinker.
6. Well-run meetings are enjoyable. Any executive worth his salt should enjoy them too.

Various Type of Meeting

Informational

The purpose is to present ideas, data, techniques, etc., to the; people concerned in a minimum possible time.

Methodology : Lectures, guided discussion and demonstration.

Visuals : Films, charts, slides, posters, stickers, models, etc.

Participation Style : Questions, stories, case studies, etc.

Control of Group : Activities rest solely with the leaders.

Advisory

Purpose : To gather and seek advice, information, suggestions, recommendations, etc., relating to a problem.

Methodology : Lectures, roly-poly, free or guided discussion, case method, etc.

Visuals : Charts, slides, reports, catalogue, etc.

Participation Style: Questions, case example, arguments,. demonstration.

Control of Group : Shared by leader and group, with leader being principally responsible.

Problem-solving

Purpose : To seek a decision, solution or fundamental understanding of a problem.

Methodology : Lecture, demonstration, role-play—past experience, etc.

Visuals : Diagrams, charts, models, films, slides, etc.

Participation : Free discussion, team assignment, buzz groups,, brainstorming, fishbowl, etc.

Control : Shared by leader and group, with group being principally responsible.

Informational Meetings : Communication is downward—from the leader to the group.

Scientific Objectives : To present facts, to win support, to demonstrate work procedure, to lay out policy, to interpret policy, rule or procedure and to stimulate action.

Advisory Meeting

Communication Flows both Ways : Discussion plays an important role. The leader draws upon the participants' experience, knowledge and insights to guide him in arriving at a decision. The group act as consultants and since they help in arriving at the decision are more likely to accept it or give it their wholehearted cooperation.

Specific Objectives: To gather facts, information and opinions to develop possible solutions, to draw upon knowledge of specialists, and to establish basis for greater acceptance of decision.

Problem solving Meeting

Communication Flows both Ways : Interaction among members is free. Leadership goes on shifting from person to person, where the participants have the most to contribute in terms of knowledge, experience and leadership skills. The group makes the final decision.

Specific Objectives : To bring group thinking to bear upon a problem, to suggest possible solutions, to evaluate possible solutions and to arrive at a decision.

Problem-solving Conference

Introducing the Meeting

(a) establish a friendly atmosphere.

(b) bring everyone up to date—summarise events leading up to this session. Subcommittees' interim reports to be presented at this stage.

Introducing the Problem

(a) Stating the problem—giving the background, asking group how it affects them and discussing group's responsibility.

(b) Exploring the problem—to identify the real problem and make certain—all are talking about the same thing.

Attacking the Problem

(a) Defining the problem—problem to be stated and defined more carefully and divided into subproblems, if necessary.

(b) Building a conference plan—step by step outline of what the group will do. Decisions to be made as to whether—the group should analyse symptoms, causes and remedies —it should divide into sub groups to consider different aspects of the problem —a resource person should be called in —available records and reports should be analysed —new information should be gathered.

Considering Possible Solution

(a) Suggesting possible solutions—available data can be analysed and combined in new ways to arrive at tentative solutions—open-mindedness is essential—all solutions should be judged objectively and on merits.

(b) Testing possible solutions—carry out preliminary mental tests to weigh pros and cons of all possible solutions:

   (i) How will this work in practice.

   (ii) What is past experience on similar occasion.

   (iii) What new problems are likely to be created.

   (iv) What resources are available for implementation.

(c) Arrive at a decision—Decide upon the best possible solution by consensus—voting and deciding by majority leaves the minority dissatisfied.

Acting on the Decision

Planning future action:

(i) What must be done.

(ii) Who should do it.

(iii) In what sequence.

(iv) Who should be informed of the decision.

Insight Into Conference

Definition: A pooling of thoughts of two or more persons, the purpose of which is to assist in solving a problem.

Criteria :

(a) A conference problem should be real.

(b) A conference problem should be specific.

(c) A conference problem should be of common interest to the group.

(d) Phrasing the problem—no value judgements.

(e) Should be stated in concise, understandable words.

Techniques

Group Situation

Situation	Remedy
Bright, active, responsible Resistant, antangonistic	Give it fast—Be well prepared —Ask tough questions —Pit them against each other. Find out cause and correct it. Show sympathy—Face issue frankly —Break down bit by bit—Don't bulldoze.
Slow, passive	Explain thoroughly—use side conversation to help understanding—Don't go too fast. Build on their knowledge.

Individual Situations

Talks too much	Cut across his talk and summarize— Direct question to some one else—Put the group against him. Seat him in your blind spot.
Quick, helpful	Cut across tactfully— Ask someone else a question—

	Thank him for his help—use him to summarise.
Rambler	When he pauses for breath, thank him, rephrase his statement and pass on. Ask which topic he is discussing.
Arguer	If he is naturally perverse, put him in the blind spot. Pretend not to hear—Take him alone and seek his help— As a last resort, ask him to drop out—Put group against him.
Obstinate	Does not see the point. Ask others to help you. If he is still obstinate, ask him to see you after the meeting.
Wrong subject (Off the beam) Grips about Management	Direct attention to the real subject. Tell him the problem is how best to operate under present conditions. Get another reliable person to answer him. Don't waste too much time.
Has personal problem	It is pertinent, tackle it.
Racial or political	Frankly say you cannot discuss.
Side conversationalist	Pause. Let others also listen. Walk down near him—call him and ask his opinion.
Poor voice or choice of words	Help him. Protect him from ridicule Repeat his ideas in your words.
Definitely wrong	Say "well, that is one way of looking at it..." and proceed further on.
Personalities	Ask him in what way he regards personalities he feels

	should be left out. When still there is a dispute, cut across with a direct question on the top.
Ask leader for opinion	Redirect question to the group. If no opinion, say so.
Bored	Find his interest—call on him for his experience.
Just wants to listen	Use provocative questions to make him come out with his views.
Shy, hesitant	Ask questions he can answer—Ask for his agreement—Build him in the eyes of the group.
Not disposed to help others	Tell him how much he can help the group —Draw him out on a few things—Thank him.

Questioning

Purposes :

1. Call attention to a point, an idea, fact, problem or situation.
2. Evaluate opinions.
3. Get at causes or facts.
4. Uncover sources of information.
5. Control discussion.
6. Summarize or end a discussion.
7. Call attention to another phase of the problem or discussion.
8. Reach a conclusion or agreement.
9. Control group thinking.
10. Control group behaviour.
11. Suggest action, idea or decision.

Techniques—Direction

Type	Purpose
1. Overhead (Directed to the Group)	To open discussion. To introduce new phase. To give everyone a chance.
2. Direct (address to one)	To call for special information. To involve an inactive person.
3. Relay (Refer back to another)	To help avoid giving opinion. To get other's views. To ask someone who knows.
4. Reverse (Refer back to questioner)	To help avoid giving own opinion. To bring out opinions. To help questioner think for himself.

Types

1. Factual	To get information. To open discussion.
2. Broadening	To broaden discussion. To suggest answer and get group critique. To introduce additional facts.
3. Justifying	To challenge old ideas. To develop new ideas. To get reasoning and proof.
4. Hypothetical	To develop new ideas. To suggest another, possibly unpopular opinion.
5. Alternative	To make decision between alternatives. To get agreement.

14

Index of Public Opinion

Letters in Newspapers

Who are the people who write these letters ? And what provoke them to write these letters ? What are their motives ?

Those who write such "Letters to the Editor" are invariably motivated by the spirit of public service or civil service. Just because of the urge to serve the public these people are not satisfied with the discussions they have had with like-minded people and so they take the pen and write long letters to the editor.

Such "letters to the editor" appear on nearly all subjects under the Sun be it on mosquito nuisance or on 'Centre-State Relations', or the dismal failure of Indian Cricket team in Pakistan 'Test' series. No broad classification is possible.

The writer's analysis over a period of one year reveals : first, the 'letters to the editors' deal with political; next, make some sort of suggestion and even advice ; third, make one kind of complaint or the other ; fourth, deal with matters relative to culture, religion and related matters ; fifth, make allegations about corruption, nepotism and favouritism ; and lastly, on miscellaneous subjects.

Though it is difficult to make any classification, one cannot generally fail to notice the seasonal nature of the letters. At the time of the Solar Eclipe there were scores of letters dealing with scientific probe. During times of war and elections, letters on politics and policies will be prominent ; while during students' 'unrest in the campus' letters on topics of discipline, student-teacher relations and the like grab the major part. Letters alleging corruption and nepotism and letters which give new suggestions are almost uniform, irrespective of current problems.

The letters do vary according to the nature of the publication to which they are sent. They vary from 'dailies' to 'weeklies' and from both to the 'magazine'. Most letters to the weeklies or magazines will be usually confined to the articles that appeared on their pages. Sometimes they may be commendations, at other times they may be censuring. Whatever they may be they are strictly confined to that which appeared on the pages of the weekly or magazine.

These columns are believed to be one of the most commonly read and therefore support the most natural platform for anyone with the compulsive urge to express himself. Letter writers in general have a firm belief in the impact of their communication. When a series of 'letters' by the same set of persons and others on an important subject like "Ecology" appear in the columns of newspapers, the expected result is bound to be achieved. One classical example is the "Silent Valley" in Kerala which now stands undisturbed by the Government.

Fired with a sense of purpose these writers of letters have their say—a comment on an editorial or news item or an independent thought process, an idea or a complaint, a piece of historical research on an event as fresh as tomorrow. In the final analysis, their intention is to participate in the process of Decision-making or in the formulation of public policies.

People to People Relations

Apart from connecting government and their policies with the public, "Letters to The Editor" columns connect people with people.

They play a prominent role in achieving national unity. They bring people closer together. In matters of national policy, the man from Tamilnad and the one from Kashmir or from Assam express their voices, which constantly make them understand that difference in language or in culture, does not affect their wider national interests. This gives the people an occasion to rise above mere petty parochial interests. On occasions of national crisis like the war we had with our neighbour, letters from all parts of the country flowed in supporting the nation's leader and condemning the 'enemy' and its supporters. These letters are an impetus, a boosting up of the national spirit and will certainly lead to ultimate national integration.

A nation is nothing but a collection of individuals with a common culture and civilization. But unfortunately, the individuals and their immediate problems are something generally overlooked in the country. Is it not a fact that the common man is often denied justice by reasonable authorities "If at all he gets justice, it will be often a delayed one just like T.B. patients getting admission into hospitals after their death. Bureaucracy, the world over, is generally a muddle, lagging behind by its own unending weight of redtapes. Immediate necessities will be looked after on such occasions by a mere letter to the editor.

Besides this, some papers give importance to personal grievances, too and publish the letters they receive from suffering persons. Many deserving persons get human aid by such letters.

Another important advantage gained through these columns is that they serve the print media as well. The editor will be able to perceive the impact created in the minds of the public through these letters. New suggestions given to the editor by the letter-writers often will help him to improve the standard of the newspaper or magazine.

New suggestions put forward by the letter-writers carry weight. For example, the letters suggesting alternatives to Ganga-Cauvery link appeared recently in some papers and these suggestions are valuable to the authorities.

Having regard to the vital importance of these columns, papers should try to utilize their service to the full extent possible. The slogan "Freedom of the Press" is raised everywhere now-a-days. But it is doubtful whether the public at large is aware of the merits of a free press. So, if the advocates of the slogan want it to attain some meaning for the common man, they should try to voice his demands in a better way. It is here that we understand "The Letters to The Editor" and their importance.

Techniques to Reduce the Discrepancy Between the Communicator's and the Audience's Attitudes

1. Using media most closely identified with the audience's position.
2. Using a communications source that enjoys high credibility for the audience on this issue.
3. Playing down the differences between the communication and the audience's attitudes.
4. Seeking identification in vocabulary and anecdote with the audience in an area removed from the issue.
5. Establishing the communicator's position as being the majority opinion—defining the majority from the audience itself.
6. Bringing the audience's group identifications into play when these identifications will help the development of a positive response. The converse is also true.
7. Modifying the message to fit the organization's needs—since you can't modify organisational objectives.

Effective communication means tailor-made programming specially designed for the situation, time, place, and audience. It means careful selection of media and technique.

The ideal is to keep publicity in perspective as a part of the whole process but to remain primarily concerned with the absorption of messages—the reaction.

Acceptance Goes Through Five Stages

1. *Awareness.* The individual learns of the existence of the idea or practice but has little knowledge of it.
2. *Interest.* The individual develops interest in the idea. He seeks more information and considers its general merits.
3. *Evaluation.* The individual makes mental application of the idea and weighs its merits for his own situation. He obtains more information and decides to try it.
4. *Trial.* Individual actually applies the idea or practice usually on a small scale. He is interested in how to apply practice techniques, conditions for application.
5. *Adoption.* If the idea proves acceptable, it is adopted.

Stages in the Adoption Process

1. *Awareness* : Learns about a new idea or practices.
2. *Interest :* Gets more information about it.
3. *Evaluation* : Tries it out mentally.
4. *Trial :* Uses or tries a little.
5. *Adoption :* Accepts it for a full-scale and continued use.

Six Keys to Communication

Possibly because Rudyard Kipling recognized the importance of good communication in the years ahead, he gave the clue in his poem:

"I keep six honest serving men

(They taught me all I knew)

Their names are WHAT and WHY and WHEN

And HOW and WHERE and WHO."

We shall not go wrong if, every time we make a decision, become aware of some policy or take decision affecting others, we ask ourselves, "WHAT shall I say? WHY do others need to know?

WHEN shall I say it? HOW shall I go about it? WHERE shall I do the telling? WHO should be told?

Mutual Interest

What we communicate means both, "What do I need to say? and "What do they need to know?" They are not necessarily the same. The difference is that what others need to know may invite the minimum information, whereas what one need to say should normally call forth the maximum?

There are three particular reasons for this. The first is that, although there may on occasions be some risk to security, the respect that is thus shown to the intelligence and status of employees more than offsets the risk that the more that is said, the more there is to be garbled. If someone is determined to breach security he is likely to get the information anyhow. On the other hand, in most cases respect engenders respect.

The second is that the "grapevine" will convey in an amazing way more than we like to think. Moreover, the grapevine, even though it tends to be disconcertingly accurate, is nearly always uncharitable and therefore militates against the success of normal communication channels.

The third reason for generosity in communicating is that we build up capital. If the general rule is to tell as much as possible, then people will more willingly understand and accept those occasions when only the minimum can be said. Understanding is a two-way communication and, in nurturing it, we create the climate in which communication is made. For these three reasons, then, the tendency to be secretive is both unnecessary on many occasions and harmful.

'Why' of Communication : For the first time, we now have a generation that have never known the hierarchy of authority. For the most part they have not undertaken military service. The acceptance of authority at home, in school and in daily life is no longer natural and, indeed, there is evidence that it is being consciously undermined.

Thus the manager who once was able to demand blind obedience, must now say: "I want you to do this because ..." If management does not explain what is going on, the encouragement to ask "why" will still be there either to find out, or to make trouble. Vacuums tend to be filled. If those whose task it is to explain "why" do not do so, someone else will happily assume responsibility.

From a communications point of view business organizations tend to be anything but the optimum size, so it is necessary to bring groups nearer to the ideal. This may mean establishing new entities within the existing organizations, increasing the ratio of managers and watching carefully the formal lines of communication.

The flow of information can be slowed, particularly if it has to pass through pending tray of several managers. But the need for communicating becomes greater as the obstacles increase.

'When' of Communication : The decision to communicate must be accompanied by further decisions that relate to the timing of the message, and as many heartaches have been caused by failure in this direction as by any other mistakes in communication.

First comes the decision about how many people are to be told, and because they are likely to include people of differing seniority, attention must be given to the order in which they are told. A manager, for example, will need to know about something before his subordinates. Then the question arises of informing people outside the organization.

Once a decision to communicate has been made it must be executed quickly. It is naive to suppose that secrets can be kept. The trouble when information that leaks the wrong way is that the grapevine will carry it and, since the grapevine is the fastest means of communication, beating it at any time it difficult. The grapevine can also be dangerous because, apart from its generally uncharitable message, it hardens the attitude of those to whom the message has to be given. There is nothing so impenetrable as the mind that is already made up.

The employee's first awareness of news should be from his manager and not from outside the company. If the employee cannot be given the information first, then there should be simultaneous internal and external release. Managers should, where possible, inform supervisors and senior staff in advance so that they can speak with one voice. One point that is often overlooked concerns organizations with operations in more than one country. Not only must there be clear-cut embargoes on the publication of information before a certain date, but the actual time difference between, say, New Delhi and New York, must be taken into account when synchronizing a release.

Public and individual ability to retain information is notoriously short. Therefore, in putting over important information, it will generally be necessary to repeat the message several times, using different media. It is well known that information which is conveyed both visibly and orally is retained better than that which is conveyed by only one of these means. Face-to-face communication can be reinforced by notice-boards, house journals and other formal techniques.

"How" of Communication : Language is a problem. Conversation at the simplest level can be misunderstood. Words mean different things to different people and associations. People listen to what they believe is said, not to what is said.

Language, again, has been taken too much for granted, but we can now report important progress toward understanding this gift so useful and so dangerous. Many, if not most, of the political and social problems which plague us today are at bottom communication failures. Take for instance, the big words in the headlines: "aggression", "appeasement", "coexistence", "free enterprise", "liberty", "security", "bureaucracy", "welfare state". It is not difficult to prove, using the discipline of semantics, that such high abstractions mean different things to different people, and unless great caution is taken in using them, they become not only meaningless as coin for common understanding, but actively productive of misunderstanding.

Among current problems which are in good part due to communication failure are the true menace of communism, international relations, labour-management conflics, advertising misrepresentation. Much of the trouble between man and wife, parent and child, teacher and student, is due to communication breakdown. "Talking it out" might have repaired the line before a small grievance developed into a monstrous injustice. "Reasonable men always agree if they understand what they are talking about."

In business, it is not enough that a manager understands a situation if he fails to convey this understanding to others. Understanding cannot be assumed.

"Where" of Communication : To be meaningful, communication must take place in an atmosphere where perception is not clouded by fear, suspicion and grievance, and where a degree of trust has already been created. We all tend to hear what we want or expect things within the context of our own experience.

There is seldom a substitute for face-to-face communication if that is practicable but as this can be done only with small groups of people extra time will be required to convey a message to a large number of people. Face-to-face contact makes it possible to get reactions to the spoken words and to modify the approach in the light of the changing face of the audience. In this connection, it is as well to remember that the face and gestures of the communicator are equally important.

Written communications, on the other hand, have the advantage of speed, consistency and acting as a record. There is a place for both and the advantages of both must be weighed.

Apart from the wrong choice of language, a communication can fail because it has not been thoroughly prepared, the reception has not been checked and the message has, in consequence, been ambiguous and unsystematic.

The setting of the communication is important and is a major contributor to the atmosphere which will make that communication effective. The choice is as wide as the variety of the message. It will range from a public meeting of a department to a formal interview between two people or an informal meeting outside company premises. Much will depend upon how official the communication is to be.

When the message is a general one for a number of people and concerning, *e.g.*, an announcement of some new product or employee benefit, the conference room is the obvious choice. The atmosphere of "them and us" is easily fostered.

'Who' of Communication : In most cases it is a good idea to tell as many people as possible what is going on. Even the most junior employee will work more efficiently if he is "in the know': and made to feel a participation sense in the business of the company. This way the *feeling* in each individual that he knows what is going on, and can ask more if he wants, can be inculcated. This feeling is nourished even more by the manager taking time to talk and explain than by what he actually says.

It is also important to recognize that all employees will be far better ambassadors, both in letter and spirit, for the company in which they work if they, in turn, are able to communicate an understanding to the outside world. Said Tallyr and: "Give me good internal policies and I will give you a good foreign policy."

The first rule is that if the news is bad or likely to build resistance it is the job of the manager to face the employee. It is at such times that he will have to draw on the capital of goodwill and trust that he has been able to build up. The manager should never hide behind the words "they have decreed", or "it is company policy". A manager, once he has earned that position, is identified with "them". He is the upholder as well as the transmitter of company policy.

Perhaps these points are all part of the management "touch"—that instinct that the good manager has which makes him sensitive to the requirements of each situation. Yet, whatever instinct may be there, either circumstances or lack of conscious training seem frequently to lead to failure. When they do, how often can this failure be attributed to not heeding one of these six questions? Each manager can ask how often he has not been put in the picture because his manager has not told him what is going on. And then he can ask how often has be been responsible for the experience with others.

Role in Human Rights

1. Effective communication and sound human relations are interdependent on each other; it is not what we convey to the other person but what the other person understands.
2. Free flow of communication upwards and downwards and even sideways therefore becomes an important factor for establishing healthy attitudes.
3. We must reckon with and understand an individual's will to misunderstand, to misinterpret and to distort the content of formal communication.
4. All communications, especially in industry, generally fall into three categories:
   (i) Information
   (ii) Instruction, and
   (iii) Changing of attitudes or motivation.

Information : The matters that an employee wants to know about are neither many nor complicated. In simple terms, he wants to know about his own company, how well it is doing and what its further growth will help in his career.

Instruction : This aspect of communication relates to induction and training of the employee and later to the directions of the superiors. The quality of communication at the induction and training stage may actually affect the foundations of the employees' faith and confidence in the management.

Precise and clear instructions about work not only give self-confident to the employee that he can do the job with ease and accuracy, but also give him the vitally needed faith in his immediate superior, who represents the management to him.

Motivation : This is the most important aspect of the communication programme. It is to be remembered that merely because an employee earns his livelihood from a company, he is not obligated to love it. But he may love it for other reasons for which he loves other things like his family or friends among whom he is respected as an individual or his native place, where he is recognized and he belongs. Here it is not what he does for them that earns him the respect, recognition and sense of belonging, but his human qualities.

Projects in India

Communication is the life blood of Public Relations. Public Relations utilises various communication media for reaching its goals.

Communication is coming now to our country because it has been in use, in one form or another, since time immemorial.

In modern times, our country successfully utilised Mass Communication and Relevant Communication technologies. The future assures a far advanced and result-oriented commnication system, if we approach the matter in the right spirit.

Audio-visual, electronic technology, indigenous media, and research-supported oral and extension communication at the grassroot level will help us overcome the disadvantages like multilinguism, widespread illiteracy, diversity, etc.

Research : In order to gain maximum advantage from Mass Communication in the future, certain basic defects and deficiencies in the system must be removed. Efforts should be made to reorient the communication system to serve the rural areas and interests as against its present urban and elite orientation. To achieve this, intensive research should be undertaken in respect of media and their programmes and audience profiles.

Besides, some structural changes should also be brought about to promote a free and balanced flow of information in the country, to reevaluate news values to correspond more to the developmental priorities of the rural people, to eliminate all restraints on the media and to stimulate inbuilt feedback and evaluatory processes in the communication system. This effort can activise a multimedia based, pragmatic and solution-oriented system of balanced and free communication at the village or regional level. This would also be a participatory and decentralised system which would foster the tempo of an equitable development process in the future.

***Role of Different Media* :** The newspapers in the future will have to shoulder the responsibility of preparing their readers for social changes and become organs of participatory communication, without ceasing to be watchdogs of public interest and a balancing wheel in the administrative structure of the State.

T.V. programmes must follow in spirit the pattern of the Kheda experiment, where a decentralised local transmitter was able to produce relevant programmes dealing with local issues in the local dialect and the attempt at two-way communication was made successfully. TV should follow the model of participatory programme making and solution finding.

In places where TV may still not be available even with satellite, radio can operate as the principal medium of participatory interactive regional and local information service. Science should be popularised for the common man and wider teaching of self-operating and self-repairing skills and techniques should be conveyed through radio programmes.

In the same way, films can be harnessed for integrated rural development. Rural children's films, documentaries and even feature films can be specially prepared for specific rural themes and situations. The portrayal of rural social and economic problems car also be done through the celluloid medium.

***Bright Future* :** India has soared into high technology and is touching the edge of an information society. In the coming decades, commnication will become more research based, multimedia and multi-discipline oriented. Our communication history and experience, our capacity for experimentation and open-mindedness, the flexibility of media and technology, assures us a promising future in this field.

15

Use of Language

Many persons who are not specially talented or highly educated have learned to express themselves well in speaking and writing. By using language with skill they have made their way from the inglorious life of solitary organisms to the rich life of communion with their fellows. They have progressed from obscurity in business and social life to impressive attainment. Such satisfaction is within the reach of everyone.

Thousands of young men and women go into business or a profession every year with their hearts set upon self-fulfilling careers. They need to learn now, during their years of training, how greatly their chance for success depends upon their ability to use words accurately and effectively.

It does not matter how little related to the niceties of language your business or profession may be, command of language adds to your ability and extends your knowledge. Before expressing your thoughts in words you make up those thoughts in words. The more meaningful and exact you make the words in which you think, the better fitted you are to cope with the complexities of life.

An adequate power to express oneself is not a literary frill with which to decorate the edges of life. On the contrary, it is the indispensable tool of our self-understanding and self-acceptance and of our rational contact with the world around us.

Only a few business men believe that it does not matter how they speak or write. Successful people know that the person who does not use words precisely can never be sure that he has said precisely what he meant to say. He has no assurance that his reader will understand him. If there is one thing worse than being unable to express a thought it is thinking that one has said something when he has not.

Art of Writing

If you keep in mind the two principles, clarity and precision, and write simply and naturally, you may disregard the tyranny of small critics. You do not write effectively merely by obeying the rules of grammar and syntax, but before you break the rules you should know what they are. Skilled writers study words so that they use those are fitting, and they consider the most effective way of putting them together. They observe how words affect the thinking and acting of people.

The urge to "write as you speak" can lead to a trap. If one puts into letters or print too much racy speech the resulting prose will be either an money-maker or something to be laughed at ; if one writes as loosely as he talks, his letter or essay or report will command little respect.

In any sort of composition meant to communicate ideas, the writer must consider his purpose and the need of the reader. It is irrational to sit down with pen and paper to write something that will be worth the effort unless you know: (1) what you wish to say, and (2) to whom you wish to say it.

It may be taken for granted that the thoughts of a person receiving a letter will run something like this : What is this letter about ? How does it concern me ? is this statement true ? What does the writer want me to do ? Why should I do it ?

Creative writing

Creative writing is a bridge from the mind of the writer to that of his reader. Across this bridge the writer must Send information of interest to the reader and ideas which will stir him to thought or action.

The words sent across the bridge have meaning only when they are understood in depth and breadth by the person heading them. A word or a sentence is not merely a bundle of sounds : it is also a bundle of associations. Most of the time people cannot grasp our point unless they are able to connect it with their own experience.

People respond readily to some words while remaining indifferent to others. Try to use words and language that will affect your correspondent as you wish him to be affected. Take into account the perception range of your reader : are you sure that he will read out of your letter the thoughts that you mean to inspire in it ?

If your subject is difficult, if you must take your reader through swampy land, at least throw him a rope. Give him some help toward reaching solid ground. There are times when persuasiveness consists in saying things that leave the reader believing that is just the way he would have said them himself. But be tactful : do not remind him that he didn't.

Anyone writing for a wide audience must pay attention to possible peculiarities and dislikes. An enumerator making his rounds of households before a British general election said : "A number of people can be thrown by being asked what sex their children are. They would look affronted at the word 'sex.' By and by I learned to rephrase the question as 'have you got any little boys or little girls' ?

It is necessary for the correspondent seeking to sway people to his viewpoint to be prepared with facts, a fact meaning something known to be true. The writer should have a bgger array of facts than he is likely to need. It is disheartening to make a good start and thin run out of gas. It is humiliating to have a correspondent ask for facts which the writer should have known enough to supply without being asked.

A mind cluttered up with undigested facts, suppositions and theories is in no instate to dictate a letter. Plato followed this drill be announced his subject, presented it rapidly in numerous aspects, walking all around it in the process, and then spoke in such a way as to relate his ideas to the lives of the people around him.

One sign of deftness in written work is the ability to keep to the point of your topic. Something often happens when you are writing that changes the direction of what you are saying from due north to north or west. It is not always wise to know that it is there.

To ramble in words is to confuse the issue you are discussing. Brevity is not always the soul of wit. The real trouble is that speeches and letters are too irrelevant, too dull and too slovenly. They give the impression of using a shotgun shell loaded with many words in the hope that some may hit the target. These faults make the speech or letter appear long.

Business men are aware that the ability to get along with people, to advance in their job, and to sell their goods, depends on clear communication.

Once a letter leaves your "OUT" tray it is what is in the letter that counts, not what is in your head. Before signing a letter look for the needed virtues. Is it complete ? Is it courteous ? There is no situation in which you are so right in your contention that you can afford not to be urbane. Did you end it gracefully ? It is just as important to make a first rate exit as a dramatic entrance.

Your letter is more than a statement of facts. It is an expression of your personality, a symbol of your status.

The Matter of Style : If you express your thoughts in their proper order in words that are proper to the occasion, you will be writing in a clear style. Socrates, about to drink the hemlock, urged his friends to disregard the manner but think of the truth of his words. A maxim of Horace's said that good sense is the source and origin of good style.

Light and shade are as necessary in writing as they are in sculpture, but if you overdo either one you obscure the meaning you wish to convey. Do not feel that you have to shout every once in a while. Your reader will look at a rainbow without having his , attention drawn to it by a clap of thunder.

A writer of good taste—some people would call it "sensitivity"— will take pains perfecting his style to make the reader believe that he took none at all. When the style shows in a piece of writing one feels as if he were on the wrong side of the stage scenery, with all the props and ropes and pulleys nakedly seen. Someone described good writing style as being as casual seeming as the skimming or a dragonfly.

Style is closely linked with feeling. A fact or truth may be stated so as to touch the intellect alone, or it may be expressed in terms which, without dimming its clearness, may appeal to the reader's sensibility by their harmony or energy.

Make time for stargazing in between abouts of writing. It is a way to woo ideas and to surround them with bright images. It helps, if you wish your ideas to seem inspired, to make them sound as if they were inspired.

In conveying an idea we may show what it is by giving instances of it in operation or by making contrasts. If you make a general assertion that is of importance to your purpose in writing, follow it up with proof or illustrative examples.

The most effective device a writer can use is the parable, a metaphor which presents a story to illustrate a point. We do not wish to write in pictographs as our long ago forefathers did, but the closer a word or a sentence comes to picturing what it stands for, the, easier it is to comprehend.

Words are esteemed for more reasons than the meaning they convey. If you analyse your enjoyment of a verse of poetry or a passage of prose that gives you delight, you will find that only a part of your enjoyment comes from thought of the facts or events to which it draws your attention. Much comes from the beauty of the words and sentences considered as a pattern of sound.

Poetry uses synonyms for variety, metre and rhyme, therefore poetry is a first-class place to quarry words that will add a lilt as well as accuracy to a piece of prose.

Build a Vocabulary : We do not inherit words and the tales they tell. Many times as the story of Alauddin and his Wonderful Lamp has been told, it must be told again for every child as new generations come upon the stage.

When building a vocabulary fit to express all our thoughts, hopes and emotions, we need to remember that words are symbols, standing for things. If we did not have words we should be condemned to carrying around large bundles of things instead, like the professors in Gulliver's satire Laputa.

When you improve your vocabulary it will be larger and broader, but it will also have greater depth and precision, enabling you to use the word symbol which most closely calls up the thing symbolized it will enable you to express purposefully facts, ideas, feelings and experiences. A word fittingly chosen may be like an electric switch : something that turns on the light.

Out stock of words is enlarged through the experiences that are woven into our lives. Our writing is effective, vivid and interesting when we put this stuff of our lives into it.

Close and attentive observation of what is going around us is necessary if we are to write brightly. Everyone has seen a photographer of nature subjects at work : he puts his camera lens close to the flower, or as close as he can get it to a bird or a butterfly. The lens brings out beauties that the eye cannot see and projects them on a screen. So Shakespeare sprinkled his plays with similes and word pictures that presented themselves to his attentive observation. In Cymbeline we find "Like the crimson drops, the bottom of a cowslip". Shakespeare had to pay imaginative attention to see this imperial mixture of crimson and yellow in the cup of a primrose.

Next to personal observation comes reading as a source of words. Knowledge of words does not descend upon us magically at the end of any grade in school or at the end of a university course. It comes as a matter of being acquainted with many men and women of talent through their books.

Words have Width and Depth : He is a good workman in writing who uses the implements of his craft with care and skill. He chooses words as a skilled machinist chooses the tools that will do particular jobs in the finest way.

Words are picked up by the conscious mind and made into pictures in the subconscious. When you write you are writing a constant, the ratio of the circumference of a circle to its diameter ; when you write formula NaCl you are indicating the chemical substance, sodium chloride, and it always means that substance and nothing else. Few words in common use have such limited denotations as these. Consider 'mother' and 'father'. They are extended into multiple new areas of use such as mother of parliaments, mother earth, mother wit ; the child is father of the man, father to that thought.

The interpretation we give words is bound up with the images; they evoke. "Informer" and "informant" may be said to mean, roughly, the same thing, but note the difference that may be read into them. "Informer" makes us think of stool-pigeons and talebearers ; "informant" has no such nasty frill attached to it.

Nearly every writer is tempted at times to embellish his work by using qualifying words; others are dead set against the use of words that modify words. Without doubt, adjectives and adverbs can weaken a statement or blur the meaning.

You cannot measure a writer's genius by the length of his words. Some enjoy the use of big words without paying attention to their meaning : others use gigantic words on a microscopic topic, like pinning a white beard on the face of a child, and yet others think that their dignity demands that they use many-syllable words. When Dr. Johnson was asked about a comedy, he said : "It has not wit enough to keep it sweet." Then, realizing that this sentence was not up to the standard of his sonorous prose, he hastened to give a more fulltoned sentence : "It has not vitality enough to preserve it from putrefaction."

If your desire to use big words is as overpowering as Johson's, recall what Shakespeare did to get rid of his stock of resounding nonsense : he invented Pistol, associate of Falstaff, to make meaningless speeches in magnificent verse.

Revise your Language : Everyone should revise his language habits from time to time in order to keep pace with life and custom. Language is an expression of human activity, and because human activity is constantly changing language changes with it.

There are accepted good standards of every language, and the fact that a language is changing is not a good reason for abandoning the standards. In all change there must be an element of continuity ; if that element of continuity is absent you have not change, but the destruction of one thing and the creation of another.

One trend today is toward the use of ugly words. We can do quite well in expressing ourselves intelligently without the mean and unlovely words which some writers introduce in the name of liberty, frankness, and progressiveness. A good writer put it this way : "I try to watch the words I say, and keep them tender and sweet, for I never know from day to day which ones I'll have to eat."

The whole oiliness of language is menaced not so much by the crude vulgarism of the untaught who are indefatigable in their search for gross, squalid and violent words, but by the blithe irresponsibility of the taught.

Discipline as well as purposefulness plays a part in effective communication. Do not give in to the "any word do" mentality, or scatter words as if you were shaking a floor mop. Use honest words, the sharpest you can find, to say what you mean. Choice of words by a writer deserves as great care as does the selection of a fly by the same man when he goes fishing or of a club when he is on the golf course.

Read it Over : Ask yourself "How does my writing read ?" Quite often one dock not fully know what he has written until he reads it.

Look over the letter or speech and ask whether this or that word is as serviceable in its context as some other word might be. Experienced writers make many changes at this point.

Check whether the language you used is suitable to the occasion, the subject and the person to whom you addressed it.

Have you made it clear that you are interested in what you write ? A piece of writing is strong if it conveys the assurance that the writer cared about what he wrote. It is doubly blessed if it gives the reader the feeling of believing that the writer understood him and his problems.

Boiled down to its essential, language is serviceable when it conveys things useful to be known. When a person has great thoughts and cannot express them, it is like high voltage passing through a small wire, and the only relief is to blow a fuse.

A person may be neither an eloquent speaker nor a great writer, but practice and a faithful system of reading and observation will change him into a convincing speaker and a readable writer.

He must practise as consistently as a musician. If everyone waited until he was perfect in the subject, no books would ever be written.

Instruction : The management under public and private sectors and other institutions and organizations attach more importance to the reports of public relations executive. The features that distinguish their reports from other writings are :

1. Technical nature of the subject as exemplified by emphasis on physical sciences and business practices even in dealing with related social sciences and human relations.

2. Strict adherence to the outline form of presentation developed by direct approach achieved by writing that is complete, correct, concise, clear and convincing.
3. Formal use of the third person style. Certain special considerations may warrant the use of the more familiar first and second person.
4. Emphasis upon the quantitative approach even though qualitative statements are frequently employed.
5. Established dependence upon accuracy, definiteness and reasoned analysis, interpretation and conclusion.
6. Use of medium other than words for the conveyance of thought; normally, statistical methods, tabular arrangements diagrammatic and photographic illustrations and mathematical treatment of scientific or technical or allied matter.
7. Inclusion of the original source material upon which the solution, conclusions, and recommendations are based.
8. Direct personal relationship between reader and writer through the letter of transmitted and other supporting correspondence.
9. Use of calm and judicial tone with distinctive individuality.
10. Overall criterion that the report presents the facts desired, the answer to a question, the solution of a problem, the record of prevailing conditions or other specific objectives as needed by the management or client.

Impact of Writing

The product of the mind is thought. The raw material of thought is the succession of impressions made on the mind. Impressions are carried to the mind through the senses, of which hearing and seeing are the most useful in communicating ideas. The mind gathers, classifies, stores, and recombines these impressions. Upon receiving an outside stimulus, the mind gives evidence of thought through speech and action.

One system by which the character of man's thought may be classified is based on these skills: MANIPULATION—KNOWLEDGE— REASONING JUDGEMENT CREATIVENESS.

Report writing as an art of communication may be divided into eight steps :

1. Gaining and understanding of the objectives and purposes of the report, of the existing situation, and of the qualifications of the readers of the report.
2. Gathering and organizing the essential facts and information.
3. Analysing the assembled data to the extent that proper solutions, convictions, applications, conclusions and recommendations may be reached through reasoning and logic.
4. Outlining the report preparatory to writing.
5. Writing the rough report.
6. Checking, revising and rearranging and rewriting the early drafts.
7. Final review for arrangement, style and mechanics.
8. Typing in final form, proof-reading, assembling and binding.

Detailed Outline for Body of Short Report

Object : State the purpose of the work covered by the report and the situation or events that make the study desirable.

Nature of Work : Indicate how the work was accomplished—whether the development of a theory, by research and investigation of one or more phenomena, by tests, by compiling data and drawing comparisons or by making a survey.

Definitions : Define as concisely as possible such facts as the limitations of the report, the scope of investigation, and any special words or terms are used.

Related Facts : Cite earlier work used as basis or as supporting material.

Method Used : Describe the method chosen to develop the facts and to arrive at a solution of any phase of the problem in hand.

Discuss various methods that were considered and indicate why the method used was given preference.

Types of Report

Dull Report : Bulkiness, poor quality of contents, unattractive presentation, drab or high sounding language, abundance of technical jargon, inclusion of incomprehensible charts, emphasis on highly sophisticated theories, lack of practical approach and untimely submission—even one of these is capable of deciding the unfortunate fate of a report.

Good Report : List down the major topics you wish to discuss in your report and insert, if necessary, subtopics or subheadings suitably below each. Decide the sequence of the topics according to their importance and inter-relevance to maintain a proper flow of thought.

***Size of Report* :** Give a careful thought to the size of the report. Remember a reader has little patience. His time is precious. Your report should, therefore, be brief. Nevertheless, it should include all you want to say. Skill lies in being able to convey the maximum amount of sense using the minimum number of words.

If you anticipate that your report would be bulky, make and submit it in parts, if possible. A reader prefers to handle a small, light report.

Preparation of Report

Most of us find ourselves at some time up against the job of writing a report. It may be a business report or the report of a meeting ; it may be out report as secretary of an organization, or an analysis of a situation in a factory!

Writing a report need not be the ordeal so many of us fear it to be, and sometimes find it. Like so many other things, it is not particularly difficult if we break it down into small jobs. The purpose of this Monthly Letter is to show, step by step, how to write a report. All the suggestions will not be appropriate to every report, but the principles will be generally useful.

We should try to make reports constructive. Instead of threshing old straw, or moving in a pedestrian way through an account of some convention or meeting, it is much more interesting to offer vigorous and thought provoking interpretations and ideas of our own. To prepare a good report we need to cultivate dependability, resourcefulness and patience, and do some hard work.

There are, broadly, two kinds of business reports : the information report and the research report.

The information report is to keep an executive up-to-date with events, developments and projects. The research report is the outcome of your investigation of phenomena. This may be in any branch of human activity, from politics to labour relations, from some crank's idea about taking electricity out or the air to a plan for extending customer use of the power already developed.

Any report upon which actions may be based, or which may influence executives in this or that direction, is an important piece of work, and deserves our earnest attention. There is no more engrossing job than that of exploring in search of material for such a report.

Your work starts long before you make a motion toward your pen. You must be properly briefed, and that is a joint responsibility of you and your boss. You must know exactly what is wanted and why it is wanted. Requests for reports should refer to definite and limited problems.

This simple working outline will be of help : (1) comprehend what you are required to report on ; (2) ascertain all possible sources of information ; (3) decide upon what sources to draw ;

(4) gather information and explanations ; (5) sift the evidence ; (6) synthesize the acceptable evidence ; (7) abstract what is to the point and discard the rest; (8) throw what is left into report form ; (9) summarize your findings.

There are at least four limitations upon research for a report; time, staff, money and data. It is important that the report writer should do his best within these limitations, and his report should note any short coming because of them. If the report is taken from the files years hence, it should provide evidence of the difficulties the research man encountered, so as to give a realistic starting point for following up or modernizing the report.

Economy of Efforts

Economy of effort will be possible to the report writer if he keeps a clearly defined purpose in mind, and refuses to allow himself to be drawn away by other things, however attractive they may be.

The Objective : In planning the report, serious thought should be given to the need and temperament of the person for whom it is being prepared. Some persons want great detail, others will be content with deductions ; some will want tables and graphs, while others will run a mile from a statistic. "What," the report writer should ask himself, "is to be done what data by whom." The kind of report we are considering now—one that given information on the basis of which an executive may take action—is a sort of diagnosis. It tells what is right and what is wrong, and gives an interpretation which serves as the executive's guide to the remedy, should one be needed.

There are two occasions when recommendations by the report writer are in order : when they are requested, and when the writer believes that because of his knowledge, experience, and other qualities, his voice is worth listening to.

All recommendations are touched with the personality of the writer of the report. The wise man will make a distinction between his conclusions, based upon the facts he has uncovered, and his suggestions, based upon these conclusions. The former are actualities, the latter are tinged with the colour of his opinions.

Form of the Report : Writing a report will be much easier if you work out a form, or skeleton.

A good plan for the inexperienced report writer is to start with a statement in one sentence, setting forth the objective of the study which is being reported upon. This will focus attention upon the primary purpose. Then follow with main and subheadings, growing out of the sentence and leading toward the conclusion.

It is surprising how greatly this plan helps to eliminate vagueness, fill in gaps in information and reasoning, and keep the writer on the track of competent thinking.

Although it does not hold true in every case, the success of many reports may be attributed to a well-written introduction or synopsis. If attention of the reader is seized at this point, he is likely to proceed into the body of the report with an expectant mind. Even when one is sure the report will be read, as when the topic is one of particular interest to an executive, it still is good practice to provide a summary telling what the report is about and what point it makes. It should be sharp in its diction, sparing of words, and careful to promise no more than is in the report.

When you come to your preliminary outline, it should be drafted so as to give you a fairly clear idea of the road ahead, enable you to judge what you should stress, and provide you with a test of the adequacy of your research.

It is not necessary, in this short mention of the form of the report, to go in detail about the appendix, the table of contents, the index, and such like. These are features which are required only in exhaustive and lengthy reports, and they fall into place quite naturally when their use is indicated.

Not much need be said about the various kinds of analytic reports except just to name them. The case study, while incomplete in itself because no conclusions can be drawn from one case, is useful as part of a larger project. It can be enlightening, and because of the narrowness of its field it can be thorough. The genetic study traces the development of project. It can be enlightening, and because of the narrowness of its field it can be thorough. The genetic study traces the development of its subject, stressing the causal sequence of events. The comparative method involves bringing together significant facts. Its chief impediment seems to lie in the danger of bias attending selection of the facts to be compared, and the perplexity of discriminating wisely.

Much of abiding value may be learned by report writers and research men who study military "appreciations." These follow logical sequence :

I. The object to be attained

II. Factors which affect attainment of the object

III. Courses open to

A—our own side

B—the enemy

The factors relevant to a military situation do not apply in industrial or social life, but the thorough analysis of the problem demanded by the military people is suggestive for all who write reports.

Information Sources

Collecting information is the foundation of all good reporting. Thomas Edison gave this advice : "The first thing is to find out everything everybody else knows, and then begin where they left off."

While every problem will have its peculiar requirements, certain sources of data are common to nearly all observation, experimentation, books, questionnaires, interviews, workshop and accounting records. The successful writer will be resourceful in his research activities, thinking of new approaches and seeking data overlooked hitherto.

Data may be primary or secondary. Just as in law the evidence of an eyewitness is more valuable than that of a person who testifies at second hand, so in business and other reports the fruits of observation and experimentation rate high marks. He is a wise report writer who applies, whenever possible, observation and experimentation to check the findings of others ; he is likely to remain unremarkable for his work if he merely echoes the opinions of others, believes things because others believe them, and uses only books and papers with which he is in complete accord.

Secondary sources depend for their value upon their accuracy, their acuteness of valuation, the validity of their reasoning, and the applicability of their conclusions to the came being studied.

No statement is more reliable than its source. The report writer must spend long hours in gathering facts, arranging them, interpreting them and then as much time again in checking the accuracy and worth whileness of what he has in his hand. It is useless to quote a writer unless he is known to be competent in his field. It is dangerous to give the opinion of a man unless he is recognized as being unbiased, up-to-date and in all respects reliable.

Writing the Report : The report writer needs to analyse, and group, and marshal his facts into order. He must classify and conquer the elements of the chaos around him before he can hope to appeal with any force to the intelligence of other people. In this process of viewing the whole situation and at the same time seeing its components, the writer will detect incongruities to avoid and discern a path to follow.

These are skills which come only, so far as we know, with practice, but there are some hints about the process of writing which apply in all circumstances. The report must be practical. We have loose way of thinking of a realist as one who not only sees things as they are materially, but acquiesces in them : let us rather, as report writers, consider ourselves as being realists in the sense that we understand things as we have found them, not as we would find it convenient to believe them.

The report must be complete. We must have walked all around the matter about which we are reporting, seeing the good and the bad, the perfect and the imperfect, the desirable and the undersirable. We must have provided adequate proof for our favourable findings. Do not be content with one opinion : it may be the wrong one. As Cicero once pointed out, nothing is so absurd that someone has not called it profound ; nothing so profound that someone has not called it absurd.

The report must be concise. It may be as long as a roller towel, or as short as a message on a postcard : length is not the criterion.

Conciseness does not consist in using few words, but in covering the subject in the fewest possible words that will express what is in the writer's mind.

The report must be clear. Only the careful organization of facts and interpretation will enable the reader to follow what is to the writer a clear-cut line of reasoning. The art of good prose resides not so much in the swing and balance of the language as in the marshalling of argument, the orderly procession of ideas, the disposition of parts so that each finds its proper place. The writer misses his target if the idea in his mind is not received with understanding. As Alice said after reading labber wocky : "Somehow it seems to fill my head with ideas—only I don't exactly know what they are."

Use of trite expressions shows that the writer is in a rut. If he has no imagination in his language? is it likely, the executive will ask, that he exercised any imagination in his analysis of this problem ? There is no place in good writing for proverbs, saws, and tinkling aphorisms.

Foggy language detracts from the force of writing, and use of words loosely may well vitiate all usefulness that might have been incorporated in a report. We say nothing against trade, occupational or professional jargon so long as the report is solely for people who are on speaking terms with it. That sort of talk is not infrequently the only kind in which a writer can convey the true meaning of his thought to a particular audience. But jargon has no place in reports which may be read by the uninitiated.

The report must be intellectually honest. The facts must be scrupulously weighed and properly evaluated, and the writer must sincerely attempt to present something that has a judicial quality. He will draw a distinct line between what he has found to be factual, what is his opinion, and what he sets up as a hypothesis.

The report must be readable. We cannot afford to assume that our report will be read because the boss is interested in the subject. We should try to add to the clarity of our presentation something that will lift it above the ordinary.

There may be an whatever disposition toward decorum, leading us to think that research requires a depersonalised manner of writing. The truth is that nothing written is useful unless it is attractive enough to be read. We are entitled to be as brilliant and interesting as we can be, so long as we observe the requirements of correctness, relevance and the objective.

Having written it, the writer would be well advised to forget about his report for as long as time permits. If he tries to make corrections and improvements as soon as he has finished the writing his memory of what he meant to write may be so strong that he will overlook the shortcoming of what he actually wrote.

Here are some questions to ask at the time of revision : is my report fair, broad-minded and dignified ? Have I used enough imagination in presenting the facts ? Have I answered all the pertinent questions likely to arise in the reader's mind ? Does my report read as if a human being wrote it ?

It is well to read the report aloud : if it is easy to read you may bank upon its being easy to understand. If you hesitate over a word, a phrase or a sentence, take a second look.

The writer who achieves distinction of expression, conciseness, directness—and, if the nature of his work permits it, dramatic quality, beauty of rhythm, and some adventurousness of phrase and idea—has not done something miraculous. He has worked hard and intelligently.

16

The Correlationship

Corporate Relations

1. The core of corporate public relations is that humankind has now moved into "We" generation from "Me" generation: Which means that in the past man has pursued a philosophy of "Every man for himself and the devil care the hindmost".
2. In the whole of the Vedas and Upanishads we have no prayer for "I" but the whole community. They, in effect, said "When I, a man, see a fellow man in rags, in filth, starving in slums, unless I raise him, I have not raised myself'.
3. What does India's prayer, "Gayathri" say : "Lead us and enlighten. God, who inspired us by His intelligence—US, not me or thee. That is the social and civic sense. There you get the conception of Community Service which tells us that unless we strive to elevate all, the elevation of a few is the country's degradation and decay. Our "Gayathri" reads like the stirring lines of the English poet who prayed, "make no more grants, god, but elevate the

race at once". Poverty anywhere is a threat to prosperity everywhere.

4. Again, the Bhagavad Gita Chapter Three (2.13) says "Those sinners who cook (and eat) only for themselves verily eat only sin".

5. John Ruskin in his book "Time and Tide"—December 14, 1867— pleads:

   (a) "The profits which are at present taken as his own right by the person whose capital or energy or ingenuity has made him the master of the establishment should be divided in some proportion among the subordinates. The system of management of an establishment shall be such as to increase the facilities of advancement among the subordinates, to stimulate their ambition, to enable them to lay by, if they are provident, more ample and more early provision for declining years and to form in the end a vast class of persons wholly different from the existing operative: members of society possessing each a moderate competence; able to procure therefore not indeed many of the luxuries but all the basic comforts of life; and to devote some leisure to the attainment of liberal education and to the other objects of free iife.

   (b) "It is the merest insolence of selfishness to preach contentment to a worker who gets thirty shillings a week while his plotting and covetous master gets three thousand a year. In this, as in other points of mental discipline, it is the duty of the upper classes to set an example to the lower.

   (c) "By this I do not mean that all bank workers, for example, should become masters, soon, but they should consider themselves members of a national body, answerable as a society for all deposits, and that the private business of speculation with other people's

money should take another name than that of banking".

(*d*) "An arrangement may be supposed by which every subordinate shall be paid sufficient wages according to his rank by which due provision shall be made out of the profits of the business for the sick and superannuated workers, and by which the master, being held responsible as a minor king or governor for the conduct as well as the comfort of all those under his rule shall, on condition, be permitted to retain to his own use the surplus profits of the business which by the fact of his being its master may be assumed to prove that he has organized by superior intellect and energy".

Legend

1. Public Relations is a management tool by which the management strives to earn the trusts of its publics—not just their business. The task may seem to be simple as gaining their goodwill. However, a true corporate citizen does not forget that trust is earned by doing it not only right but also inspiringly every single time to every, kind of public ; and he does not also forget that goodwill goes where it is well received and stays where it is well treated.
2. When a business corporation says it "stands" behind its publics, the corporate public relations manager's duty it is to see how many of these public keeps on "standing":

Elements

The discipline of Corporate Public Relations practice can be summed up as follows:

FIRST, foundation of business is credit

SECOND, foundation of credit is confidence

THIRD, foundation of confidence is character

FOURTH, foundation of character is reputation

FINALLY, foundation of reputation is laid by PUBIC RELATIONS."

Social Relations

Meeting social costs makes for Business Statesmanship.

It is the shareholders who own the business corporation; they, the owners, elect the Board of Directors; the Board names its managers; thus the managers have the rights associated with property by 'Natural Law", the professional obligation of managers to protect and serve the public interest is not a fortuitous by-product, but an integral part of their managerial function.

The great majority of business and industrial enterprises in the private sector have not in the past considered as part of their aims any function other than those directly involved in the manufacture and sale of their products, and services. Even today, many of them seem to believe that if they make a good product, sell it at a fair price; pay their taxes and decent wages; they will have discharged their obligations to the community.

The technical resources and managerial talents of industry in both public and private sectors have a function in society and obligations to the community much wider than the discharge of their primary business functions.

One of the sad attitudes of modern times, notably in our country, is the abdication of social responsibility by the business community, barring a few pleasant exceptions, which has tacitly accepted that it is also the function of the Government to look after the social welfare of all the people. Within the limited resources at the disposal of business, we cannot expect to tackle all the social problems confronting the community at large. Nevertheless 'business' can try and make an arbitrary allocation of even limited resources for social purpose activities. It is the responsibility that a 'business' or any similar or other organization owes to society, which nurtures it and enables it to function and operate.

The strong view of the Traditionalists notwithstanding, the need for a new approach is fast gaining acceptance, even inevitably, in our times. The reality of our times is that demands are being made on companies, demands that business obligations be expanded to include a whole range of social obligations. And pressure groups have today established their power to force companies, organizations, and even the government, to fall in line.

Thus it follows that to ensure its contribution to society as a Corporate Citizen, to cope with pressures mounted increasingly by pressure groups, to harmonize company's economic goals with the nation's aspirations, there is obviously need for a distinct, top-level managerial function.

Philosophy of Management

Quality of Work Life (QWL) is a philosophy of management that accepts the legitimacy of existing good 'Unions', that believes cooperative relationships (with those Unions) are worth encouraging, and believes that every employee has the ability and the right to offer intelligent and useful inputs into decisions at various levels of the organization. Quality of Working Life is a *Process* to involve employees at every level of the organization in decisions about their work and workplaces. QWL also refers to the intended *outcomes* of practising this philosophy and process, with improvements in working conditions, environment, and practices, and in the general climate or culture of the workplace. This same process also brings organizational benefit of cost reduction and quality improvement and personal development benefits which are also integral parts of the QWL concern.

The Goals of QWL

(1) To help businesses, State and Local Governments, and other organizations to increase their effectiveness in providing lower cost and higher quality goods and services.

(2) To help increase personnel management efficiency, develop joint problem-solving, and improve the quality of working life.

(3) By these means to help existing business to stay, prosper, and expand and new business to be attracted here, leading to more .and better job opportunities, higher incomes and increases in State revenues.

Justice in Society

"BHUNJATE to tvagham papa ye pacantyetma-karnat."

=Those sinners who cook (and eat) only for themselves, verily eat only sin.

The Bhagaved Gita : Chapter Three (2.13).

To amplify the concept of Quality of Working Life, it is perhaps appropriate to quote the observations of the Supreme Court of India : vide (SCALE 1982 (2) 114):

> "...In fact, the owners of capital bear only limited financial risk and otherwise contribute nothing to production while labour contributes a major, share of the product. While the former invest only a part of their moneys, the latter invest their sweat and toil, in fact their life itself. The workers therefore have a special place in a socialist pattern of society. They are not mere vendors of toil; they are not a marketable commodity to be purchased by the owners of capital—nay very much more. They supply labour without which capital would be importent and they are, at the least, equal partners with capital in the enterprise."
> "...Unlike the shareholders, to most of whom the shares they hold represent mere investments and to some of whom, the means of control over the affairs of the company, to the workers, the life of the company is their own and its welfare is theirs. They are so intimately tied up that their interest in the survival and well-being of the company is much more than the interest of any shareholder—be he an investor, a 'Corporate Commander' or acorporate manipulator..."

> "...this capitalist instrument should observe "socialist" purpose of our Constitution. No doubt it is the creative genius of the bourgeoisie that invented the corporations and the companies, invested them with a corporate soul and a juristic personality and called them legal entities in order to meet the growing and complex demands of modern industry and management, to conduct business and commercial activities more conveniently and efficiently and, essentially to foster, consolidate and stabilise the capitalist system of society under whose aegis alone the exploiting class could thrive and continue to exploit the working class ... (However) the movement is now towards socialism. Workers want the control and direction of their lives in their own hands and not in the hands of industrialists, bankers and brokers. Our Constitution has accepted the workers' entitlement to control and it is one of the Directive Principles of State Policy..."

This classical 'Judgement' speaks for itself as to the legal and moral responsibilities 'corporations' of all kinds owe to their employees so as to bring about 'social justice' relative to 'man management'.

How Business Functioned in the Past closures. Until some three decades or so ago departments in industry seemed to operate within watertight compart meats. Production department made what it thought best; the sales tribe jollied up the customers in order to sell what 'production' was making ; the publicity manager produced advertisements, very often without reference to the sales manager and sent off press releases about new products or services which excited him.

And what of the board of directors ? The 'board' also was insulated from reality. As long as they' could pass a satisfactory dividend once or twice a year, all was well. They generally did not know what went on behind the factory gates. The accountants who supplied the balance sheets, which were, perhaps, the only record in which the board was interested, also lived apart from the daily round of producing and selling. Sometimes the board was unaware of whether the corporation made a profit or a loss during the year until the balance sheet was produced many months into the new year.

That such a world did exist seems almost incredible, now. However, the situation now prevailing is very much better. Corporations in private and public sectors, government departments, universities, non-profit organizations and others are actively engaged in examining the need to establish a favourable 'image'.

It may not be incorrect to aver that such a happy state of affairs could be brought about by Sanchar Committee. Its report has induced our Parliament to-take-deep interest in the wider disclosure of financial and business *information* by commerce, industry and others.

Development and Growth

"The Trusteeship Concept held by our businessmen, today, should have the fine flavour of baronialism generously tinctured with *noblesse oblige'*.

The concept of corporate relations has evolved over the last two hundred years. The Industrial Revolution around 1750 A.D. marks the beginning of the end of the feudal economy. The elaborate structure of responsibilities built over the several thousand years of feudal economy started crumbling. The resultant changes can be summarised as under.

Means of Producation : In the feudal economy, land for the farmers and handicraft tools for artisans were essentially the means of production. And the tools were generally owned by the 'masters'. The production was carried out as a matter of contract between the tenant and the landlord (master) or between the artisan and the trader and direct 'employment' was minimal restricted to the employees of the landlords or the State. Such employees had feudal ties with their employees who were responsible for them from 'cradle to grave'. Samples of such 'tradition' are still available—"Bonded Labour".

In the industrial economy, there came into being a large class of 'employees' who were hired only for their working hours and the industrial employer was not responsible to look after them once they were "off the job". The owners of the new means of production, viz., factories, thus accepted very limited responsibility for their employees. Manufacturers of Safety Matches being run as "Cottage Industry" and also 'Biris', blue metal crushing, to name a few, may be cited as examples.

Consumers and Suppliers : In the feudal economy, most of the goods and services consumed were produced 'locally' and often exchanged on barter basis. Thus, consumer and supplier relationships were interchangeable and mutually responsible.

In the industrial economy, the consumers were far removed from the producing factories. Similarly, the suppliers to the factories rarely consumed production of the factories to any appreciable extent. Thus, the responsibility of the producer to his suppliers or consumers could not be directly looked after.

The Community : In the feudal economy, the community was an integral part of the feudal structure and the feudal landlord was generally the overlord of "his" community, and was considered responsible for their welfare. He often was given the statutory authority to "govern" the community.

In the industrial economy, the industrial unit had no *locus standi* with respect to the community, and did not consider itself directly concerned with its welfare.

The State : In the feudal economy, the state was a distant entity for most people—essentially responsible for law, order and national security, its activities touched upon the activities of the common man only occasionally.

The Investor : The industrial economy brought forth this new class as controlling agent of the industrial units. For many years, industrial units considered themselves responsible only for the welfare of their investors.

Thus when corporations came into being as operators of the industrial economy, the only corporate responsibility recognized was that towards their investors. This was the situation in the first hundred years after Industrial Revolution.

New Trends

The turn of this century witnessed remarkable change in the concept of corporate responsibility. The change started with the responsibility for employees. Partly this was due to the paternalistic attitude which was steadily developing among managements to "take care" of their employees in the feudal fashion. However, largely this was due to changes in the socio-political arena where protective measures for employees became the platform of all "progressive" parties. The statutory changes over the last 100 years acknowledged the role of employees as shareholders in the corporation—almost on par with the investors.

Similarly, laws were passed to protect the consumers and this also became a corporate responsibility, particularly for items of present risk like medicines, baby food. The consumer movement has widened this responsibiiity to include many consumer durables.

The advent of pollution also created another area of corporate responsibility, *viz.*, the 'community'. The community also figures incorporate responsibility when some corporations took over the community development as a part of social service.

During these 100 years, many States assumed responsibilities for industrial development. Consequently, the corporations had increased responsibility towards the government since industrial development at the micro level had to fit in the planning at the macro level.

Thus, at the end of the second 100 years, we see that corporations find themselves responsible for the following :

(i) Investors (iv) Suppliers

(ii) Employees (v) Community

(iii) Consumers (vi) Government

Corporate Performance

Corporate performance is the perceptible and measurable performance with respect to the stockholders. For example, in the case of investors, it would be in the form of dividends and also corporate growth. In the case of employees, it would be in the form of wages, working conditions and related perquisites. In the case of consumers, it would be in the form of quality goods and services at reasonable prices supported by after sales service. For the suppliers, it would be in the form of objective and steady purchasing policy with invariably regular payments. In the case of community, it would be in the form of minimizing the pollution and maximizing the job opportunities. In the case of government, it would be in the form of paying taxes promptly, and carrying out industrial activities in harmony with the National Plan.

However, these performances cannot be considered adequate to sustain the image of the corporation. In fact, the corporations all over the world regularly get attached for failing in their social responsibilities. Technically speaking, any commercial organization which accounts for surplus and pays its taxes fulflls its social responsibility since various social activities ranging from government administration to defence, hospitals and educational institutions depend on the revenues collected from agricultural and industrial surplus.

Social responsibility is basically a slogan originally coined by politicians to create a sort of guilt complex among industries and commerce. And politicians cannot be underrated at any time especially in a country like India!

However, in any situation where human beings come together, politics is inevitable since they will continually seek to establish their influence. Projecting public image is a task which essentially requires political ability, *i.e.,* the ability "to win friends and influence people!"

It is not only the high quality that satisfies the consumer. Often his ideas are subjective. Till a few years ago, many items of bath soap and some allied items were produced in the same plant but marketed by different organizations. The customers were ready to pay a higher price for the leading brands and felt they were getting the best!

Thus it would seem that it is not only a high wage level that satisfies the employees. In fact, the unit paying the biggest wages is likely to have maximum trouble from labour. The employees feel that they have no alternative but to stick to the organization and cannot vote against it by resigning and finding another job, with the same or better emoluments. Consequently, the employees with grievances stay on to spread their discontent.

The pressure on corporate managers to keep abreast of politics is not their making. It reflects the way in which industry and commerce have been politicised with the result that no question can be discussed, let alone decided, without regard to the political context. However, sight should not be lost of the fact that all those who take some kind of political roads with respect to corporate performance cum-political performance are likely to suffer from the Utopian delusion—that omelettes can be made without breaking eggs; that causes have only the intended effects, and that economics has no unbreakable law. Bad money drives out good, and bad industry has exactly the same effect.

Markets can be rigged or interfered with in many ways; but in the end all economic life depends on the market, on the exchange of resources for other resources. The 'market economist' merely points to the delusion of those who think that the exchange can never take place at less than full cost—somebody always pays;

and that somebody is usually the masses, working people and their families.

Personal wealth is the price paid by society in exchange for services rendered. If perfect equality were achieved, the result would be the same as if all prices for all goods and services were identical. Many people and products would disappear from the economy and the market.

Thus it will be apparent that in each case discussed it is not merely the corporate performance that generates the greatest reputation. Unless the corporate performance is coated, lightly, with political performance to project the image and influence the stockholders, it is not easy for the organisation to gain reputation.

In the past, quite a few managements have neglected this political performance task—which is essentially a top management task. It is possible to improve technical performance by strengthening the junior and middle management levels, but it is only the top management that can deliver the goods in terms of political task.

What can happen if the political performance is inadequate, can be seen from the current plight of multinational corporations. In terms of technical performance the industries have a good record Many of the consumer items produced in the world are available in India at prices which are of-ten-times lower than those in the world market. And yet, the industries' public image is not as it has been or has to be, because the top management unwittingly neglected the "political task".

The doctrine of social responsibility espoused by Government should not be a mere overt propaganda device by which it can hope to maintain power by covert relations with 'business'.

Establishing the Department

There can be no rigid type of PR department; indeed, flexibility should be one of its chief characteristics. It needs to be ready to tackle any and every PR requirement and able to adapt itself to changing situations without much loss of momentum. There is nothing static about PR—it is essentially a dynamic function both in the character of the work it does and in its attitude of mind towards that work. However, the character of this work differs from company to company. In some firms the emphasis is on employee relationship, whilst in others employee communications are divorced from PR and are the responsibility of the labour and personnel departments. It is, however, becoming increasingly evident in a large number of industrial companies that PR is being recruited as an aid to marketing, making possible improved communications with customers, suppliers, stockholders and the creation of a favourable public image that is able to influence the attitudes of specific groups of people towards the company.

There are some companies that look up PR mainly as a means of contacting the Press with the object of interpreting policy and communicating information about products and new developments ; this is the narrow view.

Whilst some degree of specialisation is inevitable, the proper function of PR in an industrial concern is to help improve communications with all its contacts, including labour, customers, suppliers, stockholders, the press, community neighbours and the public, and to provide management with advice and assistance on all matters which have a PR aspect.

The organization or structure of a company PR department depends on the character as well as the volume of work and the policy of the Board towards PR, *i.e.,* whether the directors regard its functions as crucial to the well-being of the firm and encourage its management to give PR opportunities to improve and extend communications, or whether they look upon PR narrowly and rate the PR man rather low in the hierarchy of the firm. The pattern of industry changes year by year and there is a constant shift of emphasis so that whatever type of organisation is devised to cover the functions of PR there must at all times be a readiness to modify this to meet the new needs of management as they arise. And some of these needs may call for special skills.

For example, where employee relationship is a major responsibility of the PR department, as it might be in a large steel works or one of the nationalised industries, then personnel may have to be recruited with some experience in this field. The old idea that any competent journalist can do PR work is entirely wrong today and the person best equipped to communicate to employees should have had some experience in labour relations, as well as an ability to write and also to be able to speak knowledgeably and convincingly on subjects of interest to staff and payroll. Similarly the new technologies and complexities of so many industries call for PR personnel with an academic or technological background so that they can talk the same language as the technologists, scientists and engineers. In other words, the communication problem has first to be solved at the PR end, if its personnel are to be able to communicate effectively with others.

Responsibilities : The following breakdown covers most the PR functions likely to be carried out by an industrial concern :

Press Liaison : Responsibility for all company relations with the Press ; preparation and issuing of press releases and handouts, arrangement of press conferences, initiation and writing of articles for the press and the editing of material prepared by company staff, copy writing of prestige or institutional advertisements in collaboration with the advertising department ; commissioning and supervising all photography required for PR, arranging facility visits of the Press to factories, laboratories, etc., arranging interviews of the press with, among others, drawing up and keeping up-to-date press lists for different groups of publications, checking, filing and recording all press notices, circulating to top management selected press cuttings or summaries of press coverage.

Whilst the PR man himself would have the overall responsibility for press liaison, dictating policy and laying down procedure, he would delegate most of the day-to-day work to his press officer.

Publications : Internal responsibility for the planning and preparation of employee handbooks, works newspapers, staff magazines, staff bulletins, pay envelope inserts, posters and other publicity material.

External : Annual reports.

Recruitment publications.

Publicity releases covering products, company policy.

Brochure, handbooks and other publications issued by the marketing departments.

Company magazines and publications issued regularly to customers.

Visual Aids : Responsibility for the planning, direction and production of films, special displays, notice boards, charts, product exhibits, etc.

Information : Responsibility for answering general queries ; supplying information of an educational nature to schools and colleges, arranging speakers from company staff to speak at clubs and organisations of various kinds; circulating to shareholders the publications prepared by the publicity section of PR.

Control : Responsibility for administration, preparation of the yearly budget and the actual running of the department.

Research : Responsibility for planning and organising opinion research amongst employees, customers, community neighbours, shareholders and members of the public so as to determine their reaction on company policies and to report the findings to top management.

Although the pattern of PR as outlined in this kind of organisation is excellent, covering as it does most of the major PR activities that one would except to be carried oul in a large company, it should be possible to effect economies by streamlining some of the actions and to collaborate with other departments in certain operations ; for example, some of the work of the internal publications section might well be undertaken by personnel and labour departments. Similarly some of the work of the external publications section, notably that concerned with annual reports, could probably be passed over to the secretary's department, it might also be argued that the production of customer literature is primarily an advertising function and could best be done by that department.

A department organized on these lines would require a minimum staff of 10 including the manager or PR man, his assistant who would be the press officer, section heads and juniors. The head of the department's chief function would be planning and direction of operations, coordination of all PR activities, administration and, most important, liaison with top management. In a large complex concern with a number of factories or manufacturing units or divisions, there might well arise a need to have PR advisers or liaison officers stationed at the various plants to give assistance and advice to local managements on handling PR matters (including, of course, employee relationship), to maintain contact with the local press and to feedback to headquarters, *i.e.*, the central PR department, information about company activities and problems that have a bearing or may influence future PR.

The minimum scale of operations for a mediumsized company is indicated below :

Publications and Visual Aid : Responsibility for the planning, writing and publication of air types of company literature to be circulated to employees, customers, shareholders; and so on. Production of firm's display notice boards, charts and special product exhibits needed for conferences and seminars.

Press Liaison and Information : Responsibility for all contacts with the press including the preparation and circulation of all press releases, handouts, organisation and running of press conferences, interviews and facility visits, supply of information of a general nature to all enquiries, including those from educational establishments, contact where necessary with suppliers, shareholders, and others.

Control and Research : General administration including budgeting and carrying out of research.

For such an organisation, one well qualified PR man to run the show, two assistants and juniors should be just about sufficient, although it is agreed that they would be under some pressure to fulfil all requirements. The PR man would naturally assume direct personal responsibility for all press matters and information and his two assistants would look after the other two sections. A couple of really good secretaries would be needed to cope with day-to-day work, although for special exercises additional assistance would be needed.

Close Liaison with Marketing Essential : To be really effective, the PR man must be allowed to work on a large canvas and be free to recommend and to use the media of communication that he considers likely to be the best suited to the situation.

If PR is looked on by top management as essentially a marketing function then there must exist a very close liaison with the marketing departments. On the other hand it, would be total for PR to come under the control of marketing as this would rob it of all independence of thought and action, and PR thrives on freedom. The PR man must not be tied down to systems or regulations but able to switch methods and to change procedures so as to meet any new situation that arises, and marketing conditions are highly fluid. Ever uppermost in the mind of the PR man must be the likely effect on sales and the company image of every important decision that top management makes ; how customers react to it ; the effect of it on the competition, suppliers, shareholders, employees and the public. If PR work is always carried out in cooperation with marketing so that every one connected with selling is aware of what is happening, then the maximum effect is likely to be achieved. It is when PR is carried in isolation, as so often happens, that the results are so disappointing. Therefore, before a major PR exercise is implemented it is vitally important to sell it to all branches of management to secure first their approval and interest and finally their cooperation.

Staff and Qualifications : While it is true that the ability to pass the examinations set by the Institute of Public Relations for its associates and members is an indication of the candidate's knowledge of the theory and practice of PR, to be a successful practitioner requires a great deal more than this. It calls for the somewhat rare ability to think clearly and objectively and to be able to communicate information in a way that will create the maximum impact, using the most suitable media of communication. The PR man needs to be experienced in dealing with people and able to secure the ready cooperation of all types, from the man on the shop floor to the Chairman of the firm. An extrovert, but one whose personality earns him the respect both of his colleagues inside the firm and the many contacts outside, he must have the courage to express his opinions, even when they are unpopular, and be ready to make decisions and to accept the consequences if they prove to be the wrong ones.

This is not the picture of a superman, but one who has graduated in the hard school of experience and achieved success in the profession because of his ability, personality and mature judgement. And most PR men are either journalists or advertising men, some have academic qualification, a few have technological background but the majority have gone into PR largely because of their natural aptitude for this kind of work. Industry is becoming increasingly complex, the new technologies have a language all their own and even modern business procedures are not easy to understand. This means that those engaged in the actual operation of industrial PR must, if they themselves are to communicate effectively with their colleagues in the some scientific, technological or marketing experience.

This does not necessarily mean that the PR man himself needs to be a technologist or a scientist, although it would be helpful if he had some technical knowledge or background, but he would be well advised to recruit staff that is best suited to the particular type of business carried out by the firm. If, for instance, it produces electronic components and devices, a man with some knowledge of electrical engineering would be invaluable ; similarly a company manufacturing plastics would ideally need some one who knows his way around the tongue-twisting polymers. Just as a PR consultancy recruits special skills to suit the client's accounts, so too should the PR man in building up his department. Ideally, it should be the Press officer who has the technological background as he is the one who is called upon to translate the jargon of the chemist or the engineer into easily understood press notices and articles, and to be able to do this with any degree of competence calls for an ability to understand the language of the specialist. The press officer cannot be expected to be an expert, that is not his job, but he loses the respect of his colleagues in the firm unless he has a reasonable grasp of what they are talking about. There are some fortunate people who are blessed with technical appreciation. Although not technologists, engineers or scientists, they possess a mattering of knowledge on a variety of useful subjects and a great deal of common sense that enables them to follow a technical argument and to converse not un-intelligently about technical subjects. Such men and women make invaluable PR assistants

However, to sum up, the first essential is to study the pattern of business undertaken by the firm and then to try and recruit personnel with some experience or knowledge of the particular technologies that are involved, plus, of course, the ability to do their jobs as PR assistants.

Responsibilities to Board of Directors : If PR is responsible to too many bosses the inevitable result is confusion, frustration and irritation, all of which sap the strength and destroy the effectiveness of the PR man's work whilst he should have ready access to all members of the Board of Directors, from the chairman downwards, his problem and queries receiving a high degree of priority. He should be responsible to one senior director, preferably a marketing director or the commercial or sales director. In some concerns where there is a great emphasis on employee relationship, PR is the responsibility of the personnel director. This is not altogether a good move as it slants PR too much in one direction and encourages the viewpoint that it is primarily a personnel activity. There are also objections to the responsibility for PR being in the hands of the managing director as he is usually so preoccupied with high finance and questions of company policy, and under such pressure from departmental managers that access to him proves difficult and quick decisions are not easy to secure.

It is important, for the smooth running of the PR department that the director in charge is reasonably static because PR is a job that demands quick decisions and prompt action. There is always a sense of urgency about PR matters and some executives resent this, complaining that the PR man is constantly holding a pistol at their head. However, this urgency has to be accepted and top management must look upon it as part of the price to be paid for ensuring rapid communications. There is, of course, a reluctance on the part of some directors to have anything to do with PR. They fear the repercussions in the board room when questions are asked about the advisability of making this or that statement to the Press. For this reason there is a tendency for directors to duck the really tricky questions and to refer decisions to the managing director or chairman. These tactics mean delays, failure to meet Press deadlines and the missing of opportunities, all of which result in loss of confidence in the PR man and general deterioration in his relations with the press and other media.

It is always an advantage if the director responsible for PR is also responsible for advertising and promotion and that is why the marketing director is the ideal executive. He is able to ensure that responsibilities are clearly defined, that collaboration is of a high order and that all PR activities are closely geared to marketing.

Corporate Public Relations Manager

Duties and Responsibilities

Reports to Managing Director or Chief Executive

Basic Function : The Public Relations Manager formulates and presents to the Managing Director for approval, the major objectives in respect to the company's public relations programme involving the general public, shareholders, employees, public institutions, customers, opinion makers and government circles. Liaises with the representative bodies of the industry in evolving and implementing industry PR programmes. Keeps abreast of trends in the economic and political field, particularly Government's thinking and policy concerning industry and advises management from time to time of such developments as are likely to have a bearing on the company's present operation and future growth. Implements approved plans and policies so as to most effectively achieve company's PR objectives, within the limits of approved expenses.

Responsibilities : Within the framework of company policies and procedures and within the limits of the approved budgets and programmes, the Public Relations Manager is responsible for and is vested with commensurate authority to accomplish, *inter alia,* the following tasks:

1. In line with the MD's corporate objectives, develop and finalise PR objectives, have these approved by Management.

2. Initiates and recommends to management specific plans and programmes for the conduct of the company's public relations activities and, on approval, implements such programmes so as to most effectively achieve the company's PR objectives.

3. Prepares annual PR budgets and plans on the basis of PR objectives and ensures that these are organized and carried out as scheduled, within the approved budgetary limits and are also made known to all key managers so as to seek their support and involvement.

4. Participates in industry PR activities through representative bodies and helps in developing and implementing industry PR programmes.

5. Keeps abreast of developments in the political, economic and other fields and advises management from time to time of such developments as are likely to have a bearing on the company's present operation and future growth.

6. Maintains liaison with the press, MLAs, MPs and other VIPs and supplies such information on the company or the industry which will improve understanding.

7. Organises Annual General Meetings of Shareholders and other shareholder relation programmes including visits to plant.

8. Develops and initiates designing, production and distribution of company's Annual Report, Chairman's Speech and other shareholder communications, with appropriate publicity.

9. Arrange contributions and donations of money and medicines and organises other service projects.

10. Initiates and implements programmes to improve customer relations with the assistance of the respective marketing divisions.

11. Directs internal communications and employee relations activities. Keeps employees informed through internal communication media about company's and industry operations and contributions.

12. Organizes participation in professional and other associations which are of benefit to the company.

13. Submits regular reports to Management on public relations activities and other topics of interest.

14. Supervises designing and production of corporate and divisional stationery. Ensures appropriate identity and good presentation of signboards, company cans, packaging material, etc.

Accountability : The Public Relations Manager is accountable to the Managing Director. He may, at his discretion, delegate such portions of his responsibility to appropriate personnel together with proportionate authority but he may not relinquish his overall responsibility for results or any portion of his accountability.

Qualifications and know-how Desirable

(a) *Academic, Scientific or Technological*

- Preferably a Masters Degree in Social Sciences or Humanities with Psychology as one of the subjects. Should have knowledge in literature, communication, journalism.
- Desirable: 5 years experience in advertising, marketing and journalism.

(b) *Techniques*

- Should know technique of advertising management.
- Should know technique of Public Affairs Management.

(c) *Skills*

- Should have skill in dealing with the Press.
- Should have skill in dealing with Government officials.
- Should have skill in dealing with high dignitaries.
- Should have skill in dealing with Associations and other bodies.
- Should have skill in dealing with shareholders.

(d) *Problem Solving Dimension*

Thinking Environment

- Opportunity of on-the-spot spot observation of value adding activity does not exist.
- Introspection time is limited to one day.
- Range of discretion extends to one year.
- Range of vision and conceptual ability needs to be high.

Job Challenge

- Influence representative bodies to progressive action.
- Influence company policies.
- Influence political and financial groups and media in favour of company objectives.

- Produce and implement revolutionary themes.

Job Performance Standards

Within the areas of accountability

Industrial Image

- Incidence of effecting changes in policies of representative bodies.
- Perspective changes caused in political, economic and industrial trends towards the industry.
- Incidence of representative bodies and other companies asking for advice.

Company External Image

- Incidence of appreciation letters and phone calls after P.R. action.
- Incidence of acceptance by shareholders of company policies and plans.
- Incidence of congratulatory and exemplary references in press.

Company Internal image

- Number of new schemes evolved for employee awareness and participation.
- Number of employees leaving company with dissatisfaction.
- Incidence of employee justifying company stand.

Job Challenge Areas

- Incidence of change in policies of representative bodies.
- Incidence of change in policies of the company.
- Incidence of change in trends in political, economic and financial thought.
- Incidence of implementation of revolutionary themes.

Social Audit

Social Audit is one facet of corporate public relations activities. Those who are invited to perform this sensitive function make honest efforts to discover whether in their attempts to live up to the tenets of Corporate citizenship, corporate executives not only discharge their obligations underlying 'social justice' but also seen to be discharging.

What is social justice"? Live and let others also live is the soul of social justice. As Mahatma Gandhi used to point out time and again, "There cannot be happiness for any of us until it is available to all." Man is interdependent and so individualism has its limits.

The simple and significant word for social justice is "dharma"—in effect a deep concern for the welfare of those with whom you live and work. This is central to the moral life of corporate citizens without which no country can endure. Frequent references are made in Mahabaratha and in Plato's books, too, stressing its importance. This is now evident in the patent failure of democracy to function as originally envisaged.

Why this 'audit' ? Pressures are developing from government, from Parliament and Legislatures, from various statutory authorities, from financial'institutions, from trade unions, from trade and professional organizations and a variety of external groups. In planning corporate strategy, business has to take a note of these pressures.

All human institutions in society have to accept that social responsibility is a necessary corollary to social accountability. It is in this context that 'business' needs to willingly submit itself to a "social audit".

Every corporation should examine its performance against exhaustive checklist of demands, needs and aspirations of its employees, shareholders, customers, ccmmunity, government and the public at large.

A corporation should examine its performance against an exhaustive checklist, as mentioned above, and review at regular intervals to know how far it is living up to the expectations of the various 'publics'referred to above. Conditions relative to social, economic and political changes might call for revision of the said checklist.

The government and Parliament would like to see a corporation working towards the betterment of its employees, and would also like to see how far it helps in contributing to the nation's economic development, and to meet the current economic and social objectives of the government and the country.

The 'audit' is conducted by a panel of the members of which are generally competent men of highest integrity who could understand and appreciate the operating problems of business, and the genuine interests of the government and the country at large. These personalities are empowered to ask for such records and information as they deem fit from the top management and others connected with operational cadre so that the audit could be conducted quite successfully.

The broad terms of reference to social auditing are:

1. What people look for from businessmen today is a combination of professionalism and humanity and this is what gains respect in modern industry.
2. In order to achieve a satisfactory reputation with its customers, shareholders, workpeople—in fact the public at large—whether the corporation makes genuine effort to gain respect by a deliberately planned and sustained effort to establish mutual understanding between itself and the public ?
3. Does it adopt a four-stage programme to create a favourable reputation for its own organization in particular and the capitalist society in general.
   (a) First and foremost to reduce business abuses, if any, by upgrading standards. If businessmen expect society to improve its standards of behaviour, the lead must come from businessmen.

(b) Help mitigate and ultimately eliminate the effects of poverty.

(c) To reduce pollution of our environment.

(d) To develop international institutions which will contribute io the improved use of the world's resources and, as a result, to world peace.

4. Whether there is any instance where the corporation wastes time trying to make itself good although it does not possess the required attributes. If a firm is slapdash and inefficient, or ruthless and overbearing, it is no use expecting that "public relations" will somehow or other create an agreeable and impressive corporate image. Power demands a social conscience and big corporations are taking on more power, in some cases more than governments. Therefore it is vitally necessary that they play the role of a catalyst in aiding society's problems by their social involvement. This involvement should be in specific areas of social life such as the areas of communal relations, upliftment of the economically weaker sections of society like, backward and depressed classes, education and training.

5. Whether in the creation of goods and services it takes into account not just the production of profit for investors, but also the effect they produce on the total design of society ?

6. Whether the corporation avoids the 'battle' that generally takes place between the economist and the ecologist by duly recognising public interest at large ?

Economists see technological change as the factor in society which is responsible for stimulating the economy. Ecologists, on the other hand, look on technical change with a misgiving. The change in agricultural techniques, for example, made possible by the introduction of chemical fertilizers and insecticides, has increased agricultural productivity. But it has done so only by imposing costs on society as a whole—in terms of chemical pollution—the scale of which is only now becoming apparent.

To an ecologist it is obvious that the large-scale interference with the environment, involved in producing ever larger flows of goods, will interfere in harmful way with those processes which together sustain human life. And we cannot afford to tilt the balance between human life and wild life.

Improving the environment should not stop just at building schools or improving roads or cutting out pollution. To improve the overall quality of life, business must not neglect the broader social problems created by the existence of underprivileged minorities.

7. Does the corporation perceive that people work to satisfy the needs which are today more sophisticated than the mere bases of physical survival food, warmth and shelter?

Satisfaction in work is provided principally by six elements called motivators. These are achievement, recognition for achievement, the qualities of the work itself, responsibility, advancement, and self-development. The presence of these elements, the theory suggests, will influence the person doing the job to want to work, their absence, however, will not make him dissatisfied, just indifferent.

8. Does the corporation appreciate the factors which contribute to employees' satisfaction, such as:
   (a) the work they do and how it is organized; the equipment they work with.
   (b) the training or retraining provided, and the general opportunities for development;
   (c) the company : its reputation, its concern for employees, the security it offers:
   (d) the cooperation between various parts of the organization;
   (e) the extent to which they are informed about the company's plans, and other aspects of communication which may have a bearing on their future;

(f) the payment systems that are in operation;

(g) the physical working conditions:

(h) the amenities and welfare provisions.

9. Whether there is awareness of the fact that social environment outside the factory is becoming increasingly liberal and permissive with the breaking down of all class barriers; thus it becomes increasingly difficult for people who are treated like human beings outside factory, to knuckle under once they get through the gates of the factory.

10. Whether public relations work is handled by an executive who has authority in his right, possesses a senior title and is close to the real head of the organization. He should be in the complete confidence of the chief executive, knowing the entire background of every situation which he handles.

Since the complexities of big company management often remove the chief executive from the general public, the public relations manager must interpret to the chief executive what the mass of people think of the company—as well as interpret the company to the people.

11. "Love thy neighbour". Granted that we should love our neighbours as ourselves, the questions under modern conditions of trade practice remain for solution are, 'who precisely are our neighbours ? and, how exactly are we to make our love for them effective in practice ?'

    In our modern way of corporate public relations practice, such traditional social doctrines had no specific to offer, and were merely repeated, when, in order to be effective, they should have been thought out again from the beginning and formulated in new and living terms.

12. "Although it is right and proper that we should as honest corporate citizens give the clearest and most accurate information to shareholders in our accounts, the pressure

to furnish more and more information in their report to shareholders, although politically attractive, should be resisted, as it may make company accounts more difficult to read". —SIR CAMPBELL ADAMSON, former Director-General of the Central Bureau of the Industries in the United Kingdom.

How does a Typical Social Audit Report Read ?

"It is with pleasure that we present this report on the Social Audit of Bapuji Iron and Steel Company Limited. Few committees are so fortunate as to be able to look into the affairs of so well managed an organization—even if it be in the matter of social performance.

While we have been unable to follow rigidly some of the systems of elaborate evaluation followed in US.A. and the West, as these systems are unsuited to conditions in India at present, we have tried to the extent possible to be guided by some of them.

"First, we have found the following inadequacies which may, in time, be attended to :

(1) At the time of allocation of funds towards the various items of social welfare, the allocating authority should call for greater details of each head of demand and determine the estimated benefits therefrom. This should be stated in the budget so as to be useful when the next yearly accounting and budgeting comes round. Merely stating heads of grant is not enough.

(2) When the next annual budget is prepared, the previous years' performance in comparison to the expectations and details of expenditure should be closely scrutinized in order to enable the allocating authority to determine :

   (a) whether the aid has reached the persons for whom it was meant, and

   (b) whether the allocations among different items require any change.

(3) A larger appropriation towards education of children, particularly girls and socially backward, is of vital importance. Since a programme of rural uplift has now been undertaken, such education should be carried to the village folk within the area set apart by the company for its effort.

(4) In allocating funds for social welfare, care should be taken to :

(i) foster self-reliance in the community, and

(ii) give priority through a process of consultation.

(5) The problem of pollution from the chimneys has assumed serious proportions and requires to be controlled early and, if possible, eliminated. Since the cost of pollution control is likely to be very heavy, even for a Company like Bapuji Iron & Steels, the effort may be spread over a period of years. In the meanwhile, units or locations where the ill effects of pollution are concentrated call for immediate measure of alleviation.

(6) The dividends paid during the past few years appear to be somewhat meagre and since the Company is constrained by executive instructions to limit them, the Company should make the necessary application to Government to be allowed to increase it. (As we concluded this report, we were happy to learn that such an application has been made to the Government.)

(7) "Subject to what weave said above, we are satisfied that the social performance of this Company is of a high order and in its magnitude, is perhaps unequalled in India. We are satisfied that the Company has amply fulfilled the objective contained in Clause 3A of its Articles of Association regarding its social and moral responsibilities to the consumers, employees, she reholders, the local community and society.

(8) "The credit for this outstanding social performance of the Company goes to a number of persons—past and present—

but in welding an effective team together and inspiring with a sense of larger purpose the role of X is so outstanding that it deserves special mention. He has presided over the destinies of the Company for over 45 years now and has shown unceasing care and anxiety for its employees and all those associated with it. He is usually one of the first to assist in setting right inequalities or injustice in whatever field they appear. Through all this, he has helped build up the social conscience of the Bapuji Iron and Steel Company.

(9) "Under the leadership of X, the Company has not merely fulfilled the dream of its founder for the Company which he planned and for his country, but has gone far beyond it. The Company spends in all about Rs. ... crores per year upon its social welfare programmes. It has encompassed,within the ambit of its activities and financial aid, not merely the worker and his dependants but the community among which they live and indeed society in general in far-flung corners of India whenever *a* calamity or a disaster has struck. At the same time, it has taken care to see that the consumer who buys its goods gets value for his money and within the limitations laid down by the Government and other compulsions within which it operates, the share holder, whose money it uses, gets an adequate return."

Corporate Objectives

"Corporate Planning" in India is still in an evolutionary process. As it is undergoing dramatic changes from time to time, it cannot be adopted overnight and become an instant success.

Different people will look at corporate planning from different angles giving rise to divergent views, commentaries and explanations. The concept generally deals with futurity of present decisions in terms of (i) setting clear-cut goals and objectives and developing strategies to achieve them, and (ii) translating strategies into operational programmes. Besides profit planning, capital budgeting, research and development, corporate image, social welfare and employee welfare—all need greater attention.

Corporate planning deals with the long-term future of a company within its existing environment and "SWOT" analysis will be of much use in this area. Strength, weakness, opportunities and threats to the organisation should be listed first and analysed.

The concept helps the organisation to survive and record a sustained growth. All business decisions and actions have to be taken after "SWOT" analysis. It has also to be seen whether a new decision will be of help to the company in the long run.

Corporate planning is carried out in the following sequence:

(1) Determination of the organisation's objectives.

(2) Preparing the demand forecast for the products of the industry in which the organisation is operating or wishes to operate.

(3) Working out the demand and supply gap of a particular product and assessing whether the product will fill the gap and the scope for export, and

(4) Identifying the constraints to or the key limiting factors for achieving the objectives. Solutions to overcome the constraints have to be found after a scientific analysis. By keeping all these factors in mind, the organisation has to work out its corporate strategy.

The corporate goals are to be fixed not merely in quantitative terms such as sales, net income and net worth. The company should also try to satisfy two important qualitative goals : First, it should aim to be a good corporate citizen and contribute to societal goals in the area of national priority. Secondly, the company should benefit every constituent of its own business environment —*(a)* shareholders *(b)* employees *(c)* vendors *(d)* the government *(e)* the trade and *(f)* consumers.

A survey of India's most respected companies in 1987 assessed their respectability on the basis of various factors such as the quality of management, the quality of products, service, innovativeness, financial soundness, quality personnel, community and environmental responsibilities, profitability and willingness to work for the company.

The basic strength for any organisation should be its people working for and with the company and they should contribute to and nurture the company's culture of character and competence. They should share a vision for the future and be made committed to its objectives, philosophy and principle and give more to the organisation than they take from it.

Thus, corporate planning is not just for projecting the future, but for deciding the objectives and actions to be taken to achieve the goals. The role of a corporate planner is to introduce, a decision-making system and not to take a decision by himself. He has to get the planning system going and ensure that it gets going. He has to install a system and ensure that the obvious pitfalls are avoided.

Corporate planning has to be done by one who is in touch with reality and is going to play an executive part in carrying out plans. He must understand at what level *(i.e.,* the Top Management, the Middle Management or the Lower Management level) decisions are taken.

Top Management **(Board of Directors) :** Here, the decision-maker develops the objectives and allocates resources to achieve them.

Middle Management : At this level, decisions dealing with the process, which assures resources and their effective and efficient use, to accomplish the objectives, are taken.

Lower Management : Here, decisions are taken on short-term day-to-day operations. The objective here is to ensure that specific jobs are carried out efficiently and effectively.

The corporate planner has to ensure that the managers are in the know of the objectives and get to know the views of the top management on all important issues. Out of the five main basic management functions—planning, organising, staffing, directing and controlling—planning is the prime one. The planner can assist the executive and supervise the whole process of planning. His task will be continued in (i) assisting other executives to draw up plans, *(ii)* helping them to identify the appropriate plan ensuring that the forecast and analysis of problems are of a high standard the system commands, and (iii) alerting the Board of Directors when rescheduling of plan is required to close gaps.

Thus, the corporate planner's Job is to see that planning and execution are done well and accepted at all levels of the organisation.

17

Industrial Effect

An active social conscience, and individual recognition of social responsibilities will compel us, as individuals, to test every managerial practice, measure every policy by a single yardstick: Not what does it mean to me, but rather what will this mean to my employees as people, to my customers, to my suppliers, to my shareholders, to the community in which my factory is located, to my Government, to the industry to which I am a part, to the economy as a whole". —MORRIS SAYRE, a former President of the Corn

Products Refining Company, U.S.A.)

The Perception

We have borrowed the term "democracy" from the political field. The Greek word as we all know means a system of authority deriving from the people. It involves a sharing of power among the members of the society. If we are to be true to the basic definition as we look at the workplace, we are considering a sharing of power among those who deal with the firm's product. The three principal participants are the Corporation's managers, its workers and the consumers of its product. This discussion will focus on the industrial relations process between workers and management, leaving the question of the consumer involvement aside ; the role of the consumer is a separate complex issue worthy of a study in its own right. Here we will focus on the role of corporate management in the process, recognizing of course that the worker's interest is inextricably involved in management's approach to industrial democracy.

The term industrial democracy is fraught with emotional overtones. This is understandable because the issue of sharing power is always controversial. It is controversial in the basic human social dimension. The psychologists have taught us that the process of human maturation involves the growth of the child from total absorption with his own needs into concern for the needs of others (the super ego). Each of us is constantly struggling with the tension between our desire to exercise total control over our environment and our realization that we cannot have that total control if we are to live in harmony in the social environment which we also seek. No better example exists than the human family where we constantly find the need to modify our own short-term desires and interests so that other members of the family also can achieve some of their desires. Living in the social environment of the family or of the workplace requires some abdication of control over our own life. Some men have opted not to make that compromise : hermits and autocrats. Most of us do not take these options because hermits and autocrats have to live in isolation and loneliness.

The term industrial democracy is also worrisome to us because it raises issues of parallels with political society. Some fear the introduction of radical political ideas which propose the complete loss of power by management in the economic business of the firms. But industrial democracy does not mean total worker control or total State control. It means the same thing it means in the political arena of democracy : a sharing of power and authority through accepted channels so that the greatest good reaches the greatest number. Thus there is nothing inconsistent with a system of firm management practice within the context of industrial democracy. The key element of industrial democracy is that all elements of the corporation in society, managements and labour, have a voice in the welfare of the corporation, because that welfare is important to the well-being of all.

Egalitarianism

Essential to the concept of democracy is a concept of egalitarianism. There is much confusion and debate about this concept. Over two centuries ago Thomas Jefferson penned an immortal phrase which is still a live topic: "We hold these truths to be self-evident, that all men are created equal." It seems to me a futile interpretation to assume that Jefferson prophesied a simple society in which every man's labour and every man's talent would be standardized to some predetermined mould as if every human were product of an assembly line. No, but as per the present social concept Jefferson was talking about a state of mind when every man would appreciate the dignity of the personality, talent and contribution to the general welfare of each of his fellows. The application of the principle of egalitarianism to the workplace involves acceptance that each person in the production process has a vital and appreciated contribution to make to the enterprise whether his work be manual or intellectual.

Industrial Democracy

The manager's role in the promotion of industrial democracy is to create the environment which permits a sense of participation in decision-making by all elements of the production units. In order to do that he must subscribe to the underlying assumption of democracy a belief that all workers have a claim to equal dignity. The Medium for working toward that difficult state of equal dignity is communications, horizontally and vertically in the corporation's work-force.

The manager does not have to fear the industrial democracy concept as some net subtraction from his task to maximize the efficiency of the operation. Rather he can look at industrial democracy as a process which will make the Corporation more efficient. A worker's sense that he is a vital part of the production process and that his labour is appreciated increases his own happiness and therefore his own efficiency. Open communications which reduce the sense of superiors dictating to inferiors also reduces the psychology of class conflict which debilitates the production mechanism. Finally the manager who is open to suggestions and communications from below will find that some of the greatest contributors to more efficient production will be the workers themselves.

Part of the Democratic System

As we have discussed political performance rather than about the principles governing the practice of industrial democracy. However, it has to be noted that the two cannot be totally divorced. The workplace is a fundamental element of a worker's life. He spends more of his waking hours there than in any other single place including his home. His perceptions of the society around him are shaped by his experience at the workplace.

If it is a happy place in which he has a sense of value and dignity, his view of the world will be an optimistic one. Therefore the managers of the workplace have a heavy responsibility in the shaping of the perceptions by which a worker views the world. If the worker has his sense of the dignity ground down at the workplace he will see society as a place which needs radical change. Therefore, it seems to me, in a democracy the manager has a vital role to play. It has been said that people get the government they deserve. One may paraphrase that to say that managers often get the work force they deserve. If the work force is truculent, confrontational and uncooperative, management should examine itself as closely as it examines the protestors.

The manager in a democratic system is one of the stewards of that system. If it fails, he is one of the principal culprits. He has the opportunity to offer the people he manages an optimistic view of their world, of the opportunity for their fulfilment of their aspirations. We therefore would offer you the prospect of industrial democracy as a great and exciting challenge to the manager's sense of patriotism and social commitment. He is one of the key elements ia making democracy a vehicle for mankind's dream of economic and political freedom.

Selection and Training

The supervisory system is the key to production. Skills for this task are often more important to production than even the technical skills of the individual worker. Management most assure that its supervisory staff is committed to the concept of industrial democracy. Formal training is often necessary to indoctrinate the supervisor in the goals of the company and its policy of enhancing industrial democracy and worker dignity. Supervisors must learn that time spent in explaining tasks or listening to grievances is not wasted time but a vital element of long-term efficiency. The company therefore just take a long-term view of production by realigning that supervisory time spent on training and discussion with subordinates is not wasted time. A brief curtailment of the day's production to perfect communication may pay treble or quadruple dividends in the time ahead. Selection of supervisors is critical. A man with supreme technical competence may be a disaster as a supervisor if he had no patience for the task of communication. The Bell Telephone System in the United States for many years has used a comprehensive and expensive system for selecting its supervisors and middle management from within the company. Candidates for promotion are put through an exhaustive battery of tests and simulated workplace personnel problems. The test result show whether a person can perform effectively as a communicator and therefore as a supervisor.

Industrial Relations

Before coming to the issue of industrial relations in the organized sense—collective bargaining—We would to emphasize the important responsibility management has within its own system to contribute to industrial democracy. But in our complex industrial societies, trade unions are a necessary element in the evolution of industrial democracy. If management has taken care to provide the framework of a workplace with open communications, it also can learn to deal harmoniously and productively with a sensible trade union movement. The union can actually be a facilitator of communications. If the leadership is convinced that management wants a workplace in which dignity and just prevails, it can play a constructive role in guiding management. There always will be some tension between management and labour as there is in any structured social system. The union can point management to ways in which this tension is minimized because often workers will share grievances to the union that they will not share with management. But more than a cooperative approach is required. Good industrial democracy and good industrial relations require structures. Together management and labour must work out a system which provides rapid and just settlement of grievances. Often they must go to outside parties for help just as sometimes in a family we call in an intermediary to help us over a dispute with a relative. Mediation machinery and ultimately arbitration machinery is a highly useful channel for such resolution. And we should explore ways whereby this can be made informal and voluntary so that settlement of problems becomes the goal rather than skilful litigation.

The Employees

All conscious actions by all of us are need-based, or, ultimate aim of all actions is to satisfy some need. All personal interactions and the interpersonal relationships are, therefore, need-based. When instructions, orders and messages are conveyed, the action is backed by an objective, an objective of achieving something. When one talks to one's friend, complains to one's boss, or clarifies from a supervisor, the intention is to achieve certain satisfaction. These and similar actions are the constituents of interactions which result in interpersonal relationships.

Viewing from within the periphery of Industrial Relations, two kinds of relationships commonly exist. Relationship between the employer and employee and that between employee and the political forces. This situation is specially true in case of India.

Raja-Praja System? : Let us deal with the first. What kind of relationship between employee and employer one does find in India? It does not need elaborate study to find an answer. A close watch for a certain period is adequate. One will find, in majority of the organisations, public or private, two watertight compartments; the employer or management in one and the employee in the other. Consider the attitude. The management conveys orders and the employees are to obey them. Of course, there are certain liberal organisations. They are democratic in approach, where the command is 'first obey, then complain'. They would look into the complaints at leasure. Talking to a worker informally is something that can not be thought of by the managers. Informal get-together with them, therefore, is out of question. Wages are determined depending upon the union strength and not skills or quality of work. These are only secondary considerations. When there were no labour unions, the wages could not even support mere subsistence. This is very much true even today in many of the unorganised sectors, say, agricultural labour, casual labour, and so on. The management, therefore, rules according to their might. The employees are, then the ruled.

Why is it so ? Why this casteism in Indian organisations ? Speaking plain, the answer is not far to seek. Sociologically, Indian Society is a highly segmented amalgam with discriminating contours caused by caste system, clanisms, regionalism, linguism and religious followings. Some are born high, in a caste or clan and some low. High society members look down on the ones belonging to the lower strata.

All the employers, managers and employees belong to this segmented society. One answer to the question is : this social attitude is carried into the organisations and practised there.

The other answer is socio-psychological, every one selects and accepts, consciously or unconsciously, a lifemodel, for one to follow and to become. This social-model is picked up from one's own society, based on the social values. The less privileged looked up to the well to do and try to imitate their beliefs, attitudes and behaviour patterns. In India, we had the zamindars, the Rajas, and the Colonial rulers. The serfs, the poor, the prajas and the slaves (that is what we were under the British rule) picked up their masters as their lifemodel. This model selection also affected the behaviour pattern within the industries, commercial houses and other organisations. To begin with, only the privileged people from privileged sectors of the society could afford education and hence become managers and officials. Again, only those could start industries and businesses. They treated the workers, who were then, the downtroden like in the society. As for the workers, the life-models were those managers and officials. That is why even when a person belonging to the less privileged segment, becomes a manager or official, the starts behaving like the model he had in mind and ill treats his own category of people, or in short, they forget their root.

Need for Rethinking : Can we continue to nurture this traditional pattern of interpersonal relationship in our organisations ? The answer is an emphatic No. Not any more, if we have to build our industrial output, desirable if we are looking for lasting industrial peace, and cannot be tolerated if we have to compete in the world market. The concept of cheap labour, existence of a sellers' internal market, continued use of obsolete machinery and the operation of unjustifiable and unkind industrial relations policy, have caused considerable harm to our industrial growth and national economy. Strikes, lockouts, work-slow-downs etc. have become a common feature of the Indian industrial scene. While we see many smaller nations, who entered the industrial field much later than India, surpassed us many folds in technology, quality, quantity and hence in export trade. Japan and Korea are examples. They do have strikes, but do so by producing more. The interpersonal relationship in their organisation is not based on organisational casteism. The vehicles are parked together, they eat together, and they live like in a big family, like an Indian joint family, so to say.

One predominant question that comes to our mind is that why should the management spend time and energy to pamper and make friendship with the employees ? The managers who are hardpressed for time, could use the time that spent to make friendship with the workers, to do something good for the organisation. Unemployed people were given a job, a secure job in some cases, and thus a livelihood. They should be thankful for that.

The argument contains a lot of convincing facts. Nevertheless, when we view the issue from a broader perspective, it lacks in many respects.

An employee needs food, shelter, clothing and in adulthood must have sex. These are essential for his physical well-being. These needs are absolutely basic, for, they do not much differ from the animal needs. These needs are not created artificially by him. These are natural or instinctual. When we contend, therefore, that the employee should be satisfied with the means of livelihood provided by the organisation, we are treating him at equal footing as the animals. Human beings are, but, rational animals, with intelligence, and ability to observe and learn ; reason out to identify good and bad, right and wrong. In the process, his needs increase. Managing the human beings, unlike the animals, thus necessitates more forethought, tact and ability.

Food, shelter and clothing obtainable with the wages given by the employer, no doubt, satisfies him. But, beneath this satisfaction there exists a strong flame of fear, a fear of uncertainty. He fears about the day when he could be deprived of the job and the income. He fears about the subsequent struggle to search and find another means of livelihood. To take off this fear, he needs a secured job, help in case of sickness, accidents and on retirement. In other words, his source of income is to be preserved. This is also done by many of the organisations.

Man is a gregarious animal. This is the cause for many other needs and problems. He loves company. He wants to love and be loved by someone. He wants to belong to some group which creates in him strength, confidence and a sense of security. If he has to live with Joneser, he has to keep up with them, in his living standards, dressing, material possessions, educating the children, social customs and many more. Otherwise he would feel out of place, and probably, he may not be welcomed in the group interactions. A significant characteristic of these needs is : they constantly keep changing and also increase as the society progresses.

These socio-genic needs are strong forces, which if not dealt with prudence and tact could create havocs for the organisation. Usually; the management has no time to find out where the employees live, what their social standings are, whether they are happy in their social and personal life and so on. One point to be remembered here is that the employees spend whole day, or most of their useful time in their daily life, working for the employer. They therefore cannot spend time elsewhere to find means to satisfy their socio-genic needs. If these needs are not satisfied, they remain unsatisfied. An unsatisfied man spends considerable amount of energy thinking about it which, in turn, adversely affects his productivity and efficiency. When the organisation fails to give credence to his sociogenic needs, and fails to help him to satisfy them, a certain gap is created between them and the employer. This gap is often exploited by unscrupulous political parties and selfish trade union leaders, by promising to fill the gap, giving them wrong information, advice, guidance, which generally are confusing. They create mass appeal by trigeiring mobaction. Mob-psychology says that mob-behaviour is based on emotions and sentiments rather than on reasons.

This is mainly true in case of large organisations, where the depth and width of the gap between the employees and management is too large.

Let us consider, for the sake of discussion, that the employee is fully satisfied of the above needs, at a particular point of time. Does it mean that he has no more needs now ? No ; still he has a few more instinctual needs for the satisfaction of his ego. These needs motivate him for action, the intensity of which will depend upon his intelligence, education, energy and physical strength.

Every individual has a desire to be important, at least in his/her own group, by being superior or distinct in some respects. Such persons would like to be assertive, independent and like to lead, than to be led. A highly motivated person will do anything to satisfy this need. The egoism is so strong in them. In the interest of the organisation, and also to utilise such highly productive individuals for the best advantage, the management has got to identify them. For these category of persons rewards and publicity are more important. In the; absence of which they could be thorns in the flesh.

There is yet another category. They work quietly. They throw a challenge to themselves and continue to better their own ability, output and efficiency. They are not bothered about recognition or rewards, but their pursuit should not be hindered. This is important. They are trying for self-accusation. That is, they believe in what one can be, one must be : or one must bring out more and more, what one is. They help the organisation, much more than any one else, while they help themselves.

Abraham Maslow had grouped these needs in an hierarchical order because certain needs are common to all individuals, while others are only found in some individuals. Basic needs of food, shelter, clothing, job-security etc. and socio-genic needs are common. Egoistic needs and self-accusations needs are examples for second category. These are higher needs as per him. The places of various needs in the ascending order are : Basic, Security, Sociogenic, Egoistic and Self-accusations. From this grouping, one could draw an important conclusion that some needs are more important than the others and hence less important needs could be sublimated for higher ones. Thus an individual, who is highly motivated to achieve positions, power or self-effectiveness, may not bother about the meagre benefits, food, rest, permanancy in the present job etc. Some managers do not wish to have such people in the organisation. Mainly because, these persons are a source of headache to their own capabilities. Only capable managers could handle them. They are the best asset to the organisation, provided the organisation has the right climate for them to work and grow.

Diagnostic Syndromes : Every employee, as a matter of fact, requires the right climate to work and grow. To put it differently, the employees must have the confidence that they are cared for and the organisation is concerned about their well-being. They are accepted as useful members of the organisation. This will be achieved only when the employer-employee gap is reduced or totally bridged. To remove the gap, the management must be able to understand the employees by taking interest in them. The management also must be able to study the employees through their behaviour. This is not a difficult task, provided the managers know a few facts about the causes and effects of employee behaviour.

It has been stated earlier that the human or employee behaviour is need-based. All conscious actions are directed to satisfy some needs. The needs are of two types. Some needs can only be satisfied with the help of external factors, say, with the help of other persons or resources. The second category of needs are psychological in nature and hence internal to the individual. Failure to find reasonable satisfaction to these needs therefore results in frustration or conflicts.

Let us consider a few examples. An employee is making an effort to meet the manager directly to make a request for a loan which he requires very urgently to meet the medical expenses of his wife. The supervisor, angry on bypassing him, stops the loan. This action of the supervisor frustrates the employee. One office assistant draws all his savings to conduct the marriage of his only daughter. While busy with the arrangements, his wife falls ill and enter into a serious condition. He has to spend a sizable amount for her treatment. If he does that, the marriage cannot be conducted. With the limited resources, he has to do two important things, which is not possible. He gets frustrated. In another case, an employee resigns from his present job and joins another organisation, expecting better prospects. On joining the new job, he finds that his information was wrong. The result is frustration. These are three different categories of situation in which an employee gets frustrated.

What is the effect ? Immediate reaction is anger ; therefore, anger is a sign of frustration caused by external interferences by other individuals or lack of means. The intensity of anger will depend on a few factors, such as how important the goal is, to what extent the interference is going to cause damage to individual and how frequent is the interference. Nevertheless, if the interference is reasonable, *i.e.*, the employee is reasonably convinced of the reasons, then the intensity of anger will be less. When person of lower status, rank or service is the case for interference, the intensity of anger will be more and when person is higher in status, etc., the anger will be comparatively less. Anger will be more when the interference is caused by persons not concerned with his work or from outside the hierarchy. An employee would express his anger in many ways. When the intensity of anger is more, the employee is emotionally disturbed, anger could result in violence. If the person who caused frustration is stronger by virtue of his position, physical strength or support, the violence may be substituted by verbal hostility. If this is also not possible, then the concerned person is likely to resort to sabotage in order to frustrate the opponent. Circumstances, in case, do not permit even this, then he might withdraw to himself and resort to self-criticism and fantasy.

Conflict, as mentioned, is a psychological process, and caused by one's value systems. The value systems vary from person to person due to various reasons, say, education, upbringing, the company one keeps and so on. A person, for instance, may not be very much concerned if he gets an amount under the table or when a small favour is done for a gain, in return. Whereas, there may be another person who is totally against bribery or favouritism.

Conflict occurs in a situation when the employee is required to choose two equally attractive offers, for instance, the dilemma of a man whether to marry the girl whom he loves, without dowry or the one arranged by his parents with a lot of dowry. Or a decision whether to accept promotion and get transferred to a remote place or refuse promotion and stay back to treat and care his ailing parents. Another situation is that the employee is caught in between two totally unacceptable alternatives.

A Purchase Manager has been asked, let us say, by his Director to buy a huge quantity of substandard raw material at a higher price so as to favour some of his relations. The Purchase Manager is against such unjustifiable action. If he does not listen to his Director, then his job is at stake. Such situations, in extreme cases, often cause neurosis in the person. The third situation is the result of attraction and repulsion values of a single object. For instance, an employee is in dire need of finance. He cannot get it from any normal source. He could, if he decides, get it by brow beating the customers or clients, without the knowledge of anyone in the organisation. But he has not done it. He is not a person of that type. He is sandwiched thus in between the emergent need for money and the desire to preserve his values. Result, the person turns into an introvert, giving a confused look, with lack of concentration and disinterest in work. Same is true in the first situation mentioned earlier.

It is difficult to diagnose the problems of the employees unless their superiors are concerned about them. This requires an attitudinal change. The employer-employee gap in interpersonal interactions within the organisation will have to be considerably reduced, if not totally eliminated. For this, the managers will have to find time, in the midst of their busy schedules, for an informal chat, a sincere chat, with at least their own subordinates. They must understand the syndromes, study the causes and try to help them. If cannot help, at least show the willingness to help and sympathise. These are the ways to human bondage and unity in an organisation.

Good Relations

Most executives agree that good employee morale is important to the success of a business. However, not everyone agrees about what creates good morale. Again and again, studies have short that employee morale is not simply a matter of money. A sense of being appreciated and a feeling of "belonging" are at least as important.

But how is recognition imparted? How is feeling of belonging fostered among such diverse groups as plant workers, clerical staff, branch office managers, field salesmen ? Should there be a company magazine ? An annual picnic ? A labour management committee ? How does management show its interest without appearing patronizing or insincere ?

There is no one "right way" to establish good employee relations; there are only basic principles to use as guidelines. Essentially, this is a belief in the worth of each individual, and recognition of his need for personal dignity and self-respect.

For an employee relations programme to be successful, there must certainly be communications—both ways. But how you communicate depends on employee attitudes in your company and information gaps which may exist. Only after the level of employee understanding and awareness has been determined can steps be taken to boost morale and efficiency by correcting misconceptions.

Look for particular trouble spots, or opportunities. Are new employees being properly indoctrinated ? Is a projected company move to another city creating insecurity and bewilderment ? Are unfound rumours circulating ? Is the food in the canteen being well prepared and served? Are individuals being cited for good work ?

Since employee requirements are no different from the normal human requirements, a company that meets its employees even halfway is sure to generate strong loyalties. The key to good human relations is that people react to what they believe the facts to be, not what they are. More than anything else, a policy of fair dealing in all circumstances will keep employees happily and permanently wedded to a company.

Guiding Principles for Employee Communications : Below is the checklist containing very useful points :

(1) Do the right thing, then earn awareness and understanding of your actions.

(2) Make supervision people the main channel of employee communication.

(3) Give bad as well as good news.

(4) Use simple language.

(5) Have definite reasons for communicating, whether the issue involved is short or long-range.

(6) Provide for two-way communication.

(7) Know and reach the worker's family.

(8) Find out what employees want to know and, as fully and frankly as possible, give them answers.

(9) Emphasize events of significance to employees.

(10) Employ the best possible communications tools; use several for conveying major messages.

What Employees Want to Know : They generally want to know ; What are other locations doing ? How do government regulations affect us? What is company policy ? What is management doing to keep jobs secure ? What new job openings are there ? How is the company doing financially ?

They prefer to work for a reliable firm that makes promises it can keep. They respect an employer whose motives they have of to trust.

Getting Across to Employees : Whatever means of communication are used, employees prefer specifics rather than generalities. A good communications programme reaches an employee in terms of "what it means to me". It will be a continuous effort—not just an emergency stopgap. And the timing and integrity of statement will be reflected by company actions.

How should management communicate with employees :

(1) The spoken word (on radio, television film or in a speech) has great impact.

(2) A company with a long established communications programme and a record of reliability is most successful in presenting its side of an issue.

(3) Letters from company chairmen or high-level executives usually are well received by employees.

(4) Booklets are effective only if the language is easily read and understood.

(5) Company publicity in local newspapers has a high degree of believability.

Based on these guidelines, a successful communications programme can make use of any number of vehicles, from bulletin boards and handbooks to pay envelope staffers.

18

Art of Motivation

Management can encourage worker support by (1) providing opportunities for individual recognition, leadership and status, and (2) showing concern for the workers as a group.

Good employee morale is created both when material needs and non-material needs are satisfied. When employees understand what their company is trying to accomplish, they develop an emotional interest and a pride of association. This, in turn, leads to higher production rates, better quality product, and improved customer relations.

No relationship in society generated by motivational process will ever be continued for long unless the relationship is rewarding to both parties : we are friends with another only for gain or reward at minimum cost. The nature of the aim or reward comes from such intangibles as self-esteem, heightened morale, increased insight financial help, material gifts.

"The Mysteries of Motivation" : "There is a lot more to motivation than the fabled carrot and stick, especially at a time when workers have become more assertive."

"Low level motivators equal low level effort."

To get people to do mediocre work, one need only derive them, using coercive and reward power in a manipulative way.

To elicit their top performance, one must get them to drive themselves.

It is not the satisfaction that drives but the desire.

'High level' motivation resulting in high level performance must come from within an individual. It is the sum of a person's aspirations, values, self-esteem and sensibilities.

In his classic work 'Motivation & Personality' A.H. Maslow divided the range of a normal person's needs into five broad categories, *viz.*, basic creature comfort, security, social instinct, ego gratification and living up to one's image on oneself.

No one has an entirely equal complement of Maslow's five varieties of needs. It depends very largely on his or her temperament and background. The intensity of one need or another within an individual will vary according to circumstances.

The person most responsible for a person's motivation on the job is his or her immediate boss.

The results of surveys of workers' attitudes show that present-day employees place a strong emphasis on challenge, opportunity and recognition of performance. They are more willing than their counterparts of a generation ago, to quit a job that does not offer these things.

The most successful leaders are always those who pay most attention to the people who follow them. If a leader cares about what happens to his followers will care about what happens to him.

Psychologists stress that Work is a major source of self-esteem.

The most fiendish punishment, the military mind can devise initial having a prisoner do something entirely useless, like scrubbing his cell floor with a tooth brush or painting a pile of rocks. They must be made to feel wanted within that system.

The bosses who are most concerned about their subordinates get the most out of them in the form of high quality work.

Practical Pointers

Your Role in Motivation : Managers, as we all know, "get things done through other people". Next to planning, directing, controlling and the other textbook defined roles you play, motivating is an unspecified yet critical part of your management function. You set an example for your employees and your own motivation—or lack of it—is obvious in your behaviour and work patterns.

Motivating is not something you can schedule from 9.00 to 9.50 on Wednesday mornings. Rather it is a process that requires your continuing commitment, and objective view of your own management style and an understanding of your effect on your employees.

Today's employee is no longer a cog in a massive work force of synchronized behaviour, as Alvin Toffler states in The Third Wave.

Workers still want money—especially with the current inflation rate and cost of living. But money does not have the clout it once did in motivating people. Workers are more seriously considering family, life-styles, and personal goals. They don't feel compelled to give blind obedience to the organization employing them.

Employees went respect, a sense of accomplishment, recognition, responsibility, advancement and personal development among other things, etc. They're probably the same-things you want.

Set an Example : Demonstrating your attitude by playing the lead is a good move ; more likely than not, your employees will follow suit. If you are not prompt, conscientious and consistent, you should not demand those qualities of your staff.

Communicate : Keep employees informed about what is going on in the organization. People resent having information dumped on them after the fact; they like to feel they are trusted with information as it becomes available.

Speak plain English. Avoid jargon and obscure terms that may intimidate or inhibit people. Demonstrate your willingness to explain a task or request that was not clearly understood and be alert to indications that you are not getting through to someone. Make your expectations clear and follow the old adage, "Say what you mean and mean what you say".

Actively listen. Listen to what people are really saying—not what you want to hear them say. Make time available to staff so you can meet without interruptions.

Got to know your staff. Do they have career aspirations of which you are not aware? Do they have outside activities or talents that are interesting? The workplace is not someone's entire life. Have an awareness of the person as a whole, rather than as cog in your machine.

Involve Your Employees. Allow flexibility in decision-making, especially in areas directly affecting your employees. Giving them the opportunity to make their own choices can increase their personal commitment to the organization and their feeling of control over their jobs. Such decision-sharing can include work schedules, task production activities such as setting deadlines, logistical decisions, day-to-day activities and any other areas determined by you and the employee.

Include employees in the goal-setting process. Encouraging their participation allows them to have more of a stake in helping accomplish the goals set.

Interact with your employees as regularly as possible. Make yourself available for give and take. And, don't do all the talking all the time.

Allow opportunities for employees to feel a sense of accomplishment. Let them know how their work fits into the organization by helping them understand how their tasks relate to organizational goals. People like to feel their work is significant and that they are making a contribution.

Respond to Your Employees. Give frequent feedback. You don't have to wait for appraisal time. In fact, whether' your comments are positive or negative, letting people know how they are doing is most effective immediately following the performance that warrants it.

Be Supportive. Write a praise memo for an employee's file.

Help workers reach career goals by offering your advice, and expertise.

Demonstrate respect for your employees. For example, avoid making staff sit in your office while you are on the phone (their time is as valuable to them as yours is to you); avoid cancelling or scheduling meetings at the last minute (they also have schedules to maintain) : and don't ever admonish an employee in front of others (especially their peers).

Recognize and reward staff. Help them get awards when you can. If you can get a raise or promotion for a deserving employee, make every effort to do so.

Invest in Your Employees. Some managers contend that motivational techniques such as bonuses, job enrichment programmes and other institutional incentives are satisfactory. Yet, in our society's changing social and economic structures, it is still important as managers to remember that employees are individuals. Many managers agree that little can replace motivating on a one-to-one basis.

Yes, this is time-consuming and no, you can't spend full-time of motivating your staff. But you can develop your motivational skills and assess your opportunities to use them. Think about those things you can honestly say you already do and those you would feel comfortable trying. Think of alternative actions for these that just don't seem to fit your style. These suggestions neither pretend to offer innovative insight nor discount new approaches being attempted. They simply reiterate that the Golden Rule can be as effective in the workplace as anywhere.

(A successful man is one who can lay a firm foundation with the bricks that others throw at him.)

No Big Lies

"By and large Corporate leaders do not tell lies but sometimes some of them omit some facts in their talks or speeches; but not in Corporate disclosures as they know it is risky."

In recent years, there has been an increasing interest in the disclosure of financial and business information to a much wider variety of corporate stockholders and interested parties than in the past.

Traditionally, information contained in companies' annual accounts has been directed towards shareholders and creditors, but changes in the social, economic and political environment, particularly over the past decade, have brought into question the role of the corporation in society, along with a consideration of its rights and obligations.

From this has evolved the notion that the reporting responsibilities of the corporation should be extended to encompass its wider obligations, which in turn has stimulated debate concerning the amount and type of information that should be disclosed and how such disclosure should be secured.

One result of government legislation has been that in recent years, greater efforts have been made towards the presentation of financial reports in a way which makes for greater appreciation and understanding, particularly by people with limited financial knowledge.

Clarity and simplicity combined with adequate disclosure are the essential objectives of good financial reports. The basic purpose of financial statements is to transmit reliable and useful information to interested groups both inside and outside the company.

People Interested in Financial Reports :

I. Inside a company:

(a) Shareholders : They are primarily interested in dividends, the retention of profits and growth prospects.

(b) Management: The concern here is with evaluating results and using financial reports as a guide to controlling the business.

(c) Employees : They hold shares if the company has a profit-sharing scheme. They may also, for example, be concerned with the relationship between profits and wages earned and use the balance sheet information as a basis for wage negotiations through their trade unions.

II. Outside a company :

(a) The Inland Revenue : The share of profits in tax is high and the correct determination of taxable profits is of great importance.

(b) Creditor, trade creditor : They need to know about the financial stability of the company and the prospect of receiving payments for debts owing to them.

Debenture Holders : Although their loans are generally secured on assets, they are interested in the realisable value of those assets.

Banks and Financial Institution? : They also lend funds and are concerned with the information contained in financial reports before making loan.

(c) Potential purchasers : Anyone interested in buying a company or menrine interests wishes to have information regarding the realisable value of assets, goodwill, and records of past financial performance.

(d) Other outsiders : Government bodies, research institutions and trade associations may use balance sheets to establish trends and conclusions regarding particular industries, products or services.

The two traditional statements shown in the annual reports of companies are the balance sheet and the profit and loss account or the income statement.

The balance sheet reveals the financial condition or status of a business reflected in the accounting records at one particular moment of time, usually the close of business on the day indicated by the date of the statement.

The income statement of a manufacturing or a trading concern shows primarily the revenue realised from the sale of goods or services and the costs incurred in the process earning the revenue. Also, the statement reveals the net income or net loss resulting from the operation of the business during the period covered by the report. It is a statement of activity and the results of that activity.

The profit and loss account is concerned then with financial transactions over the whole of the financial year. On the other hand, the balance sheet looks at the state of the business at a particular moment of time usually the end of the financial year.

The balance sheet is, therefore, rather like a photograph of a railway train, which does not normally reveal anything about the speed of the train, if it is moving—and the direction in which it is travelling. It gives a snapshot and not a moving picture of the business.

In recent years, the profit and loss account has been regarded as a much more important financial document than the balance sheet, as most of the asset figures shown in the latter statement are based on historical costs rather than current values.

The balance sheet itself is not indicative of current economic realities. It records costs of assets purchased at different price levels lumped together without adjustment and, therefore, without regard to the unequal value of the rupee in different years of acquisition.

The growth of inflation implies an adjustment of historical costs to rupees of current purchasing power and this in turn is leading to the production and publication of supplementary reports showing the effects of inflation on capital values and earning.

Inflation accounting, therefore, is a vital necessity at times of escalating inflation. Philips of Eindhoven (Holland), the electrical giant, has used a system of 'replacement accounting' for over 20 years in order to compare the performance of its overseas branches on a realistic basis.

A few large companies in India have started this practice and it is hoped that more will follow suit before long as real profit can only be measured on the basis of the current purchasing power.

The funds statement is in no way a replacement for the profit and loss account and the balance sheet, although the information which it contains is a selection, reclassification and summarisation of information contained in those two statements.

The objective of such a statement is to show the manner in which the operations of a company have been financed and in which its financial resources have been used and the format selected should be designed to achieve this objective.

A funds statement does not purport to indicate the requirements of a business for capital nor the extent of seasonal peaks of stocks, debtors, etc.

A funds statement should show the sources from which funds have flowed into the company and the way in which they have been used. It should show clearly the funds generated or absorbed by the operations of the business and the manner in which any resulting surplus of liquid assets has been applied or any deficiency of such assets has been financed, distinguishing the long term from the short term.

The statement should distinguish the use of funds for the purchase of new fixed assets from funds used in increasing the working capital of the company.

The funds statement provides a link between the balance sheet at the beginning of the period, the profit and loss account for the period and the balance sheet at the end of the period. This statement should form part of the audited accounts of the company.

Many large and medium size companies disclose such a statement in their annual accounts in European countries.

In recent times social problems have tended to move to the centre of political debates and the search for solutions to social problems has assumed importance.

The interest in social responsibility accounting is a response to this development. It widens the scope of conventional accounting by considering the social consequences of corporate decisions.

The areas which should be covered by social accounting include pollution control, equal employment opportunity, charitable contributions, plant safety and employee benefits.

The advantages of social disclosures, briefly, are:

(a) Increase in personnel morale,

(b) a large labour pool from which employees can be chosen,

(c) improved public relations, and

(d) a better corporate image.

Annual Report

Every year, major corporations spend exorbitant amounts of money on an elaborate ritual called the annual report. And every year, a large percentage of stockholders, securities analysts and others who receive these reports litualislically file and forget them—sometimes in the nearest waste basket. Ironically, many public relations practitioners, at least subconsciously, do not view the annual report as a communications tool, subject to the same canons of readability and pertinence that dictate other written communications. Instead of relating to their main audience, the broad financial community, they relate only to a select group—members of their own corporate boardrooms.

While two of the three basic elements of an annual report, financial disclosure and the president's letter, provide standard fare from year to year, the third element, discussion of operations, provides a golden opportunity to tell the company's story to both the professional and casual investor. This section in often the only part of the report the casual investor reads. The professional analyst looks here for information that goes beyond law requirements. The opportunity to influence both of these broad publics, however, is often squandered.

Doing the job right means more than just presenting surface facts. It means discussing what inputs go into making day-to-day management decisions, why these decisions are made, and how they are executed.. In short, a sound discussion can pique the interest of the uninitiated, and reinforce the faith the present investors have in the company.

Once a solid bedrock of goals is decided upon, the public relations practitioner can then stretch his creative imagination to the limit in developing a format. In other words, selecting a format should always follow the determination of objectives and nature of content. Doing the opposite would be tantamount to tailoring a made-to-order suit before measuring the wearer.

The Advantages

In assembling current financial year's annual report, one format is—a question and answer session with each of the company's operating managers. This format can easily backfire, especially if the manager is allowed to write his own question, *i.e.;* interview himself. However, if the questions are based on field research, the format can yield a high impact, information laden presentation.

First of all, using this format provides a means of acquainting stockholders with management. Showcasing the men who actually make the decisions establishes a one-on-one relationship with the reader, particularly effective in reinforcing the average stockholder's trust in the company.

Stylistically, the format enables the writer to make quick transitions from one subject to another without seeming to be abrupt. In an expository framework, it is necessary to set up each topic with introductory and transitional sentences. On the other hand, consecutive questions can deal with different topics. The net result is that more information is provided in less space. Economy in presentation is becoming increasingly important, as the financial disclosure section continues to take up more and more report space each year.

Stylistic advantages can be frittered away, however, if the material presented is equivocal, misleading, or propagandists. We encourage our managers to specifically address problems and explain grey areas of company policy. They sometimes had to reveal some painful facts. For example, manager of our real estate division, when asked why this area of business was not going well, admitted that management had miscalculated in forecasting the real estate market. He pointed out that there would be no new investment in this business segment. The manager of our water treatment equipment segment, when commenting on record earnings, warned investors not to look for the same level of increase for next year. The question and answer format gave our financial vice-president the opportunity to explain our policy on investment, in the process giving insight into the company's rationale for diversification.

Implementing Format : Based on our experience, we would like to propose some ground rules that might be followed in implementing this format. They are not hard and fast, but they can help you avoid spilling some blood and sweat while assembling the report, and some tears afterward.

Keep your "ear to the ground" throughout the year for questions addressed to your company's chief financial executive by analysts and other investors. Continuing contact with the financial executive who maintains day-to-day contact with analysts should enable you to build up a log of pertinent questions by operating area.

Before plunging in, have a solidly established financial public relations programme already in place. We have used analysts' and bankers' seminars to acclimate operating managers to a "firing line" situation, in which they are asked the type of meaty, tough questions that we would want them to answer later in the annual report.

Use a formal survey for querying key analysts, and possibly a sampling of stockholders, to determine interest in the format, and what kind of content would be desirable.

Sit down with each operating manager personally before the interview is conducted, and assure him that the questions are not designed to embarrass him or cast doubts about his management capability. Be firm about objectives, however. A manager's ego should not be allowed to interfere with the need to describe the company in its totality. Explain that problems should be referred to along with methodology for solving these problems. Stress the importance of candour.

Even if you take this final precaution, there is a good chance you will probably receive some mundane or equivocal answer on the first attempt. In our case, the president decided that some of the questions were not tough enough. Therefore, we went through the interrogation process a second time. At a time when corporate credibility desperately needs shoring up, a brand of personal candour that transcends barebones disclosure can go a long way toward bolstering individual company's image. Answering critical questions in an annual report framework can do the trick. The key word is "critical", be sure the questions are worth answering, and most importantly, that your audience is interested in the answers.

19

Financial Public Relations

Rapid economic growth in the 'developed' countries has to a fair extent produced its own impact on 'developing' countries like India. Our economic growth is slow. Nevertheless, it has created a somewhat large middle class having some discretionary funds available for spending or saving. One result: investing in securities is no longer regarded as a privilege of the wealthy. Another is the steady emergence of specialized financial PR counsellors to discriminate and interpret facts to present shareholders, and to the rest of the financial community.

When it comes to a single company's financial relations, the investing public can be divided into two categories: (1) actual shareholders of publicly owned corporations, and (2) professional financial opinion leaders. In the first group, many owners of securities are new investors seeking a better return on accumulated savings; many are novices in financial affairs, unfamiliar with the specialized language of the financial community. The second group consists of the security analysts, mutual fund researchers and managers like Chit Funds, investment counsellors, insurance company analysts and executives, bank officers—stock and share brokers who influence the judgement of other investors.

The Advantages

The growth of financial public relations can be traced to many factors. Among them : the need for equity financing arising out of the tremendous postwar growth, educational campaigns by the Stock Exchanges to encourage investment in publicly owned corporations; the existence of a broad group of individuals looking for ways to put their money to work.

Financial PR is not a means to "push up" the price of a company's securities. While informed stockholders and professional analysts may indeed help maintain a better stock price, good financial public relations can limit the ability of raiders to take over; increase the company's ability to borrow funds; attract and hold key personnel; lead to more favourable terms when arranging corporate loans, or issuing stock.

Besides circularising information on a company's position in its industry, its current activities, earnings, future prospects—so it can be evaluated as an investment—a programme of financial PR leads to a broader base of stock ownership, a stronger bargaining position when acquisitions are made through the exchange of stock, and support from stockholders and the financial community during a period of adversity.

Shareholders can often become customers too, or at least salesmen of goodwill for the company. Articulate, loyal shareholders work in a company's interest—buying its products, urging others to do so.

How to Communicate ? : Few active investors have the time or knowledge to analyse the comparative merits of securities. Some rely on what they read in journals devoted to 'commercial intelligence', market letters or Stock Brokers' Bulletins; some depend on recommendations from their investment advisers, bankers, brokers, security analysts, trustees of estates; some weigh the information in annual reports.

A corporation must prepare an audited financial statement for its stockholders once a year. But in today's competitive money market, it is a rare company that stops at the legal minimum. Most companies use personal visits, telephone calls, mailings, and supplementary reports to keep shareholders informed, interested and satisfied.

The Shareholders

Problems of communication have led to increased use of surveys as management sought more information on stockholders' characteristics, knowledge, attitudes, and motivations. Initially, the questions were simple : Who are the stockholders ? Are there more men or women ? What are their occupations ? What is the average number of shares they hold ? How long have they held them ? In how many other companies do they invest ? How shareowners first learned about a company and what prompted them to acquire stock; why they maintain their holdings; why they might sell in the near future; their age, education, occupation and family income; whether they buy company products; how they feel about dividend policies; how they characterize management; whether they are satisfied with the information they receive about the company. Such attitudes and opinions within the financial community—among security analysts, brokers and dealers, investment bankers, and the financial Press—are often assessed in these ways.

There are many ways to cope with survey results and reinforce or change the stockholder attitudes they reveal. Such communications may include reports on the annual meeting, dividend enclosures, magazines, special mailings, financial Press releases and periodic correspondence.

A few companies in India mail their annual reports to the stockholders, the Press, suppliers, libraries and selected persons in the financial community; and each new stockholder receives a personal welcoming letter encouraging him or her to ask questions at any time. Yet a few other companies send out reprints of speeches and magazine articles by company officials, copies of the company internal or external house publications, special fact books contain in statistical information on the country as also brochures on the company. Companies often arrange for interviews and plant visits by interested analysts.

Business and financial editors do an excellent job of reporting and interpreting corporate news. But space for financial news in even the largest metropolitan newspapers is limited, and much of it is generally devoted to market reports, tabular listings of earnings, and dividend sections furnished by services. Moreover, we have in India only a handful of newspapers and journals which have special business and financial pages.

How Does the Investing Public Choose the Right Company to Invest in : Investing in a company is very much like being a top-flight executive who is faced with an option of choosing one of various job offers.

The name of the company is important. But equally, or even more important, are the answers to the questions : Where is the company going ? What are its growth prospects ? And will I be able to grow with it?

Here are the guidelines for the 'investor' :

1. Take a good look at the 'profit and loss statement'.

   If you are looking for a growth-oriented company to invest firstlook at the sales and profitability record to gauge the soundness of the company's business strategy and its execution.

2. Study the 'balance sheet' carefully.

   You should know about the sources and utilization of funds.

   Supposing the company has doubled its gross fixed assets over the years or anywhere near it, it indicates that the company has been, steadily increasing its capacity to earn more.

   Similarly, if the 'reserves' too show such a trend during the same period, the company's capability to invest in additional productive capacity in the future. This indicates continued growth.

3. Consider the intrinsic value of the share.

   The secret of being successful investor is not merely to invest in a "BlueChip" company but to invest in a company before it becomes "BlueChip".

   Only then do you have more to gain.

4. Find out from the experience of existing shareholders.

   If they convince you about continuous payment of substantial dividend, then you are in for a sound and profitable investment in the company you have decided on.

5. Judge the standing of the company in the industry it is in.How does the company, you plan to invest in, rate, with the others in the field? Are its aspirations realistic? Does it have infrastructure and the professional inputs to realize them ?

6. The company's contribution to the community.Examples:

   (i) Contribution to the national exchequer, by way of correct and prompt payment of the tax dues.

   (ii) Foreign exchange earned.

   (iii) Health care of the community.

   (iv) School programme aimed at educating school-going children from low and middle income families.

   (v) Community service programme to improve the quality of life in the community like :

   Encouraging Fine Arts and Culture, outdoor recreational activities amongst the youth in particular, and other projects which may benefit the under privileged and the handicapped. Going for Public Issue.

Since the Financial PR has a lot to do with public limited companies, it is necessary to take a look at the way they are promoted and the way they go public and secure share investment from the public. This would be clear if we take up any public limited company. For example: Allwyn Nissan.

Allwyn Nissan is a public limited company promoted by Hyderabad Allwyn and has started its operations recently. The company has been set up to manufacture light commercial vehicles of 3-tonne capacity each.

The financial structure of the company envisages that the promoters of Allwyn Nissan would hold shares, and also offer a part of the shares to the public. Offering shares to the public is generally known as 'going public'.

What the company does is that it determines the total financial outlay for the organisation and works out the quantum of equity (share investment) and debt that the company can have. Generally debt equity will be in the ratio of 2:1. This means that company can borrow from financial institutions, such as, Industrial Development Bank of India and Industrial Financial Corporation of India twice as much as the share investment. As has been mentioned earlier this share investment comes from promoters and in this case it is the Hyderabad Allwyn Limited as also the general public.

Securing share investment from the general public is where public relations has a role to play. The PR focus is on informing potential shareholders about the company. Financial public relations is a planned, organised communication effort to gain recognition for the company and its policies. The underlying motive is to gain their acceptance for the company, its goals so that they eventually become the shareholders of the company.

Once a decision is taken about going public there are certain requirements under the Companies Act of 1956 which are mostly of statutory. These are taken care of by the Company Secretariat or the Finance and Accounts Department of an organisation. However, the Public Relations Department of an organisation has a key role to perform, prior, during and after a public issue.

Support for Public Issue : Prior to public issue, while the company is fulfilling statutory requirements, PR provides the necessary interface by creating a climate or an environment where the public issue will be a success. This is done by building the corporate image of the organisation, by disseminating information among prospective shareholders on such aspects as the history of the organisation, policies, programmes, product range, market share, growth prospects, anticipated profitability. Dissemination of this information can be done through corporate publications such as booklets, brochures and audio-visual presentations. However, by far the most effective means of disseminating information about a public issue is through the media of newspapers, financial dailies and magazines.

Public Relations Departments plan and secure coverage for the organisation at the time of pre-issue through news media by organising press conferences at leading share market centres such as Bombay. This news coverage in important daily newspapers helps one who is looking for share investment opportunities information on an organisation and who may be eventually influenced and persuaded to buy shares. This type of "build up" in media is almost invariably attempted by organisations planning to go public. The press conference gains in importance, since it is addressed by the chief executive of a company. As it happens, the press conference and the resultant media coverage generate a great deal of interest and need for information in prospective shareholders. This is where the corporate publications mentioned earlier can fulfil the information needs of the public.

Public relations has a role to play during the period of public issue by sustaining public interest in the ongoing public issue. Given a good corporate image, the public issue is bound to succeed.

It is after the public issue that the role of public relations becomes even more pronounced having to address "Welcome Letters" to the shareholders, establish a channel of communication with them and sustain the communication link. While the company secretariat or the finance department would mail to the shareholders the share certificates, it is the PR department that would send out the welcome letters. With creative orientation, public relations can contribute a lot to making the shareholders feel happy with the company.

Annual General Meeting : In public limited companies it is mandatory that once a year a meeting of all shareholders is held to review the performance of the company, to appoint directors of the company as well as auditors for the next financial year. This meeting is known as Annual General Meeting. While, here again, the company secretariat calls for the Annual General Meeting, the PR department provides the necessary interface by evolving suitable communication material covering financial highlights of the company, new product developments, and other related information which will make for appreciation of the company, its policies and programmes.

The Annual General Meeting provides an opportunity to the PR Department to provide an overview of the company and also an occasion for the shareholders to get information relating to various aspects of the company's performance. This is generally in the form of question and answer session with questions posed by the shareholders and answers given by the Chairman of the company.

Open House for Shareholders : Shareholders would be interested in knowing what production facilities the company has, how products are made, how the quality of the products is ensured. They would generally want to know about the working of the organisation. This aspect is taken care of by throwing open the company to the shareholders who can inspect it. The open house for shareholders is planned and executed by the PR Department.

Shareholder Newsletters and Annual Report : Different companies have, different approaches to shareholder newsletters. While in some companies this may be a monthly newsletter, in others it takes the form of quarterly reports or even half yearly review reports. At any rate, all the companies provide annual reports to shareholders. It is necessary to understand the distinctions between these different types of reports.

The Annual Report is a document brought out by companies providing information as per statutory requirements, whereas monthly or quarterly or half yearly reports are not governed by any statutory requirement. Public Relations Department plays a key role in the presentation of such reports. Indeed, most companies' Annual Reports are designed by Public Relations departments with considerable creative input in them. Here again, the Public Relations Department has to work in coordination with the company secretariat and the Finance and Accounts Departments.

Article 46 of the European, Economic Community's Fourth Council Directive states that:

1. The annual report must include at least a fair review of the development of the Company's business and of its position.
2. The report shall also give an indication of:
   (a) any important events that have occurred since the end of the financial year.
   (b) The Company's likely future development;
   (c) activities in the field of research and development;
   (d) the information concerning acquisitions of own shares.

The Downfalls

Unlike man, a business firm might be expected to live for ages. However, statistics of voluntary liquidations and bankruptcies, merger notices and posters announcing a 'closing down' sale tell a different story.

In many ways the life of a company is similar to a human being's. We can distinguish a number of common phases in the life of a commercial enterprise:

- The prenatal phase
- infancy
- adolescence
- maturity, and sometimes, a sad forewarning of the end,
- senility.

Difficult Situations

At the start of the prenatal phase the outside world notices little or nothing of your future plans. As the founder, you will be fully occupied with negotiations with financiers, attorneys, architects and contractors, government departments and important suppliers. At any time during this phase you can decide not to proceed further. Outsiders only become aware that your business is taking off when a start is made with alterations to your premises, recruiting to staff and other activities.

During your company's infancy you will probably spend most of your time increasing your number of business contacts, customers, and range of products and services you offer. When you have overcome a multitude of difficulties and points of friction, inside as well as outside the business, you have reached adolescence, 'You seem to be doing very well' say outsiders.

At the zenith of your company's existence everything seems to be going nicely. You have built up a stable circle of customers, your turnover shows a steady annual increase, and profitability is maintained at a healthy level. Nothing indicates that this happy state of affairs will not endure for ever.

Every phase has its own characteristic risks and problems which may create special dangers for your company's future. We still have to meet the entrepreneur who has never been worried about how things might turn out.

What are the most critical phases in the life of a business ? If you wish to determine the critical phases in the life of man, you can consult official population statistics. You will soon discover that at certain ages the probability of deaths is greater than at others. It is also possible to discover the most prevalent causes of death. In our experience we have time and again found that the rare certain typical causes of business death, which tend to occur at specific points in its life span.

Three Mortality Peaks : Just as people, a business can die at any age. It is possible, however, to discern certain peaks, one of which is two to three years after its official birth, for which we take the date of its registration. No information is available about the cessation of activities during, the prenatal phase—what one might call termination of the pregnancy.

A second but less marked peak occurs eight to ten years after the company was founded. At that time more enterprises tend to fold than during the immediately preceding or following years. The third and lowest peak often is found during a period of 25 to 30 years after the company's inception.

Naturally these peaks must have causes and it is interesting that each is often the result of a fatal combination of circumstances during the company's infancy. This lasts only for a limited number of years, but may repeat itself. This happens if you embark upon a fairly radical change in products, markets or technology—your company rejuvenates itself, and once more is exposed to the characteristic childhood ailment.

First Peak—Fatal Starting Errors : The causes of death during the childhood of a company are often the result of cardinal errors made at or near the time the company was founded.

Unattainable objectives, *e.g.*, an unrealistic assessment of the size of the market for the products to be manufactured.

- A start on too grand a scale relative to the available funds, so-called under-capitalization.
- Insufficient reserves to cushion the impact to unavoidable adverse periods.
- Short-sighted shareholders who want to dispose of their shares too soon or expect immediate, exaggerated dividends.

- An un-business-like attitude by the owner, manifesting itself in excessive cash withdrawals.

Each of these can be fatal in itself, and when more than one of these unfortunate circumstances join forces, the result is seldom in doubt.

Second Peak—Growing Pains : The second mortality peak, about eight to ten years after the company's establishment, is usually found just after the middle of its adolescence. In this case, however, the causes are of an entirely different nature.

- Cut-throat competition from older companies who have become progressively more worried about the newcomer's success.
- Competition from new companies who are trying to emulate the success of your company.
- Failure on the owner's part to adjust his sight as the company grows.

In many cases the founder of the business will have started as the sole owner-manager. His views have prevailed, no matter whether he was right or wrong. As the company grew it became more difficult to attend to all matters in the degree of detail required. The development of the enterprise now demands that he reconcile himself to the necessity of delegating part of his authority to capable colleagues who specialize in a particular field. If he persists in doing everything himself, matters will get out of control and his ablest colleagues will leave him. Wrong decisions or—equally bad no decisions are taken. In short, the transition from owner-managership to multimanagership does not take place. Even the healthiest business can succumo to this well-known phenomenon.

Third Peak —Misguided Conservatism : The last, low peak is a frequent consequence of the retirement or death of the owner/founder. Assume that as an enterprising young man he started his own business in his early thirties. He has guided his company astutely through all phases to the summit of its existence. After some 25 or 30 years of intensive work he has the choice of slowing down or of becoming another statistic among those dying of heart attacks.

In either case he is forced to leave the business to others or to sell out. He may let his son succeed him, even if in his heart he knows that this is not the best choice. Enter the Trojan horse. From maturity the company rapidly moves into *senecence*, with the usual terminal result. If he sells the company, it still remains to be seen if the new owner will be able to emulate the founder's success.

An alternative explanation may be found in the owner's constrvatism which during his lifetime has already led to the company's deterioration. Possibly the founder has become progressively less open to suggestions for new possibilities, or less readily prepared to venture into new directions. "We've been trading successfully for thirty three years now. Why should I now suddenly change? Circumstances change and demand adaptation. The penalty for misguided conservatism in business is no different from that found elsewhere in nature. The company becomes extinct.

Corporate Security

Several kinds of factual material are used by analysts as yardsticks in comparing one corporate security with another. Among them are :

(1) Statistical data over a 510 year period on such items as sales, cost of sales, net income before and alter taxes, earnings per common share, number of shares outstanding, common stock dividends and reserves.

(2) Nature of capital expenditures (to learn if a company is keeping abreast of competition in modernization and expansion).

(3) Scope and direction of research, and the relationship of new product development to research programmes.

(4) Relationship with unions and the terms and expiration dates of current contracts with labour.

(5) How inventory accounts are being handled: what portion of a company's sales are for Government (defence); how much money is spent on advertising.

(6) Foreign operations, and how they relate to domestic operations.

(7) New markets, new methods of distribution, changes in marketing policies, and new products.

Generally, analysts are concerned with the long-term market outlook, not short-term patterns. They examine company performance, management competence, and general business conditions, using balance sheets, annual reports, prospectuses, and personal interviews, they first determine a company's position in its industry, and then the position of that industry in the economy as a whole.

Some good rules to follow when dealing with analysts are the following :

(1) Make sure the analyst understands management's policies and the reasoning behind them.

(2) Do not regard an analyst as a competitor; some information you have labelled as "classified" need not be kept confidential from him.

(3) Do not withhold information unless you absolutely have to because of company policy.

(4) Do not attempt to conceal bad news; your action will be held against you when the facts come out.

(5) If there is a startling development in the company, let the analyst know by mail or telephone.

(6) Do not play favourite; try to remain impartial.

(7) Do not try to force conclusions on analysts; conclusions are his business.

Annual Meetings : Unfortunately, many companies in our country go about them in such a way that they have nearly degenerated into a ritualistic farce: whereas, those overseas believe that the idea of an annual meeting is basically sound, that the annual meeting offers management a special opportunity to state its case, and the annual meeting of stockholders' "day in court".

Some companies are continually seeking new and more effective ways to use annual meetings to inform and educate stockholders, to explore investor thinking, to test new ideas, and to introduce new products.

For every company using the annual meeting as a vehicle for product demonstration or promotion, or to show films acquainting shareholders with company capabilities, there is another which believes in quick and quiet annual meetings. Their arguments : let's do away with frills and put "business" back into shareholders meetings; the annual meeting is a legal forum and not a picnic; stockholders come to learn whether their investment is being properly managed."

The following is the kind of checklist a public relations counsellor uses for the annual meeting :

(1) Site selection—convenient to stockholders, near a major transportation centre (or perhaps a travelling meeting).

(2) Announcement—invitations, proxy statements, advance publicity.

(3) Agenda—making the meeting well-paced, swiftly moving and efficient.

(4) Role of officers—review, of accomplishments.

(5). Equipment—microphones at convenient locations, ushers with hand mikes, special displays (if any).

(6) Refreshments—box lunch, buffet, cocktail party, or nothing.

(7) Traffic control—check rooms, seating arrangements, directional signs.

(8) Press coverage—invitations and accommodations.

(9) Contingencies—overflow of crowds, bad weather, underattendance.

(10) Follow-up—post-meeting report to all stockholders.

The best "training school" in the world for a Financial Public Relations Executives is in their attending the other companies' stockholder meetings. It will also be a good idea if such executives and others responsible for annual meetings buy token amounts of stock in both competitive and non-competitive companies to keep abreast of the way these companies handle stockholder relations.

How Companies Hold Meetings? **:** Companies abroad generally take to the road—rotating the annual meeting from city to city in an effort to tap buying power or to help educate shareholders in smaller cities and towns. But many companies hold annual meetings where they maintain plants or facilities.

20

Corporate Citizenship

"In the field of modern business, so rich in opportunity for the exercise of man's finest and most varied mental faculties and moral qualities, mere money-making cannot be regarded as the legitimate end. Neither can mere growth in bulk or power be admitted as a worthy ambition. Nor can a man nobly mindful of his serious responsibilities to society, view business as a game, since with the conduct of business human happiness is inextricably interwoven."

"Real corporate citizenship is to be found in achievements comparable rather than with those of the artist or the scientist, or of the inventor or the salesman. And the joys sought in the role play of corporate citizenship must be like their joys and not the mere vulgar satisfaction which is experienced in the acquisition of money, in the exercise of power or in the frivolous pleasure of mere winning:..."

Minds are tough to change. But trends do change. With it 'business" is changing—faster than a lot of people's attitude towards 'business'.

Indian business is steadily coming out to invest more money year after year in strenuous efforts to communicate the benefits of competitive enterprise.

Yet survey after survey reveals that public, like political sentiment, sometimes tend to be critical about big business.

Such a trend suggests a common problem. And a credibility problem at that.

It also suggests some possible corrective steps towards more effective communication with the public.

Since, as we all know, public opinion is ultimately the controlling force in our democracy, an informed public is really one of the costs of building the business further. That would naturally involve 'business' in the task of restoring its credibility. And that is to level with the public. It is here that Public Relation as an arm of management function emerges.

With the catalytic role that public relations professionals are, of late, playing in the realms of private as well as public sector enterprises, there has been a perceptible shift in public relations emphasis in the direction of a more intensive involvement with the operational side of the company's business. The trend is towards an involvement with short-term and long-term operational problems to enable a company to function at its optimum capability in an environment that may not always be sympathetic.

Corporate managements of today are pursuing more tangible objectives than mere "images" and increasingly the public relations professional in the organization is seen more as a corporate 'reputation' ("image") builder. For, as many of us know, large business corporations everywhere in the world are being given increasing scrutiny. This is understandable.

A sizable economic enterprise is a matter of justifiable public interest—sometimes concern—in the community and the State, and the country at large in which it is located. And when substantial amounts of goods, services and capital flow across State and national boundaries, the public interest is, logically, even greater. For, the public judges business corporations in human terms and assigns to them human values. How?

Many corporate personalities stem from the one dominant personality by whom the corporation was originally founded. For example, Jamshedji Tata, Ghanshyam Das Birla, T.V. Sundaram Ayengar. In some multinational corporations the shadow of the original 'Founder' will hang over the decisions that are made. In some cases, this is of great benefit to the corporation, but in other cases it may not be.

Whether the corporation's personality originates in part from its founder or has merely created it, a recognizable personality for good or for ill, it is up to the management to discover what this personality is and to see whether there are benefits to be gained by its exploitation or changing it in order to bring it up to date.

Nothing is offered gratis in this very pragmatic world, not even life itself for which many pay dearly. We must never forget the basic principle of a free society which is this: For every privilege granted to the individual citizen there is coextensive responsibility which should be voluntarily assumed.

This is especially true of all business and non-business corporations. Each one of us must have constantly before him the thought that what society has granted, society can take away.

Man's control over the material world has grown to be far greater than his mastery of himself. Man, not material, is the chief problem of the world today. Man, not merely machines or material objects, should be the chief subject of our future study and research.

Against this background, business throughout the free world needs to perceive that the creation of goods and services take into account not just the production of profit for investors but also the effect they produce on the total design of society. And that is the only step to earning the title of "Good Corporate Citizen".

Therefore it is that business corporations set forth their own *beliefs* based on ethical convictions and international business experiences that date back to the turn of the century. This can be self-imposed code and it need not attempt at prescribing actions for every business encounter. It could be an attempt to capture the basic, general principles to be observed by good businessmen every where. To the extent their actions match these high standards, such can be a source of pride. To the extent they don't, these standards should be a challenge to each of them.

Personal Code of Corporate Ethics

I. "Our first responsibility is to our customers :

1. Our products and services will always be good. We will strive to make them better at lower costs.
2. Customers 'orders' will be promptly and accurately filled.
3. Our dealers will be helped to make a fair profit.
4. Our "after sales" service will be dependable, and our relations with customers will be cordial.

II. "Our second responsibility will be to those who work with us —the men and women in our factories and offices:

1. They will have a sense of security in their job.
2. Our wages will be fair and adequate commensurate with the social and economic environment in which we operate.
3. Working hours will be conducive to production, and working conditions clean and orderly.
4. There will be opportunity for advancement for those well qualified and experienced.
5. Each employee will be considered, first, as an individual, standing on his or her own dignity and merit.

III. "Our third responsibility is to our Board of Directors.

1. Our executives will be persons of talent, education, experience and ability. They will be persons of common sense and full understanding.

2. Promotions and incentives to employees will be on the basis of 'how good are they to the Corporation' ; not how good are they to individual bosses.

IV. "Our fourth responsibility is to the 'communities' in which we live.

1. We will help maintain the character of good corporate citizen by supporting good works and charity, and bear our share of taxes.
2. We will endeavour to generate the feeling that all the properties we are privileged to use are ours, first.
3. We will participate in civic improvement (promotion) programmes : health, education and good government, and acquaint the community with our activities.

V. "Our fifth responsibility is to our shareholders : Business must make a sound profit.

1. Reserves will be created, research will be carried on.
2. Adventurous programmes developed, and mistakes are not repeated.
3. Bad times will be provided for. High taxes paid—instances of heavy tax burden will be represented to the Government via the good offices of the Federation of Chambers of Commerce and Industry.
4. Outdated machines written off and new ones purchased to ensure quality and efficiency of production.
5. New factories built, new products launched, and new sales plans developed.
6. We will experiment with new ideas.
7. When these things have been done, the shareholders will receive fair return."

Corporate Image

The 'Random House Dictionary' has 20 definitions for 'Image'.

Let us imagine, for a moment, what will happen when this word "image" is scattered around 20 Board Rooms of major corporations—with its 20 definitions, of course? A sort of confusion is apt to be the result!

To many businessmen, it is panacea for all corporate ills, a magic communications elixir to whitewash all spotted reputations. Others ascribe it to a fictitious creation of ingenious "copywriters" prompted solely by rewards in the form of advertising commissions. Yet, to many thousands of businessmen, it is a hard uphill task of trying to get its public to think of them as they should be thought of.

Image is basically a mental representation or a conception. While an image may be clear in a person's mind, reasons he or she gives for holding such a view are often hazy, vague generalizations. Yet, these summations make up what is known as the "image".

Is 'image-building' just a fancy description of Public Relations work ? Public Relations is undoubtedly involved work but the building of a reputation—"image building"—is not the exclusive preserve of any one communications skill or department. It is a part of every facet of the company's activity that involves communicating and dealing with people.

Undoubtedly, it is a, glib term, a cliche and it is considerably misused, abused and overused, and, yet, we cannot overlook its strategic importance. As Peirre Martineau says: "The business executive cannot afford to scoff at the subject of images, because people are acting towards his company on the basis of them and not on the basis of facts and figures." Impressions once formed get stereotyped and are difficult to change. They are emotional filters that are used by people who are seeing and listening. They tend to cause us to reject what we do not agree and tend to pass material which, is agreeable, unchallenged. Thus a good image has a halo effect and nothing succeeds like success.

The practical way to project a clear persuasive corporate image begins by focusing it on the corporation itself. Each phase of corporation's activity adds meaning to the picture in the public mind. Nothing is perfect, but management and public relations men may have to face up frankly to several internal problems before any face-lifting is effected.

What can you, as management, expect from the public relations man in this area ? Is overall image really his responsibility ? Can indeed anyone hope to coordinate all of the diverse happenings in a corporation into a clear understandable corporate image ? The answer is yes. It does fall to the Public Relations man to assume this responsibility. He is usually in the best central position to mobilise and synchronize all internal and external resources and factors necessarily involved in company-wide actions and decisions.

The most direct way for a company to project its character to the public is indeed advertising—institutional advertising—and yet there are infinite number of meanings and situations that cannot be approached by advertising. For instance, the format of the annual report, the sales policy, the leadership of the executive management, the climate surrounding the company environment, its participation in local and national problem-solving and many other countless considerations that provide the functional dimensions to advertising.

Hence, Public Relations programme needs to be developed in the light of each firm's circumstances and business and has to basically cover the whose, the whats, the whys, the wheres and the whens of a company. Questions need to be asked as to who are you now and what is your present image? First, You must determine the character of the company before you sensibly weigh the existing image. Does the company have corporate objectives? If you can unearth them somewhere in the archives, they are probably out of date. Once you find them, can you truly challenge the *status quo*? You have to take out insurance against unpreparedness. Overconfidence spells out obsolesence. It is not enough to have well-manicured projections. It is important to determine the abstract values inherent in future growth.

Once you have looked closely at your image either through research or surveys or any other means, chances are that you will get some rude shocks. You can talk all that you want about being a good corporate citizen and yet what your public feels and what you think they should, may be miles apart.

The next question that one has to ask oneself is why do you want to change your image and what kind of image would you like to project ? The company that asks these questions is certainly the most virtuous of all companies. There are some general guidelines. For instance, to the customers, it makes the best products. To the shareholder, it is the best financially managed company. To the employees, a benevolent management. To it neighbours, the leading citizen and so on. These are the goals which ape the same as those of almost every other company. There is no argument about it, but that is where the problem lies. By saying that we should fall in with the Joneses you will not solve the problem. Be more specific or perhaps more candid about your goals. You must recognize that a company cannot be all things to all its public. What has to be determined is what is important to you. This will help you to set the foundation of corporate goals in the Public Relations context. And this is where the role of Public Relations department centres around.

When you have gone through this exercise, the next question that comes to your mind is what should be done to freshen up the company's image and where ? There is no best way to open on this attack. It must be diversified and it must be with almost a religious fervour. Whatever you do and whichever is your course, do not forget the "folks at home"—the employees. Difficult as it is in convince outsiders that the company has made a change for the better, it is even more of an assignment to convince the employees that it is so.

There are many pitfalls in the process of improving the corporate image. First of all, one must guard against too much optimism and too high ambitions. It simply cannot be achieved overnight. There is "no instant package" and anyone who suggests it is really a charlatan. The excess hardsell to win favourable image is both unrealistic and dangerous. It cannot be achieved by a heavy hand, by gimmickry or by far out advertising slogans or by corporate window dressing. Nor is the cure effected by simply endorsing the process of analysis and programming. Whether or not a corporate image is successfully changed depends, in the final analysis, upon the daily companywide effort to sustain this attitude. This is the seed of a new reputation. The job is not that of a Public Relations man alone, but it is his job to prime it.

From the foregoing, it will be evident that "image building" does not mean glorification. We know of at least two instances—one, Indonesia and another Ghana where their essays in self-glorification in foreign affairs have come to grief. Mature countries, including Soviet Russia, do not pursue their ideologies at the expense of their national interest.

You cannot create an image out of nothing; it has to have a substance. The influence that we exercise abroad is in direct proportion to the respect won for our achievements at home. "Prestige", said Lord Cromer, the Governor of the Bank of England, "is earned, not bought, least of all on borrowed money". In the matter of projecting a good image of our country, what is important is not what we say abroad but what exactly we do at home to provide enough food, clothing and housing to the people, and not what we are planning to do. Continuous plans which do not help the poor, and continual 'talk' about them by those in charge of the governance of the country will only erode the trust and confidence the voters place in them.

Corporate Identity

Company Emblems : A company identifies itself by its visual and non-visual contacts with its public. Some visual and non-visual contacts have become very popular. Some visual contacts are as follows:

The corporate name.

The logotype (lettering typography and/or graphic arrangement of the name)

The emblem or symbol.

The house colour or colours.

The characteristic—often tangible—common look of a company's products :

The uniforms, badges, flags, etc.

Printed matter (stationery, office forms, sales promotion, publicity material)

The displays, exhibitions and stands.

The audio-visual aids, films, etc.

In other words, everything carrying the explicit or even implicit 'company signature'.

The non-visual contacts are numerous, though not always as continuous as an organization's permanent visual manifestations. Amongst them there are both personal and impersonal forms of contact and communications, such as:

Personal contact (in sales, service, correspondence, telephone contact, etc.)

Impersonal contact by verbal communications (advertising, publicity, information through all media).

Direct or hearsay experience with its manner of doing business (pricing, delivery, reliability, speed of operation, integrity, informality or formality, flexibility, helpfulness, etc.)

These visual and non-visual contacts make up the corporate identity.

Corporate identity is a term used to describe the total identity and personality expressed and conveyed by an organization, both externally to the outside world and internally to the staff and executives of that organization. Ideally, the corporate identity should reflect the inner truth about the organization; what it stands for in terms of integrity and purpose, the sector of business in which it deals and the true value of its products and services. It is the amount by which the image can be improved by expert knowledge, and the importance of this to an organization's future development, that has led the practice of corporate identity into becoming a specialist function and one of the basic and fundamental tools of the modern marketing man.

Corporate identity is essential as a means of inspiring confidence among consumers, as a help in launching new products, as a means of attracting and motivating staff, as a reassurance to shareholders.

Corporate Image and Corporate Identity : There is some confusion about understanding 'Corporate Image' and 'Corporate Identity'. Some think that a name block or symbol is a corporate image. This is not so. The easiest way to explain corporate image is as follows :

> Everything we buy helps us to express our personalities, helps us to say to the world around us: 'This is the kind of person I would like you to think I am.' We buy products to assist us in this projection of our personalities. In effect, we see a mirrored image of ourselves in the products we buy. Image—a reflection of personality. Corporate bodies project recognizable personalities and people choose between competing brands very largely because the brand reflects their own personalities.

Corporate identity, on the other hand, is how you identify yourself: on your advertising, on your van sides—so that a symbol or a logotype can be part of corporate identity.

Therefore, corporate image is what people think about you and corporate identity is how people identify you.

A 'house style' is only one part of the corporate identity. Corporate identity saves money. This applies to the small man as well as to the multinational corporation.

Projects and Developments

Effective public relations coverage may be achieved through the exploitation of recurring activities, projects, and happenings which may regularly take place in any region of the corporation's operation during the normal course of any year. Most of these developments can be readily directed to national, and also international attention through various techniques of the public relations practitioner. The following are examples of news-making activity which are usually accorded coverage media almost everywhere:

Archaeological Digs : Often with an influx of foreign experts or student volunteers— proving, among other things, long identification with a region— calling attention to glorious roots.

Ecological Projects : Returning minerally exploited areas to greenery, preserving the ecology of industrial areas, etc., constitute important news and features almost everywhere.

Urban Renewal Project : Illustrate progress by a society through achievements in and; attention to a subject of national concern.

Transportation : New Rail roads, tunnels, subways, urban traffic solutions, new forms of public transportation hold worldwide interest, and often are also an attraction to potential investors and study missions.

Religious Life : The assumption of an important ritual by any religious leader is a recognized international story, along with decisions on religious doctrine and findings and ancient references, well received by foreign publics and usually treated with some deference by the press.

Senior Citizens : The care of the elderly is another subject of international concern in which public relations can benefit the client host country or organization, in terms of goodwill, respect and investment.

Agricultural Fairs : Wide interest in farm associated happenings is almost universal and illustrate the solid protective side of a nation or people—with which many audiences with roots in the soil can happily identify.

Medicine and Health Care : Health is another subject of worldwide attention, at every level, which can bring extremely positive results for single unit or collecttive public relations. Public relations describing new treatments, medical devices, drugs, research, disease control, all carry built-in international impact.

Opening of New Universities or Faculty Chairs : Exploit a worldwide regard for higher education at various halls of learning— or otherwise.

Historical Tourist Projects : Restoring and/or maintaining historical sites and offering them to a worldwide visiting public can produce international admiration, friendship, and investment in the framework of publicity achievable from news, feature, human interest, political, travel content.

Government : The traditional framework of a nation's governing bodies and processes; ceremonies, changing of political guard, inaugurations, opening of parliamentary or cabinet sessions, all can be utilized— wherever pertinent—to demonstrate democracy, stability, accepted governmental institutions. They exercise an inherent security for all who have political business or other interests in such a country, or have been approached for assistance or alliance.

Minorities : Programmes to advance minorities and immigrant groups, politically, economically and socially, always creates coverage, especially where viable progress can be illustrated.

Sports : Sports also offer the organized focus for hosting foreign individuals and groups, while achieving news space devoted to results.

The ASIAD held in New Delhi in December 1982 is an example.

Corporate public relations is almost an advanced professional weapon of extraordinary potential value not only to corporations under public and private sectors but, to a reasonable extent, to any individual or group, public or private body, wishing to influence minds and consciences and actions across their States as well as their national frontiers. Basic knowledge of its effect and applications can be a matter of considerable importance to those who are or will be concerned with information policy, marketing, sales,, promotion, exports, investments, joint ventures, capital, personnel, recruitment, overseas contracts, philanthropy, weapons acquisition for peaceful purpose, political agreements.

Although relatively new in terms of formal designation, calculated corporate public relations can boast both systemized procedures, and proven achievements in almost every field of publicity and geographic region. A studied examination of its practice should be required of all individuals involved in national and international information efforts of every type.

These include staff of government-supported institutions Information Services, the Spokesmen for official Bureaus, State Department Foreign Ministry personnel and official and quasi-official bodies of every type, and Fund Raisers, Corporate Executive in-charge of Public Relations and Marketing, Export Managers, Directors of International Philanthropies and their Publicity Chairmen, Advertising Personnel, Specialists in the Arts, Films, Music and Entertainment, University Faculties of Journalism and Communications. United Nations Common Market and staff of other regional multinational organizations, officials of binational Chambers of Commerce, of World Trade Centres, Investment Authorities, executives and public relations representatives of Cultural, Social Service and International Sports Federations.

Strategy for Publicity

"Two things indicate weakness—to be silent when it is proper to speak and to speak when it is proper to be silent."

Management is usually quite pleased when an article about its company appears in a trade publication or newspaper. When the story brings inquiries that result in new business, their reaction is usually one of surprised delight.

Unhappily, the matter is usually dropped at this point. This is regrettable because there are many more benefits that an article can provide if it is reproduced and used in the form of reprints:

> Reprints can make substantial contribution to a company's marketing programmes. When they deal with products or services being marketed, they are very valuable for salesmen to have as support for their sales presentations. They also give extra credibility to his statements and provide valuable reference information for later use by the prospective customer.

When an article is published in several countries, reprints tell an impressive story of worldwide press endorsement. This makes them even more effective as sales promotion literature.

They can be sent out in sales folders with price lists and catalogues. They provide a powerful dimension of increased believability when used with direct mail campaigns.

When available in different languages, they are usually useful as literature in trade shows. Multiple language reprints are not uncommon. Public relations firms with international press connections can and do arrange for this kind of publicity.

Foreign language reprints are also quite useful for out-of-country visitors coming to the head office.

When used inside the countries where they are published they not only tell a strong marketing story but tend to overcome the sales resistance that comes from being a foreign corporate citizen in a strange country. In addition, they are valuable to distributors in those countries. However, experience shows that distributors must be taught how to get the most benefit from them.

Both foreign and domestic distributors should be advised of the publication of any article before it happens. This should be done at the time the journalist does his interview or when the public relations firm advises that the story is about to be published. Such advice eliminates possible embarrassment if the saleman is asked about an article that has appeared and he hasn't read it. Afterward, the saleman should be provided with copies of reprints for his own use.

Advertisements used in local and international publications can also be supported by reprints. Statements taken from published stories can be included in advertising copy to show how successful use of the products and services is being reported by editors. A composite advertisement showing headings of an article as it appears in many countries is a particularly compelling means of putting a message across.

While some articles appear by "accident" when editors decide on their own to write them, many result from the efforts of public relations people employed by the firm being publicized.

A great deal of time and effort is needed to produce the right kind of article. It must not only interest an editor but give a good description of the company's products or service. A particularly useful type is the case history that describes the successful experience of a user or users. Such an article indicates that the editor of the magazine endorses its validity ; something that is not possible through any kind of advertising.

When articles are submitted to foreign editors, it is desirable to have the material translated into the appropriate language in advance. This is necessary if the foreign editor is to judge its suitability for his readers.

However, a word of caution: It is wiser to submit an English language text (hoping that the editor or a member of his staff can translate it) than it is to offer him one that is poorly translated. Few editors have either the time or the inclination to study, read and rewrite material submitted to them in a badly translated form.

It is also important that the stories be translated into good journalistic language. This can usually be accomplished by a translation agency or a multilingual journalist in the country where the editorial is to be published. This ensures that the language will be suitable for publication and the cost is almost always less than that charged by local agencies.

Some firms give such a story to their out-of-country distributor to translate or edit. Translations of this kind are almost always unsuccessful. Even editing can be dangerous because unacceptable material plus spelling and grammatical errors may be included. If distributor editing is needed for any reason, the text should be checked by the translator again to be sure the language and the message is editorially suitable.

Copyright laws if they are not understood, can cause problems. The magazine can demand compensation for reprints if it owns all copyrights. No such problems occur if the editor is offered "first publication rights only" for the story. This means that all rights to publication after his first use are retained by the writer and his client. The publishing journal can't claim payment and it can't sell reprints without prior permission from the writer.

Reprints should carry the date of publication, the name of the magazine and the country of origin. They should be printed on a convenient paper size for mailing and distribution. Effectiveness may be enhanced if coloured stock is used to make the documents easily visible in office files. It is often useful to include information like the names and addresses of distributors in foreign countries and the prices of the products described. This information can be typeset separately for inclusion in the reprint.

Usually the typesetting as published in the journal or magazine can be directly reproduced by offset printing. The copy is usually cut and pasted upon a new background to eliminate advertisements and to fill an even rectangular shape. This becomes "camera ready" art, from which the printer makes his plates. The space used for photos is left blank because poor quality results if they are reproduced as printed.

New halftones from the original photos (retained for the purpose) should be given to the printer for him to reproduce in his offset printing plates. Only in this way can good photo reproduction be achieved.

While this method of making reprints is usually the cheapest way, the job can be done most simply by buying the finished work directly from the journal that carried the original story. However, the method described above should be kept available particularly when out-of-country magazines carry the story. Obtaining reprints under such circumstances can be time-consuming, complicated and excessively expensive.

The possible uses for reprints are extensive, many more then those mentioned here. Their cost is usually a fraction of that of conventional advertising literature. In addition, they have high cost effectiveness and high credibility. This permits national and international publicity programmes to be carried out where normal advertising costs would be excessive. However, they should only be considered as a means to open up markets for products and services that are newsworthy. They should not be expected to replace advertising.

Still, they are highly useful to establish early sales and earnings in both foreign and domestic markets. The income that results makes it possible to finance an ongoing advertising and promotional budget long after the subject-matter is no longer newsworthy.

Editorial publicity in combination with the effective use of reprints provides an effective promotional opportunity that should never be missed.

21

Social Purpose Advertising

This form of advertising is aimed at promoting social causes and also in areas relating to nation-building, education, health and medical awareness, rural development, civic issues, rights, art and culture, consumer protection, rights of women, national integration, energy conservation, helping the handicapped and disabled.

Anyone, whether companies, advertising agencies, professional designers and copywriters, public bodies and even individuals can also participate.

Social purpose advertising plays, a crucial role all over the social purpose advertising plays a crucial role all over the world. Its main function is to inform, educate, inspire, motivate and if possible persuade on the evils of the society and the community we live in. It could be something as important as putting pressure on governments to stop the arms race or to make them think awhile before investing in nuclear armour, or, it could be something as vital as strengthening community relations in urban slums or supporting the spastics school next door. It may even be a campaign to fight the evil influence of drugs on the campus, alcoholism among the poorer sections of society and social injustice, of dowry, bride burning ; exploitation and misery. The kind of awareness we are talking about is like the one an advertising agency creates by a campaign when a product is launched. It has its target audience. The consumers are persuaded to buy it, try it and often stay with it. The product becomes a national brand.

Reached Impact

The reach and impact of advertising is proved by the emergence of new categories of products, new brands and new companies. The myth of India being a nation slow to change due to old traditional beliefs, with rigid behaviour pattern, is changing in urban India.

But this change is not obviously visible in rural India. Hence the challenge for the people in communication is to try and accelerate this change. Here comes the need for public service advertising. Public service advertising must be used to help alleviate clearly defined problems in different areas with sustained campaigning to achieve the desired goal. It is similar to the launching of a product. Moving people to take action is what advertising does best. It can help a local community or national project by getting a large number of people aware, interested and involved in taking specific steps to support an activity or a cause. The basic implication of this approach is that those creating public service campaigns have to work closely with organisations or groups directly evolved with the public service project.

'Adopt an 80 year-old baby. Turn old age into the golden age'— says an advertisement. 'Won't someone give him the time of day' ? 'Some antiques have more value'—'It is your turn next', campaign creates awareness among the people that old people require our care and affection.

'By the time, you finish reading this line a baby is born' to signify the increase in population and need to contain the growth of population. Whenever you see colour, think of us runs an ad to emphasise the need to care for the blind.

These kinds of advertising are very important and play a vital role in society, particularly in a society like ours with complex issues. Public information advertising exposes these issues to more and more people, so that a greater awareness is created and thus inform the people about what is happening around them and what is at stake.

Leaders, writers, politicians, the Lions, the Rotarians, the social institutions and the public sector institutions have a new peer to reckon with now in creating awareness, aimed at building a good society.

Management Information System

Broadly speaking, one can define a management information system (MIS) as a system designed to provide information needed to manage an organization. Any enterprise is managed by means of a variety of decisions made at various levels of organization. These decisions form a connected set across the hierarchy of a decision-maker and also over the period. This is complex, dynamic and interacting. Any study of this structure should centre round the analysis of decisions. Decision can be taken as an appropriate unit of analysis. If critical factors in a decision process are the information inputs, *i.e.,* the availability of a particular type of information, its relevance and timeliness, etc.

Before going into details of characteristics and nature of MIS which is so often talked now, it will be relevant to understand the role of information in decision-making. From that understanding one fundamental idea in the design of an information system will be clear, *i.e.,* information *per se* has no value —it has value to the extent it contributes to decision-making and therefore it is not always correct to say that more information given to the decision, maker, the better the decision-making—this may or may not be the case. Therefore, the primary objective in developing a total management information system should be the production of detailed up-to-the-minute summaries of the past data and the use of it to project the future activity. In essence the functions of MIS are to predict, and to compare predictions with actual results and also to produce the deviations between the predicted and the actual. Thereafter the system should use these deviations to prepare a new, updated set of predictions which can be used as the basis for management decisions. This concept is known as 'Management by Exception'. But there are only a few instances where this concept has been applied in its fullest sense.

Therefore, let us understand information in its widest range. It includes knowledge of the organisation, environment, knowledge about persons, objectives, constraints, policies, procedures and techniques, etc. In a given decision situation, selection of a particular course of action depends upon the available alternatives and the relative consequences of indifferent alternatives available to a decision-maker. A decision-maker's behaviour depends upon the information status of the decision situation and on his values and preference at a given time. The information state, value and preferences depend on (a) the decision-maker's object system—this includes knowledge about budgets, specifications, schedules, policies, interactions with other decisions and also (b) the values and preferences derived from the objectives and constraints of the given task.

Parameters : The process of arriving at a decision can be described as follows. The decision-maker estimates the parameters of the information state for a given decision situation on the basis of knowledge of the objectives and constraints (including policy budgets, schedules and interactions with other decisions). The knowledge regarding the relevant physical laws, technical processes and environmental factors is an added advantage for the proper decision-making. Values and preferences are then derived from the objectives and constraints of the given situation. The alternatives available for achieving the desired outcome are defined from the environmental factors. If the information system contains the alternatives which lead to the optimal outcome, that alternative is preferred for decision-making.

Search Process

If it does not, the search continues. The search process for obtaining more information is generally directed to obtain information such as :

(i) information regarding better knowledge of physical process and techniques,

(ii) information that generates new alternatives and

(iii) information that enables to revise the objectives, constraints and interactions with other decisions.

These points are very pertinent in designing of information systems. Thus, basically, the purpose of designing the information system is to provide information for decision-making for operating, planning and coordinating functions of an organization. It includes all the components which are involved in decision-making, coordination and monitoring. The information system also influences the data flow quite effectively. For example, in deciding a policy of inventory keeping (which is considered to be a higher level strategic decision) details of issues of stock and reorder quantities, etc., are used as information. For operational level decision-making (tactical decision) decisions regarding issues of items of stock—when how much to reorder, use higher level policies as constraints. Thus policy decision at higher level imposes constraints at lower level, it thus becomes a piece of information for operational level decision-making.

For a system to be efficient, good communication of all types is necessary. This is especially true if the system being developed is MIS. Communications essential for the system development can be broken down into four categories: man to man, man to machine, machine to man and macnine to machine. It is more conventional to use this. Without good communications a system will be less efficient. If the system being developed is MIS then any degradation system efficiency could adversely affect the cooperation.

Thus there are many aspects of communication in the design and operation of the MIS. Man to man communication must be first and must be effective for the other three types of communication to be successful. As such, communication system planning and design must be analytical from inception and dynamic through completion.

Computerized management information system (CMIS) which is often much more reliable than informal MIS, normally augments, the existing formalized MIS by providing a feedback mechanism and linking the management to the happenings throughout the organisation.

Value Analysis : Tracing back the history of the Concept of 'Value Analysis', we would recall how the concept was originated in 1947 by Lawrence D. Miles whose forceful approach and questioning attitude had resulted in cutting down the total cost in General Electric Company by 40 per cent in spite of the increasing trend in the costs of raw materials and labour.' U.S. Navy too could, then, effect enormous savings as a result of introduction of value analysis.

To put it in simple language, value analysis is an effort to compare cost with the ultimate uses and returns from the products. Even though it was a cost reduction technique, it differed from other methods like Production Planning, Inventory Control, etc.

Value Analysis is use oriented, comprehensive and aims at long-range savings. The mathematical representation of the value is :

$V=\frac{U}{C}$ where, *V* stands for Value, *U* for Utility and *C* for cost.

It can be seen from this equation that the value can be increased either by increasing the denominator, that is, cost or by both the processes.

We, in India, have to learn more about the potentialities of value analysis from countries like the United States of America, German Democratic Republic, and Japan where, despite the high costs of material and labour compared with India, the product costs are lower.

The value analysis techniques, if widely adopted, can very much help to enable our products to penetrate through the rough and tumble of competition into international markets.

Techniques of Value Analysis : If value analysis has to be a successful move it essentially requires conviction about its applicability on the part of top management.

A prerequisite for application of value analysis is the 'attitude', and the technique to decide the attitude is to analyse the function of a product from the viewpoints of its primary, secondary and tertiary or subsidiary purposes.

For example, while buying paint, it would be necessary for surface coating for protection. Hence the attitude of the value analysis should be to buy "better surface protection" than paint, is called 'primer' in the words of the paint technologist.

The attitude should result in questioning the end uses, classifying them according to priority and investigating the cost against the marginal utility, urgency, essentiality, availability, quantity and quality.

To achieve this, one who uses the value analysis techniques has to answer the following ten questions:

1. Does it contribute value?
2. Is cost proportional to utility?
3. Does it have all the features?
4. Is there anything better to the purpose?
5. Can a useful part be made by lowering cost?
6. Can a standard product be used?
7. Are quotations competitive?
8. Does the total cost equal tooling, material, labour and over head costs?
9. Are there other suppliers at lower price?
10. Is there anybody else buying similar product at less price?

Once these questions were asked for a given item, and the answers graded, then this would result in locating potential area of the application of value analysis.

The decision techniques would be :

1. Eliminate
2. Retain, or
3. Change

These three could be achieved through modification, incorporation, subdivision or substitution.

The value analysis is one of the productivity optimization techniques. It should be applied to the decision a well as every process stage and periodic review is essential.

Here it would be appropriate to mention about the 'value levelling techniques which we had occasion to observe in one or two industries in the North. By this technique, items in a group were plotted on a graph, indicating the quantities against their values. If any item deviated from the normal trend of other items in the same group, it was isolated for being subjected to value analysis.

Application of Value Analysis

Dr. Attwood illustrated the application of value analysis with the help of two case studies where the application had resulted in enormus saving. We in India should take an approach which is suited to our environments.

The first case study is regarding the manufacture of a micrometer frame. Dr. Attwood explained the "DARSIRI" method which was adopted in the case. The term "DARSIRI" is an acronym for a series of words indicating the various processes involved in the value analysis application, namely, Data collection, Analysis, Record of ideas, Speculation, Investigation, Recommendation and Implementation. The case showed how the profile cutting method recommended by the DARSIRI approach in the place of the existing milling method helped to reduce the cost per piece to Rs. 1345 from the original cost of Rs. 1888.

The second case illustrated how, as a result of value analysis, the packing cost of a company could be substantially reduced by substituting the existing wooden case with corrugated cardboard boxes.

A good value analyst should have technical background, right type of experience, professional interest and ability to communicate, ability to visualise long-term benefits, cost consciousness, creativity, ability to appreciate others' ideas and leadership qualities; and should present the value analysis findings in a brief tabulated format, highlighting the existing procedure with its cost aspects against the proposed methods and costs.

Productivity **:** Productivity is the efficiency with which outputs are produced the ratio of output and input. There are two distinct types of productivity ratios, total productivity and partial productivity.

$$\text{Total Productivity} = \frac{\text{Total Output}}{\text{Total Input}}$$

$$\text{Partial Productivity} = \frac{\text{Total Output}}{\text{Partial Input}}$$

A commonly used example of a partial productivity ratio is labour productivity which is nothing but output per manhour. Another commonly used productivity ratio is the value added index. It is calculated by removing the value of raw materials and purchased parts from the numerator and the denominator of total productivity ratio. The value added index, therefore, equals partial output over partial input.

Total productivity of an organisation can be described as follows:

$$P = \frac{O}{L+C+R+Q}$$

where

P = total productivity

L = labour input factor

C = capital input factor

R = raw material and bought out parts input factor

Q = other miscellaneous goods and services input factor

O= total output

Identifying the Areas of Corporate Manager's Operation : "More wages for less work seems so pleasant. But of course all it does is raise costs which raise prices which destroy job."

"More social security, more and bigger Government projects... higher and higher minimum wages (with obligation to earn them)... ...and ail costs of doing business become so high that incentive is strangled, and our idea of welfare State becomes weaker and weaker—the idea that everyone willing to work can go into business, and prosper."

"It looks so easy, to pass a law or amend the Constitution with the object of giving everyone everything he likes. But in this world *everything* has to be paid for—and the 'freebie in the sky turns out to be very sour and expensive indeed."—The 'Pie in the Sky' is lemon".

Realm of Operation : The categorized functions of Corporate Managers are :

Community Relations

Public relations should be responsible for :

1. Encouraging participation by executive and key employees in civic affairs.
2. Providing executive leadership and individual financial support to worthwhile causes—Red Cross campaigns, Ramakrishna Mission, National Calamity Relief Fund, etc.
3. Giving generally in both money and manpower to health and welfare, education, professional and civic fund-raising drives of a community-building nature, in accordance with corporation policy administered on a uniform basis.
4. Arrange periodic surveys of public opinion, conducted for the corporation by independent sampling organisations.

5. Maintaining a system of routine daily calls on residential customers by trained employee-interviewers.
6. Conducting periodic reviews of customer service and accounting policies and procedures to make sure that they are adequate, understandable and friendly.
7. Determining the particular "social" needs of the community and then developing specific corporation-led or company-sponsored programmes designed to help meet those needs.
8. Advertising and otherwise publicizing the corporation as "a good place to work", not only to attract job applicants but also to humanize the corporate image.
9. Taking a position of genuine leadership in area development by means of industrial expansion efforts.
10. Conducting tours of corporation facilities for organized local group—and occasion "open house" for the general public.
11. Maintaining (and vigorously promoting) a corporation speakers' bureau.
12. Keeping ahead of technological developments affecting the electric or allied public utilities, and making sure that the public is aware of the company's investment in time, energy, and money in research and development.
13. Planning, organizing and staging special events, anniversaries, and other company observances in a manner that emphasizes, above all, the identity of interest between the company and the communities and people they serve.
14. Making sure that company properties are so designed, landscaped, and maintained as to provide an example of Responsible industrial concern for the environments in the communities in which the company has facilities.
15. Instating and properly maintaining attractive and uniform identification of the company with the community.

Public Information

Public relations should be responsible for:

1. Planning, preparing, and distributing news releases concerning company and its industry developments of public interest or concern.

2. Arranging and conducting individual interviews and collective press conferences between company executive and representatives of press, radio, and television.

3. Maintaining a prompt, efficient, uninterrupted press information service that operates round the clock, 365 days a year, to answer inquiries from press and radio, TV people relative to service interruptions and the like as soon as they are received, at any hour of the day or night.

4. Publishing institutional advertisements regularly in daily and weekly newspapers and important regional magazines throughout the company's service area.

5. Planning and processing personalized mass mailings, made over the chief executive officer's signature, to newspaper editors, radio and television executives, educators, religious institutions, public officials, another local opinion leaders calling to their attention current developments on the local or national scene that importantly affect the company, the industry, their area, and the public interest.

6. Promptly and fully satisfying requests from public and school libraries throughout the company's service area for factual material concerning the policies, practices, and accomplishments of the company and the industry.

7. Organizing series of "Editorial Roundtables" between the company's top management and the editors and publishers of area and regional newspapers, magazines, and radio TV stations and networks. These "Editorial Roundtables" are not conceived as meetings for the working press. What

the company should be looking for at them is knowledge and understanding from the *policymakers* of the news media of the company's position on issues of public concern.

8. Developing and distributing widely (via televisions, speakers' bureau, and/or commercial theatre showings) motion pictures portraying the company's operations and highlighting the economic advantages of the company's service areas.

Customer Information

Public relations should be responsible for :

1. Sending "Welcome" letters signed by the chief executive officer to customers new to the company's service area, including helpful or desirable information concerning rates, procedures, and service facilities.
2. Preparing an attractive booklet summarising "what every customer ought to know" about the company, its rates, and facilities.
3. Developing a periodical customer publication to be mailed as an enclosure with each bill or timed for delivery to each customer's home with his bill.
4. Giving the company's, "contact" employees special public relations training for general guidance in meeting customers and the public.
5. Periodically reviewing the company's collection letters, correspondence forms, and the like, to make sure that they promote a friendly understanding of company policies.
8. Developing brochures and other informative material directed to specific customer segments—women, farm groups, small business proprietors, etc.
7. Preparing special mailings on company and industry problems for transmission over the chief executive officer's signature to customer-stock-holders.

Employee Information

Public relations should be responsible for :

1. Making sure that the employer publication regularly reviews' and reports on major industry developments, accomplishments, and problems of critical importance to the company and therefore to its employees.
2. Providing company supervisors with special public relations training to improve their human relations with their employees and to inform them about economic and political issues affecting the industry locally and nationally.
3. Preparing material on major company and industry developments for use at employee meetings or conferences and in conducting the question periods that follow.
4. Using bulletin boards in well lighted employee traffic centres to focus employee attention on current public relations approaches and on current problems of the company and the industry.
5. Developing for use in conjunction with the indoctrination programme for new employees, informational materials that properly stress the company's history; business and policy, an employee manual covering the aims of the company and the industry, as well as the rules and regulations of employment.
6. Providing a sound public relations approach for the company's booklets on safety, medical care, pension, and other matters of special employee interest.
7. Making applicable items among the suggested activities listed above in this section available to retired as well as active employees.

Stockholder Information

Public relations should be responsible for :

1. Explaining public relations problems and objectives of the company and industry, in terms of special current

developments, in the company's dividend folders and other stockholder communications.

2. Preparing and sending to all stockholders a transcript or highlights of the chief executive officer's remarks at the company's annual meeting.
3. Making sure that each stockholder inquiry receives a prompt, personalized response, signed by the chief executive officer, the secretary of the company, or the officer to whom the inquiry was directed.
4. Distributing to all stockholders occasional reprints dealing with developments vital to the company and the industry and making other reprints available to interested stockholders on request (the offer normally being made through the dividend folder).
5. Arranging periodic surveys to ascertain the characteristics and performances of the company's stock holders and their basic reasons for investing in the company.

Relations with Dealers : The relations a manufacturer has with his dealers, like those he has with the public, is said to be 'dealer relations'. It is conditioned by many things, though perhaps principally by three basic factors ; the quality of his products, his trading policy and practice, and the image he creates of himself. These, of course, are fundamental factors, and their significance must be given major consideration by the PR Manager. Though product quality is not his responsibility, the PR Manager, through his normal outside contacts, can help to gauge trade and public acceptability, and his subsequent recommendations based on this experience can provide a useful guide to those concerned with product development.

Broadly speaking, the actual ways of communicating with the dealer will vary, depending on the methods of product distribution. If this distribution indirect from the manufacturer to the dealer, so too will be the communications route. If, on the other hand, distribution is effected through agents or wholesalers it will be necessary for some part of the contact to be made through this intermediary channel, not only to retain what has already been established as a normal procedure, but to retain also the personal local link which already exists between the manufacturer's field representatives and his dealers.

Making contact with the dealer is, in many ways, no different basically from making contact with the public. While techniques and methods may vary and emphasis differ, contract with both is still made either through word of mouth or through established media.

Individual and regular contact by field representatives is considered necessary by most manufacturers as a normal extension of their sales effort. By this means orders are taken, point of sale material is delivered and erected, and local advertising and promotion schemes are coordinated and controlled. More efficacious than this sole method of communicating policy is periodical regional or national 'impact' meeting. Whatever is done this way could be as a marketing, sales promotion, or merely a 'get-together', it is still essentially a public relations duty to ensure that the impression it leaves on the dealer's mind is the right one, and that the total image created is successful.

Preparation can never be too thorough. Meetings can take many forms from a staged and dramatized presentation to a simple product talk and demonstration, and to some extent prior investigation into the accommodation to be used will vary in scope and detail depending on this factor. Nevertheless, investigation into the proposed venue should be thorough and pleasant.

Factory visits are of immense value and though in some cases not always easy to arrange or to administer, will repay the time and effort spent. It is on occasions of this kind that words like 'quality' assume new meaning, and what were hitherto simply names become invested with substance and personality.

Another feature of maintaining close contact with the dealer lies in providing all the dealers with regular copies of an 'external house journal'or news sheet. This should carry news and views from manufacturer to wholesaler, stockist, agent, distributor and retailer. The journal should contain advice on display, promotions, public relations, literature ; in fact, on anything that is calculated to improve the dealer's turnover and consequently his profits.

Running of dealer competitions, cooperative advertising schemes, and dealer training schemes also come under the ambit of the PR Manager.

The regional or national meeting can be supplemented by smaller and more informal locally sponsored dealer meetings followed by lunch or dinner and if it could be possible an entertainment programme ; dramas or film shows. Direct mail can be addressed in Christian name terms, advice on displays and promotions can be practical instead of theoretical, and sales training can be undertaken in the dealer's own premises or within his locality. Liaison with the local peess to further on a provincial level the relations established by the manufacturer with the national and trade press is another important function that can be undertaken by the agent or wholesaler, and in this the PR Manager should give guidance and help.

This facet of PR perscn's job can exist in four forms :

1. With customers choosing goods across a counter ;
2. With customers seeking a manufacturer's branded article from a retailer;
3. With customers buying something in which a component is made by a company different from that selling the main article—as in TV sets.
4. Customer relations exist between manufacturers selling to wholesalers or other manufacturers.

Personalities, personal service, and personal impressions play a vital role in the total customer relations of an organization. However efficient all the departments of an organization, regular contact with the customer, the person who buys (and thus keeps the seller in business) spells good PR. Customer relations is an integral part of a coordinated PR programme. So, it is advisable that a senior executive is in charge of this important portfolio.

A checklist for the PR Manager :

1. Do the customers know of the existence of the department, its functions, and how it operates?
2. Is the office planned to give the visitor confidence that he or she will meet with friendly, helpful, and efficient service?
3. Are the staff correctly selected for customer relations work or, in other words, have they the ability to handle people with empathy?
4. Is there adequate print and advertising material in the company's customer relations programme and policy?
5. Is all handling of customers on the telephone, by correspondence, or personal visit efficient, accurate, and friendly?
6. Can a customer meet and talk with a director of the company Quickly if the executive in charge of customer relations deems it advisable or necessary?
7. Are the employees of the company familiar with the customer relations policy and its programme?
8. Above all, does the customer know the extent and the nature of the service he can call on through the department?

Dealing with Complaints : Complaints made by customers are a source of deep concern to management and of irritation to the staff. It's human nature to take offence at a complaint when it is known that everyone from the man or woman at the counter up to the general manager of the firm is striving mightily to see that no preventable cause for grievance is given. But the clumsy handling of one little customer complaint by some harassed or frightened clerk may upset the earnest efforts of the whole organization.

Prevent complaints. Sense dissatisfaction. Appreciate that complaints are valuable. Do not cover up where and when it should be done. Make a constructive and positive approach. Analyse complaints. Avoid arguments. Create a feeling that the customer is right even though the fact may be wholly or partly different. A satisfied customer is like money in a bank as a deposit. Remember a customer is doing you a favour in that he or she buys from you instead of from your competitor. Try to compromise. Be courteous always. Remember correspondence is a poor means of communication as compared to face-to-face talk and a warm hand shake. Acknowledge any complaint at once, indicating to the complainant your interest in it. Make a speedy investigation; give your decision without delay.

Right to Safety

Consumerism : The core of consumerism is in the right to safety, the right to choose, the right to complain and the right for redressal. Whatever the aims and the method of operation of consumer movement organizations, results cannot be achieved in an environment of poverty and ignorance and corruption which makes the consumer bear the brunt of exploitation.

How many people die of food poisoning at regular intervals in many countries ? How could a circus tend collapse in Bangalore killing 70 school children ? Why should children die in other ways: unsafe crackers, badly made toys and grossly adulterated sweets ? Unsafe buildings collapse and kill hundreds of people; inadequate care and attention to 'preventive maintenance' of buses and taxis claim many lives of innocent passengers. And how safe is journey by rail, these days, is a question which can be answered by all correctly. Apart from regular derailments robbery on moving trains has become a regular feature.

The right to choose is limited only to certain luxury goods. Most of the services are monopolistic. The postal and telephone services, electricity, water banks, life insurance, mass media like Television and Radio are all State-owned and the consumer has no choice but to endure bad service without protest. Even if protests are made by consumers the government has a way of circumventing them. But if such protests are followed by violence the government in India, especially, relents. Where transport is nationalized, the consumers' choice for travel is also restricted.

When consumer complaints are processed many times one comes across in the law many loopholes which stalls the progress of the case. Hence it is very vitally important that a Consumer Protection Act is introduced to plug the loopholes to ensure effective protection for the consumer.

Our advertisements are generally unethical in that claims of quality are invariably exaggerated. A medical man will claim to cure all the diseases with his medicine. High pressure salesmanship has invaded even the remotest villages selling everything from soft drinks to unnecessary household appliances.

Consumer organizations alone cannot fight high pressure salesmanship, and exploitation advertising with its massive resources. Consumers must recognize that they themselves are responsible for the rise of this phenomenon, and it is their money which keeps it going. Therefore, only when consumers become more discerning and demanding, only when they realize that in this buyer-seller relationship, it is they who have the upper hand, can the consumer movement ever make an impact.

Protection Charter : Government machinery has to ensure that the manufacturers come under the ambit of a 'Charter'. It could be like the Seventeen Nation Council of Europe which has adopted a 'Charter' aimed at protecting shoppers against sharp trading practice. The 'Charter' must insist on manufacturers to accept and discharge the duty they owe to their patrons (consumers), by comprehensive legal protection and active assistance.

The 'Charter' should demand, among other things :

1. Minimum standards to protect consumers against dangers from products.
2. Protection against demands for payment for unsolicited goods and high-pressure selling.
3. Advertising must not be misleading and, if proved, must be corrected.
4. Labelling of products and the 'legend' of services must be accurate.

5. Legislative change must be considered to maks all improper trading practices illegal.
6. Children should be trained in consumer matters.
7. Voluntary consumer organizations must be encouraged, by all possible means, by the government and consulted on laws and regulations.
8. State and public services must provide for the appointment of consumer representatives to their boards of management.

Classified Components of Corporate Public Relations Work

1. *Writing.* Reports, News releases, Booklet texts, Radio, TV copy, Speeches, Film sequences, Trade paper and Magazine articles, and technical material.
2. *Editing.* Employee publications, newsletters, shareholder reports, and other communication directed to both organization personnel and external groups.
3. *Placement.* Contacts with the press, radio, and TV as well as with editors of magazines. Sunday supplements, and trade publications, with a view toward enlisting their interest in publishing an organization's news and features.
4. *Promotion.* Special events, such as press parties, convention exhibits, and special showings; 'Open House', and anniversary celebrations; special day, week or month observances; contests and award programmes; guest relations; institutional movies; visual aids.
5. *Speaking.* Appearance before groups and making the requisite plan for finding appropriate platforms. The preparation of speeches for others, organization of speakers' bureaus, and delivery of speeches.
6. *Production.* Knowledge of art and layout for the development of brochures, booklets, special reports, photographic communications and house periodicals as required.
7. *Programming.* The determination of need, definition of goals, and recommended steps in carrying out the project.

This is the highest level job in public relations, one requiring maturity in counselling management.

8. *Instutional Advertising.* Advertising a company's name and reputation through purchased space, time. Close coordination with advertising department is maintained, and frequently the advertising public relations responsibility is a dual one.

9. *Other Functions.* Gathering of intelligence, enabling an organization to be responsive to its natural constituency. Another is representation of an organization on frequent occasions in projects related to civic, social, educational and cultural advancements.

A third is the interpretation to government bodies and voters of an organization's interest in matters of public policy.

And the fourth is the training of effective spokesman for an organization.

"Today's corporate environment demands from Public Relations personnel the skills of a General who knows how to make war, the talents of an advocate who can speak for his client, the strategy of a politician who knows what strings to pull, and the knowledge of a psychiatrist who understands how crazy people are and why craziness is not so bad."

22

Community Service

Today community life is organised along ; the lines of interest groupings, whether the interest is in lower taxes, higher wages, a new civic auditörium attraction in industry, cultural facilities, or whatever. These groupings come and go, shift and overlap, each community is different anti-ever-changing. This calls for constant catalouging of the influential in community affairs and requires programmes tailored to fit the specific community—its people, history and problems.

The first step in community relations is to tag the decision-makers. Persuasion of these key individuals usually facilitates persuasion of their followers. Each stratum in the community develops its own leaders. The nominal leaders may not be the real leaders. In one town the Mayor is a leader; in another, he is a puppet. Identification of opinion leaders requires probing.

The Basic Approach : Before thought leaders or the community at large can be persuaded in a specific direction or as a unified force, there has to be an understanding of the town's mutual interests. It is necessary to know what the community wants for its well being, what part it expects each organisation to contribute toward that, and how it measures those contributions. The interest of the community will all fit somewhere in the eleven elements :

1. Commercial prosperity
2. Support of religion
3. Work of everyone
4. Adequate educational facilities
5. Law, order and safety
6. Population growth
7. Proper housing utilities
8. Attention to public welfare
9. Varied recreational and cultural pursuits
10. Progressive measures for good health
11. Competent Municipal Government.

Accepting these elements as the scope of community interests, the communicating organisation must somehow identify itself with them. It must show how it serves those interests. As a turning point, the underlying attitude of the organisation must be one of sincere interest in serving.

Organisational policies constitute a positive expression of attitude. They form the framework of a "personality" with which the organisation is endowed in local opinion. The singular personality may be in fact composed of decisions rendered by a management policy committee. Most likely, the opinions will attach themselves to the personality of the headman. He becomes the symbol. People tend to identify actions and attitudes with people, not with building in which people live or work.

Beyond attitudes and personality there is the factor of participation; The organisation cannot stand alone from the parade put on downtown by the local merchants or the town meeting discussing a new city auditorium. Nor can the officials of an organisation neglect responsibility to get into the blood stream of community life. Community relations cannot be delegated to a

on that project or topic. For, "If I give you a rupees and you give me a rupee, we each will have one rupee. But if I give you an idea and you give me an idea, then we both have two ideas."

The seven "areas" in which a group can work effectively are:

1. Leadergroup relations
2. Group drive
3. Membership qualification
4. Procedures
5. Finances
6. Meetings, and
7. Committees.

The Philosophy : Here are some of the questions that deserve thinking over and which can prove as starting points as we look over our own reasons for taking part in community activities of various kinds.

1. What is a community ?
2. What is the basis of community life ?
3. How should knowledge be used ?
4. How should we look at change ?
5. What is our part in community service ?

A community is an area which can be mapped. It includes those people who feel a sense of belonging to a centre, such as a village, a town, a city. It is not identical with any political unit since community boundaries tend to spill over city limits or even across country sides.

(For Graduates Studying Public Relations)

Roll No.

(i) Name of student:

(ii) Name of village assigned :

(iii) Period of work :

(iv) Nature of work :

(v) Survey:

PART 'A'

1. First contact with, say Sevagram, village :
2. A short history and some salient features of the village :
3. Social development of the village :
4. Problems observed in the village :

PART 'B'

1. Survey :
2. Energy study :
3. Current work and future directions :

PART 'C

Projects undertaken during 'Practice' : Date:

1. Social habits and work schedule
2. Land statistics
3. Rural indebtedness
4. Water requirements and resources of Sevagram village
5. Fishing Farm ? details :
6. Working of the village cooperative
7. Training programme for farmers.

PART D'

Statistical outline of Sevagram village :

1. List of contiguous villages
2. Statistical sketch :
   - (a) Caste pattern of families
   - (b) Age pattern
   - (c) Education pattern
   - (d) Occupation pattern
   - (e) Pattern of landholdings
   - (h) Pattern of livestock
   - (g) Composition of manures
   - *(h)* Pattern of energy consumption
   - (g) Information on wells

3. Income and employment data analysis
4. Indebtedness. Details of households interviewed at Sevagram village :
5. Caste-wise distribution of land in Sevagram village
6. Distribution of cultivable land according to the sizes of operational holdings:
7. Yearwise sale of cultivable land in Sevagram village :
8. General information about Rural Indebtedness in Sevagram village.

Proforma For the Short History and Some silent feature of the Sevagram village :

Crop Pattern

Tank

Fort (Any historical and/or archaeological significance)

School

Fields.

Proforma for Problems Observed in Sevagram village:

Agriculture

Water management

Energy requirements

Employment

Social problems :

Essential commodities

Water problem

Medical facilities ;

Rural indebtedness.

Mass Immunization

Games and entertainments

Your Camp experience.

Motivation

Your objectives.

Methodology and work undertaken

1. Topographical survey
2. Socio-economic-medico-environmental survey.

Current Work and Future Direction

Practice 'School' : Projects

1. Social habits and Work Schedule
2. Land Statistics
3. Rural indebtedness
4. Suggestions
5. Findings

Purpose	*Water Usage*	*Percentage*
Drinking	?	
Bathing	?	
Cooking	?	
Washing	?	
Animals	?	
Storage	?	
Total:		100.00

6. Working of the Village Cooperative :
   (a) Any farmer who has land can become member of the society ?
   (b) How much share each member has to buy ?
   (c) Amount of loan usually granted and the basis
   (d) Wherefrom the cooperative bank gets money and at what interest ? What is the interest charged to the farmer ?
   (e) What is the nature of the committee which operates the society : details:
   (f) Are accounts properly audited ?
   (g) Suggestions, if any.
   (h) Training Programme for Farmers :

Table I

CASTE PATTERN OF FAMILIES (Figures in percentage)

Brahmins

Harijans

Etc.

....

Total Number of Families

....

Table II

AGE PATTERN (Percentage Distribution)

Age Group(Years)	Male	Female	Persons
06			
6—15			
15—25			
25—30			
30—40			
40—50			
50—60			
60 and above			

Table III

EDUCATIONAL PATTERN (Figures in Percentage)

Categories	Percentage
Illiterates	
Primary	
Middle	
High School	
Graduate	

Table IV

OCCUPATION PATTERN	(Figures in Percentage)
Agriculture	
Trade	
Nonagricultural labour	
Unemployed	

Table V

PATTERN OF LANDHOLDINGS

Size of Landholdings	Number of Families (Figures in Percentage)
Landless	
One acre	
Etc.	

Table VI

PATTERN OF LIVESTOCK	Total Livestock Percentage
Type of Animal	
Cow	
Buffaloe	
Sheep	
Goat	
Poultry	
Etc.	

Table VII

COMPOSITION OF MANURES

Type of Manure	Area
Green manure	
Gobar	

Compost

Chemical Fertilizers

Table VIII

PATTERN OF ENERGY CONSUMPTION

Type of Fuel	Consumption (Percentage)
Firewood	
Gobar (Cowdung)	
Crop Waste	
Fuel Oil	

Table IX

INFORMATION ON WELLS

Average depth of open wells :

Depth of Tubewells

Number of wells used for drinking water

Final Evaluation and Suggestion by the Students

Fund Raising

"Mata bhumi—putro aham prithivya :"

The whole world is my Motherland—I am son of Mother (Earth)

—AtharvaVeda.

"Doctor, please----- don't let him die ! I am an old widow. I don't have anyone except this boy to support me."

It's an appeal of an old woman whose only son was admitted in a missionary hospital.

For the lady it is not just beds, operating rooms, X-ray or cardiograph machines. To people like her it is hope. For, every person who enters hospital has a "combat mission" attitude. When trouble strikes, people do not know what exactly troubles them. They do not understand that a larger laboratory, an extra piece of equipment or just more beds might swing the fulcrum of lives now hovering in balance.

Helping hospitals, homes for destitute women and children, and aged and allied missionary projects do call for funds. How could one go about it ?

Charitable bodies are undergoing great hardship in many directions. In the recent past, business and industry could afford to be liberal. But with constant inroads by politicians into their funds followed by inflation has hit them and there is more competition for less money. These situations have public relations connotations. And public relations surely is not a matter of budget or of professional training or of slick operation.

Starving children are a regrettable phenomenon of the modern world. Everybody almost without exception likes small children and wants to help them. This desire goes as far as not caring about where the children are starving, their nationality or cute. Thus in a charity appealing for funds to feed starving children, all people are public. This is an extreme example.

Putting up a memorial for political leader in a city may or may not evoke spontaneous interest among people. But when it is a question of standing by a sacred cause for which dedicated people, like Mother Teresa, are devoting themselves, the world, as we have witnessed, will vie with one another to contribute in cash and kind. The lesson, "Who is a better public relations person for the Christian Missionaries in India than the revered Mother Teresa"! When, in 1948, she started her first slums school with the blessings of the Pope, she had only Rs. 5, but an abundant faith in her service as a friend to the friendless which coupled with her faith in God brought her unsolicited and unexpected awards after awards which she scrupulously utilized for a Leper Home here, Home for the crippled and retarded children there, and so on.

Mother Teresa did not labour hard at fund raising. As a good soup needs no advertising, so Mother Teresa's service to first and last attracted funds in the shape of Raman Magsaysay Award, Pope Paul IV's and John XXIH's, Joseph Kennedy's Awards, and the Nobel Prize.

People other than Mother Teresa's type have necessarily to seek the services of professional fund raisers and public relations people.

The function of a fund raiser is to raise money by advertisements and obtaining editorial comment on the activities of the agencies; whereas the duty of the public relations person is to report on attitudes towards the organisation or agency for which the funds are raised, and report how the money raised is being utilized. The public relations person, thus, creates in the minds of both donors and possible donors awareness of the good that is being done and how it is being done.

In the way advertising is used directly to sell goods, professional fund raisers use their techniques to achieve their objectives. The normal techniques of the public relations person do not have their effect quickly enough to bring money in for deserving causes. But when once the objective is achieved, it becomes a stepping stone to further success. The professional fund raiser and public relations person can, and should, work together. Each should recognize the place of the other and not try to supplant him or replace him.

The timing of appeals must be just right. The message and the audience must be even more clearly identified. And the charity must demonstrate its ability to keep its overheads to a minimum. It is seldom difficult when preparing a list to pick out the groups to whom to aim an appeal. It is much better to make the list as wide as possible, since it is a peculiar fact of fund raising for voluntary purposes that the most unexpected source produces money. Given a list, the public relations person must now face his second problem: how much money is needed. If the charity is permanent—as might be the case for starving children—it may be sufficient to say that "as much as possible" is the total. A short-term appeal will have a limit.

Direct mail, editorial publicity, advertising, personal effort and personal contact are the generally accepted methods used in fund raising. Their importance varies in each type of appeal, and it is dangerous to generalize. The direct mail will take the form of letters and leaflets. The letters may be individually typed or produced with matched in addresses (in which the letters look as though they have been individually typed out). It is of course possible but this is seldom advisable. Remember the elements of blackmail and identification. The recipients of letters must react favourably or with interest. A stencilled and generalized appeal is unlikely to make them do either.

Who signs the letter, again, depends on the circumstances. It may be signed by the patron or president or chairman or by a notable personality such as a movie star of good name and fame. For instance, an appeal to housewives might produce a better reaction if it were signed by a famous film star or noted leader of a Women's Organization. An appeal for a sports stadium would evoke immediate interest if it apparently came from a cricket star and or a respected captain of a nationally or internationally reputed group of industries like J.R.D. Tata.

The use of leaflets produces another set of specific decisions. There are dangers in producing a lavish, we llillustrated brochure since it carries the implication that money is being spent rashly. Whatever the leaflet looks like, it must at all costs be informative and emotional. It must say clearly what are the objectives of the appeal, and as far as possible show how the money is to be spent, but it must do so in emotional terms. Remember again that the donations being solicited are spare money, that is, money return to the donor involved in any shape is not there. And remember the donor gives that money which he could spend on other things. To put it rather crudely, the leaflet must pull at his heartstrings or stir his memories. Genuine emotion will do this and its use is justified.

Other adjuncts of raising funds are : Christmas and Diwali Greeting cards, "Seals", Dramas, Music Concerts, Sports Benefit Matches, etc.

A practical example of fund raising campaign

Samanta was eleven months old in 1981. Her parents lived in North London. They were poor.

As ill-luck would have it, the first baby Samanta was born with one hand only. Being the first baby looking very charming, the parents hated the very idea of entrusting it to the care of The Home for Disabled Children. The loving parents approached an artificial limbfitting centre and sought their help to make Samanta happy in her life.

Considering the pecuniary status of the poor parents, the Centre quoted their rockbottom rate. Yet the amount of 5,000 English pounds was too large for the couple to find.

The community in North London had love and regard for the parents of bady Samanta. The members came to know of the plight of the parents. So some leading members of the local Ladies Club convened a General Body Meeting to discuss ways and means of finding the amount of 5,000 pounds required for providing Samanta with an artificial hand.

Mrs. Elizabeth Edwards, an elderly and resourceful lady, put the following suggestion to vote :

1. "Members prepare a snappy story of poor Samanta, the good qualities of the parents, and the money required for giving a "hand" to baby Samanta.
2. With the story we approach some of the kindhearted film actresses, model girls, women sport stars, and cross section of the charitably disposed housewives to lend support to a fundraising procession on a fixed day.

A very bold placard to be prepared, and that will be carried by the batches of processionists. The leading batch will be flanked by two attractive girls, a leading film star and a 'model girl' on either. One of them will be carrying the baby exposed to public view and the other will hold high the placard containing the "appeal". Appropriate slogans to evoke the sympathy and kindness of the public will also be "shouted" duly mentioning the amount of 5,000 pounds required for the "sacred cause".

The suggestion of Mrs. Eligabeth Edwards was unanimously accepted and the next day the plan was faithfully implemented. Within 48 hours more than 5,000 pounds were collected. Baby Samanta was fitted with the artificial hand. She is now a happy girl playing and running, and providing considerable happiness to her parents.

The "knowledge explosion" that has been adding momentum since the end of World War II has placed a greater burden and a greater responsibility on our youth. Many brand-new fields of activity such as space exploration and in the older, established fields of effort there is considerably more to know than most of us had to learn in our younger days.

Inquisitive parents who are curious about what their offspring are studying these days in high schools and colleges usually end up on commenting, with a sigh of relief, "I am glad I did not have to learn that complicated stuff when I went to school." That is an understandable reaction and no reflection on the parents' mental capability, because our body of knowledge has expanded tremendously in the last two decades.

There is not only more to know, but many more who want to know it. Colleges, virtually all of them with more applicants than they can handle, have had to raise their entrance requirements in order to give the opportunity to study to the best qualified. This is a far cry from the situation in the Depression Period, when all that was required for admission to even the so-called better colleges was a high school certificate.

This explains in part why we look with greater concern and more hope on the youth of today. We know that the business, professional and political leaders of tomorrow are the young men and women who are active today in Young Men's Christian Association, Young Women's Christian Association, the Boys, Scouts, The Girl Guides, Nehru Yuvak Kendra, and similar youth organizations. Groups like these are training youths for leadership, and in doing so, provide many constructive public relations opportunities. Any organization which assists youths to lead healthier, more useful and purposeful lives is respected, and those persons or corporations that provide leadership and financial support to youth organizations rate high with the public.

Help is vital : Financial support is commendable and certainly quite necessary, but it is the personal interest and participation in the work of organizations such as these that really count. All of those we have mentioned depend to a certain degree, and some very considerably, on volunteers from the ranks of business to put over their programmes and carry forward their objectives. It is a growing conviction that the future of society and our way of life depends on the next generation. Businessmen foresee the crisis. That is why corporations which turn thumbs down on many other kinds of requests for financial help will support accredited youth organizations. It is likewise that belief that makes busy men and women feel it is an honour to serve as directors of the purposeful youth organizations and to identify themselves actively with its programme. Service to youth is not only good public relations, it is also work that gives a deep sense of satisfaction for having contributed in a small way to bettering the national and world's well-being.

Many business leaders have left either the bulk or a major portion of their estates to organizations which have facilities for working with youth.

Youth organizations, including needy liberal arts colleges and vocational schools for underprivileged youths, are especially favoured by corporations in their benevolence programmes because such gifts can be localized. They do not arouse prejudices as might be the case if a large gift were made to some religious institution. Even the critical shareholder would agree that management was within its rights in using company money to insure a supply of competent future business leaders, and at the same time to strengthen the company's community relations. This is especially true in those instances where most of the shareholding is concentrated in a relatively small geographic area.

Helping youth is an activity favoured by many because it gives young people an opportunity to "learn by doing". It is likewise important that they learn, as a result of this doing. The value of making this type of leadership training available to those preparing to enter business and industry is increasingly evident.

Business organizations can help expand service to youths in three ways. First, a firm can sponsor a group and can help insure advisers by giving sincere and meaningful recognition to volunteers.

Second, a firm can support a group financially. Such Youth Groups can expand only as rapidly as it can train additional manpower and make the expenditure necessary to start a new programme in a new area.

Third, company executives can become actively and personally interested in youth groups. They can talk to business friends about it, take an active part in bringing it to a community, and bring more businessmen into the picture with them.

It is appropriate to mention here the yeoman 's service which the great Ramakrishna Mission is doing in developing disciplined leadership for our country's tomorrow's needs. Some great Christen organizations too are doing likewise.

Employees of good firms too can play an effective educational rule among the local community boys and girls. An industrial club can be formed, where supervisors or foremen from local plants can get together and discuss problems involving human relations, can help the youths to organize self-improvement programme, salesmanship, safety, speed-reading, letter writing and similar interesting kills.

College-Industry Relations can be improved by bringing about closer personal relations between business and college faculty in ambers by availing good tools of communication. Improved communications through face-to-face contacts could be undertaken. Specially, these contacts might include :

1. Educators conferences.
2. "Coop' employment of professors.
3. Use of professors as consultants.
4. Informal conferences between businessmen and educators on mutual goals.
5. Campus visits by businessmen.
6. Plant visits by educators and students.

It will certainly prove very beneficial to appoint advisory groups of businessmen who help in many ways schools and colleges.

Bibliography

Almond, Gabriel A. and Verba, S. : *The Civic Culture: Political Attitudes and Democracy in Five Nations,* Princeton University Press, New Jersey, 1963.

Altschull, J.H.: *Agents of Power: the Role of the News Media in Human Affairs,* Longman, New York, 1984.

Baehr, H.: *Women and Media,* Pergamon, London, 1980.

Bell, D.: *The End of Ideology,* Collier Books, New York, 1976.

Berelson, B.: *Content Analysis in Communication Research,* Free Press, Glencoe, Illinois, 1952.

Bhattacharjea, Ajit: *Emergency and Media,* Mainstream, 1999.

Blumer, J.G. and McQuail, D.: *Television in Politics: Its Uses and Influence,* Fabes, London, 1968.

Blumer, J.G., and Ewbank, A.J., 'Trade Unionists, the Mass Media, and Unofficial Strikes', *British Journal of Industrial Relations,* 8, 1970.

Blumer, H.: *Movies and Conduct,* MacMillan, New York, 1933.

Carey, James W.: *Communication as Culture: Essays on Media and Society,* Routledge, New York, 1992.

Chaffee, S.H. and Berger, C.R. : *Handbook of Communication Science,* Sage Publications, Beverly Hills, London, 1987.

Chaney, D.: *Processes of Mass Communication,* Macmillan, London, 1972.

Curran. J., Gurevitch, M. and Woollacott, J. : *Mass Communication and Society,* Edward Arnold, London, 1977.

Davis, Dennis K. and Baran, Stanley J.: *Mass Communication and Every Day Life—A Perspective on Theory and Effects*, Woodworth, California, 1981.

Davison, W.P.: *Mass Communication and Conflict Resolution*, Praeger, New York, 1974.

De Fleur, M.: *Theories of Mass Communication*, David Mckay, New York, 1970.

Dexter, L. A. and White, D.M. : *People, Society and Mass Communication*, Free Press, New York, 1964.

Fiske, J.: *Introduction to Communication Studies*, Methuen, London, 1982.

Gerbner, G (ed.): *Mass Media Policies in Changing Cultures*, Wiley, New York, 1977.

Gurvitch, M., Bennet, T. and Woollacott, J. (eds.): *Culture, Society and Mass Media*, Methuen, London, 1982.

Habermas, J.: 'The Theory of Communicative Action', Vol. I, *Reason and the Rationalisation of Society*, Heinemann, London, 1982.

Innis, Harold Adams: *Empire and Communication* (Rev. ed.), University of Toronto Press, Toronto, 1972.

Katz, E. and Szecsko, T. (eds.): *Mass Media and Social Change*, Sage Publications, Beverly Hills and London, 1981.

Kelman, H.: 'Process of Opinion Change,' *Public Openion Quarterly* 25, 1961.

Key, V.O.: *Public Opinion and American Democracy*, Alfred Knopf, New York, 1961.

Kornhauser, W.: *The Politics of Mass Society*, Free Press, New York, 1968.

Lazarsfeld P. F., Berelson, B. and Gaudet, H.: *The People's Choice*, Duell, Sloan and Pearce, New York, 1944.

McQuail, D. (ed.): *Sociology of Mass Communication*, Penguin, Harmondsworth, 1972.

McQuail, D.: *Mass Communication Theory*, Sage, London, 1987.

Mendelbaum, S.J.: *Community and Communicating*, Norton, New York, 1972.

Natarajan J.: *History of Indian Journalism*, Part II of the Report of the Press Commission, New Delhi, 1955.

Nimmo, D.D. and Sanders, D. (eds.): *Handbook of Political Communication*, Sage Publications, Beverly Hills and London, 1978.

Peterson, R.C. et al.: *The Mass Media and Modern Society*, Holt, Rnehart and Winston, New York, 1965.

Prasad, Bimal (ed.).: *A Revolutionary's Quest*, Oxford University Press, Delhi, 1980.

Schramm, W: *Mass Media and National Development*, Stanford University Press, Stanford, 1964.

Trenaman, J.S.M.: *Communication and Comprehension*, Longman, London, 1967.

Weiner, Norbert: *The Human Use of Human Beings: Cybernetics and Society*, Aron Books, New York, 1967.

Wilkinson, T.S. and Bhandarkar, P.L.: *Methodology and Techniques of Social Research*, Himalaya, Bombay, 1987.

Natarajan J. *History of Indian Journalism*, Part II of the Report of the Press Commission, New Delhi, 1955.

Nimmo, D.D. and Sanders, K.R. (eds.), *Handbook of Political Communication*, Sage Publications, Beverly Hills and London, 1981.

Robertson, R.C. et al. *The Mass Media and Modern Society*, Holt, Rinehart and Winston, New York, 1965.

[illegible] (ed.), [illegible], Oxford University Press, Delhi, 1981.

Schramm, W. *Mass Media and National Development*, Stanford University Press, Stanford, 1964.

Trenaman, J.S.M. *Communication and Comprehension*, Longmans, London, 1967.

Weiner, Norbert. *The Human Use of Human Beings: Cybernetics and Society*, Avon Books, New York, 1967.

Wilkinson, T.S. and Bhandarkar, P.L. *Methodology and Techniques of Social Research*, Himalaya, Bombay, 1982.